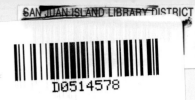

BROAD-LEAVED EVERGREENS

TREES, SHRUBS

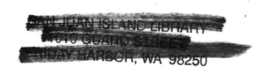

This book is dedicated to Caroline Haw

Broad-leaved Evergreens

Trees, Shrubs & Climbers

Stephen G. Haw

with colour photographs taken by Stephen G. Haw

First published 2000
by Guild of Master Craftsman Publications Ltd
Castle Place, 166 High Street, Lewes
East Sussex BN7 1XU

A catalogue record of this book is available from the British Library

ISBN 1 86108 172 3

Edited by Joanna Foster
Designed by Fran Rawlinson
Cover design by Ian Smith, GMC Publications Studio

Colour origination by Viscan Graphics Pte Ltd (Singapore)

Printed and bound by Kyodo Printing (Singapore)
under the supervision of MRM Graphics
Winslow, Buckinghamshire, UK

GUILD OF MASTER CRAFTSMAN PUBLICATIONS

CONTENTS

INTRODUCTION

EVERGREENS ARE EXTREMELY useful in the garden. The advantage of plants that do not lose their leaves in winter is obvious: bare branches look cold and cheerless compared to masses of foliage.

Evergreen conifers (pines, firs, cypresses, junipers and other related plants) have become very popular during the last few decades. Indeed, most garden centres now have sections entirely devoted to them and a number of nurseries specialize in them. Nursery catalogues usually list them separately. Broad-leaved evergreens, on the other hand, are mixed in with deciduous trees, shrubs and climbers. As a group of plants, they are generally neglected. Many are rare in cultivation. I suspect that the principal reason for this is not that they are difficult to grow, or that they are undesirable, but because many of them are hard to propagate on a commercial scale. This neglect is a great pity. It is my hope that this book will help to make broad-leaved evergreens more popular.

Even the phrase 'broad-leaved evergreens' may be unfamiliar. Broad-leaved woody plants are simply those that are not conifers or other plants of the group known as gymnosperms, including cycads and the ginkgo. Most conifers, of course, have narrow, often needle-like leaves, like those of pines and firs. Sometimes they are very small and like scales, as in the cypresses.

Most non-coniferous woody plants have larger, broader leaves, like those of the well-known natives holly and ivy. Although a few, such as heaths (*Erica* species), have small, narrow leaves, the term broad-leaved is a good generalization. If any doubt about the distinction between broad-leaved and coniferous arises, another useful difference is that broad-leaved plants bear flowers that are often, though not always, showy. Conifers and other gymnosperms do not bear true flowers at all. The strict botanical difference is in the fruits. Gymnosperms have seeds that are not enclosed within an ovary (the word gymnosperm is derived

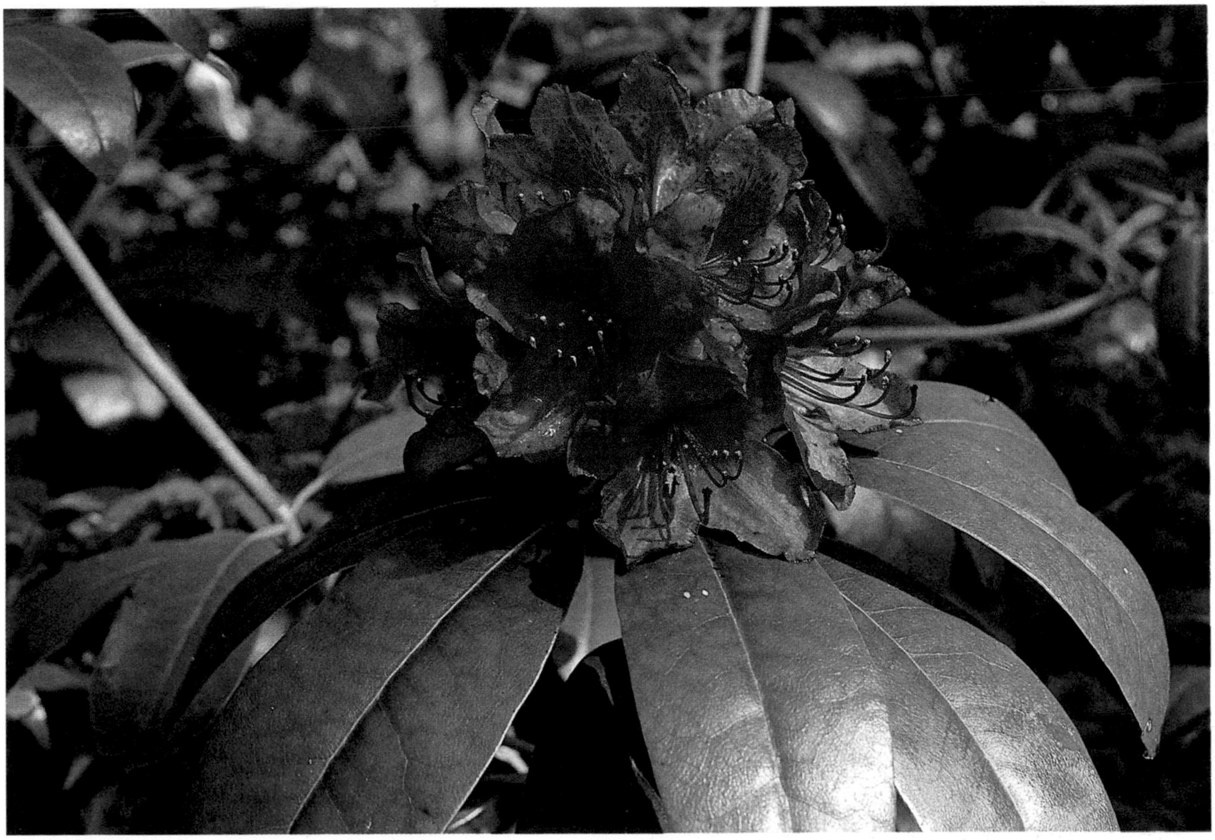

Rhododendrons are among the many broad-leaved evergreens with showy flowers

from the Greek words for naked seed). They are older and more primitive than the broad-leaved angiosperms, which produce seeds that develop inside ovaries.

HARDINESS

It is highly likely that all plants were originally evergreen. Most plants growing in tropical and subtropical regions that do not have a pronounced dry season are still evergreen today.

Plants lose a great deal of water through their leaves. Dropping leaves at certain times may well have originated as an adaptation to drought. It also made deciduous plants better able to withstand cold winters because most leaves are very susceptible to frost damage. In colder regions with winter frosts most plants are deciduous. The main exceptions are conifers, with their hard, narrow leaves that are resistant to drought and cold.

Only a minority of broad-leaved plants in colder parts of the world retain their leaves during winter. In northern Europe, for example, there are very few broad-leaved evergreens, but many more to the south, around the Mediterranean. Many broad-leaved evergreens grown in gardens come from regions with a generally warmer climate, so they are not always reliably hardy in cold winters. Even some of the most commonly grown, such as the Cherry Laurel (*Prunus laurocerasus*), are not absolutely hardy in areas with climates which have regular frost and snow in winter, such as Britain. In the severe winter of 1946–47, 20-year-old Cherry Laurels were killed outright in the Birmingham area, in central England. Even in milder counties south of London some were killed to ground level. This was a winter when many broad-leaved woody plants suffered badly, but so did the very popular and widely planted hybrid tea roses. On the other hand, hardier rhododendrons suffered very little.

Hardiness is a complex issue. It is not necessarily the lowest temperatures that cause the greatest damage. Light frosts early in autumn and late in spring often cause damage when more severe frosts during winter do not. A cool summer that does not ripen woody growth sufficiently may result in severe damage even if the following winter is not especially harsh. This is a particular problem in areas where the climate is uncertain. Morning sun falling directly on plants still covered with overnight frost is very liable to cause injury. Many broad-leaved evergreens are susceptible to being damaged by cold winds.

There is a great deal that can be done to avoid winter damage by selecting planting sites carefully. Shelter from other plants, particularly overhead shelter from trees, can make a great difference. A plant may thrive for several years only to be killed outright by a short spell of severe weather. A succession of mild winters, such as has happened recently in Britain, can lull gardeners into a false sense of security. Nurseries and garden centres now frequently seem to be offering plants that are very much on the tender side, with no caveats. I have seen many on sale at local garden centres that I would not risk planting in my own garden in central England. I fear that a bad winter now would cause many fatalities in gardens.

THE SCOPE OF THIS BOOK

As a rule, plants that are scarcely hardy have been omitted. Notes on hardiness are included in Section 3. Where hardiness is not mentioned, assume that the plant will survive all but the worst winters, particularly in generally mild areas and near coasts.

Some plants that are not very hardy have been included because they are tolerant of coastal exposure. Salt-laden winds can severely limit the range of plants that can be successfully grown near the sea. Exactly where the line should be drawn between what was hardy enough to be included and what was not was not always an easy decision. In the end a great deal depended on my personal preferences.

To keep this book to a reasonable size it was necessary to set further limits. Very small shrubs, particularly those that are really only suitable for growing in rock gardens, have been entirely excluded. Virtually all the shrubs described in this book will grow to at least 60cm (2ft) tall and most to at least 90cm (3ft). This means that I have left out many prostrate evergreen shrubs suitable for ground cover, but I considered that they would be better dealt with in specialist books.

THE NAMING OF PLANTS

This is a very problematic and complex subject which causes much controversy. Most amateur gardeners would probably be very happy if all plants had simple English names. Unfortunately they do not. There are not really enough English names for plants to go round. Books that attempt to give English names to most garden plants usually end up either failing or resorting to making names up specially.

The fundamental problem is that there are so many different plants. Some type of scientific system for assigning names is necessary to avoid overwhelming confusion. Such a system must be international. To be truly international and acceptable worldwide then it should not necessarily use English.

Until a couple of centuries ago the international language of learning, at least throughout most of Europe and countries settled by Europeans, was Latin.

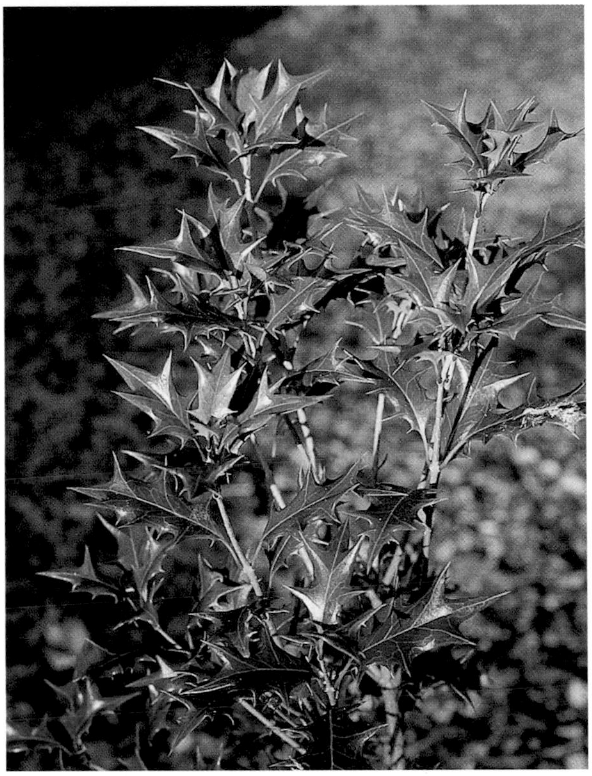

***Osmanthus heterophyllus*: its name derives from four Greek words meaning 'scented flower' and 'different leaves'**

During the mid-eighteenth century, a Swedish botanist called Linnaeus devised a reasonably simple, universal system for naming plants. He used Latin and classical Greek, to provide a sufficiently large vocabulary. This system became accepted internationally and, with many revisions, is still in use today.

An international code is published (revised at international congresses every few years) giving rules for assigning names to plants. According to these rules, any plant can have only one correct name at any one time and that name, once published, should be used throughout the world. There are, of course, many complexities. Arguments arise about the interpretation of the rules and the way in which they are applied. In general, however, they work well and doubtlessly there would be much greater confusion without them. Many problems arise because rules were less comprehensive and strict in the past and names were applied to plants with too little care. Much more care is taken now and there is probably less confusion today than at any time previously, though problems will certainly never be entirely eliminated.

The botanical system for naming plants is based on grouping them according to their relationships. The most important unit into which plants are grouped is called the genus (plural: genera). Usually it is easy even for people with no botanical training to recognize that all the plants placed in one genus are more or less closely related to each other. For example, all the various kinds of oak trees are placed in the genus *Quercus*. Even though their leaves may look very different, they all bear acorns. Similarly, all plants placed in the genus *Rosa* have flowers that look similar and bear fruits like rose-hips. Genera that appear to be related are grouped into families; for example *Pyrus* (pears), *Malus* (apples) and *Prunus* (plums, cherries and so on) all belong to the same family.

Within a genus there may be one, two or many plant species, depending on how many plants have characteristics that are similar enough for them to be considered sufficiently closely related. A species is the fundamental unit into which plants are grouped. In theory, all plants considered to belong to one species should be very similar indeed. They must be capable of interbreeding and should not – at least under normal conditions in the wild – interbreed with any other species.

This does not rule out variability within a species. Every individual is, in fact, different in some details from every other, but the variation cannot be very great and should not rule out interbreeding under normal conditions. Differences between species are often obvious, even to untrained observers. This is very clear in relation to many animals. Everyone should be able to see the differences between a horse and a zebra, or a greenfinch and a goldfinch.

Species are given names that consist of two words. The first word is the name of the genus. Thus, all roses belong to the genus *Rosa* and their names begin with the word *Rosa*. The second word of the species name is individual to that species alone and cannot be applied to any other species of the same genus. The

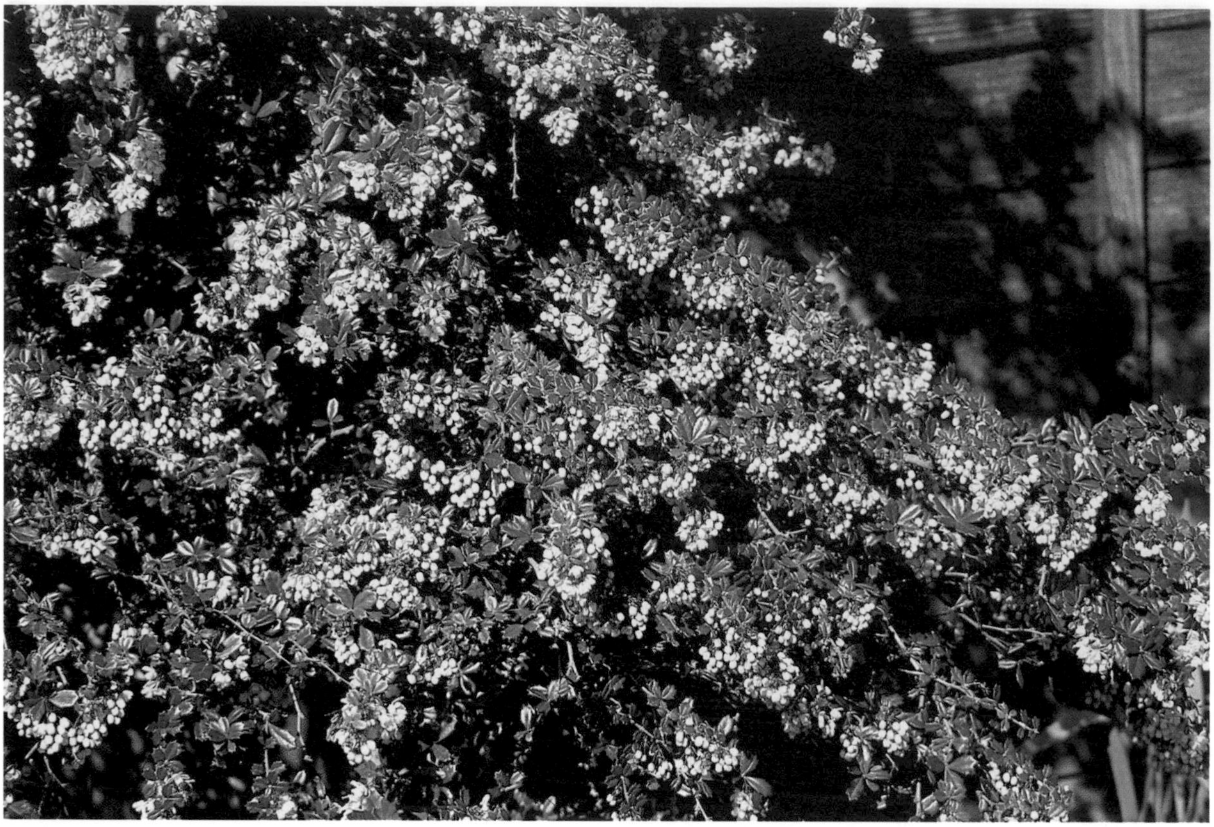

***Berberis darwinii* is named after Charles Darwin**

word may be descriptive of some physical feature of the plant. For example, *Rosa macrophylla* is so called because it has large leaves (the word *macrophylla* is derived from classical Greek words meaning large and leaf) . It may describe the geographical origin of the plant, as in *Rosa chinensis*, the Chinese Rose, or the kind of place where the plant grows, as in *Rosa arvensis*, the Field Rose.

People are commemorated in the names of plant species too. *Rosa banksiae*, for example, was named after the wife of Sir Joseph Banks, a botanist who was a founder of the Royal Horticultural Society, among many other achievements. Botanists, plant collectors and their associates are often remembered in this way. These commemorative names can often be the most complex and difficult to pronounce, because they may celebrate people from anywhere in the world. Most native English speakers have trouble with species names such as *maximowiczii* or *mlokosewitschii* and others commemorating people with long Slavonic names. We should remember, however, that Japanese or Chinese gardeners and botanists probably have the same difficulty with names like *johnstoneanum*, *campbellii* or even *smithii*.

Once a name has been given to a species and published according to the accepted rules, that name becomes permanent. The same name cannot be given to a different plant.

One problem that has often given rise to changes in commonly accepted plant names is that, in the past, it was easy for a plant to be given a name then, at a later date, for another botanist unwittingly to give it another name. The first naming may have been forgotten about or, in times when communications between countries were slower and less certain than today, it could happen that a German or Russian botanist might give one name to a plant while a British or French botanist gave it another. In such cases the general rule is that the earlier name is taken as the correct one. Where earlier names had been forgotten and a later name had come into widespread use, however, it was more convenient for widely used names to be kept. Such conservation of a name has to be agreed upon at an international botanical congress. It may also have happened that a name was given to one plant then later mistakenly given to another, different plant. In such a case, the second naming is invalid and has to be rejected.

Botanists make mistakes, like everyone else, so it should be noted that species names can be misleading. The bird we call a turkey does not come from Turkey and neither does the flower *Scilla peruviana* come from Peru. Such an error does not make it acceptable to change a validly published name, however.

Species names are often comparative, noting differences between plants of the same genus. A species called *grandiflora* (meaning large-flowered) may have quite small flowers, but the name means that they are larger than those of other plants in the same genus. Geographical names often give too narrow an impression of a plant's actual range. A plant may be named after the area where it was first found but actually occur much more widely. For example, a plant found in Yunnan province, China, might be named *yunnanensis* but occur throughout western China and in northern Burma and north-east India as well.

Sometimes two different plant species may grow sufficiently close together in the wild for crossbreeding to occur. Many plants belonging to the same genus are able to interbreed and occasionally plants belonging to different genera in the same family will do so. The offspring will be hybrids, which normally have some of the characteristics of both parents mixed together. Hybridization often occurs in cultivation, either by chance when related plants are grown close together, or as a result of deliberate human action.

Hybrids can be named in much the same way as species, but to show that they are hybrids a cross (x) is placed between the two words of the name of the species, as in *Salix* x *erdingeri*, a natural hybrid between *Salix caprea* and *Salix daphnoides*. If the cross is between plants of different genera, then a new genus is created and has to be named. The cross indicating hybrid origin is then placed before the new name. An example is X *Fatshedera*, the result of a cross between plants of the two genera *Fatsia* and *Hedera*. Plants arising from the same cross can all be given the same botanical name, but note that they will usually be variable and not all of equal interest to gardeners.

There may also be considerable variation within an unhybridized plant species. Variation within a plant species becomes clearer when compared to that of humans. We can usually recognize individual humans and tell them apart from any other, except identical twins perhaps. At the same time, we can see that every individual is recognizably human. Some differences are great and consistent enough for distinct groups, races or ethnic groups, within the species *Homo sapiens* to be perceived.

In plants, too, variation within species may be sufficiently great and consistent for distinct groups to be recognized. The highest category of difference within a plant species is called a subspecies (abbreviated to subsp.). For subspecies to be recognized, differences must be fairly great and very consistent, preferably with different subspecies of the same species occurring in different geographical areas. A lesser degree of difference, often with no geographical isolation, is accorded the rank of variety (Latin, *varietas*, abbreviated to var.). Very small differences, such as flower colour, are recognized at the level of a form (*forma*, abbreviated to f.). Subspecies, varieties and forms are given names in the same way as species. These names are added, with the rank, after the species name, for example, *Myrtus communis* subsp. *tarentina*. It is possible for a single plant species to include two or more subspecies, each with two or more different varieties, and some with more than one form. Fortunately such complex variations, which give rise to long and complicated names, are rarely recognized by botanists.

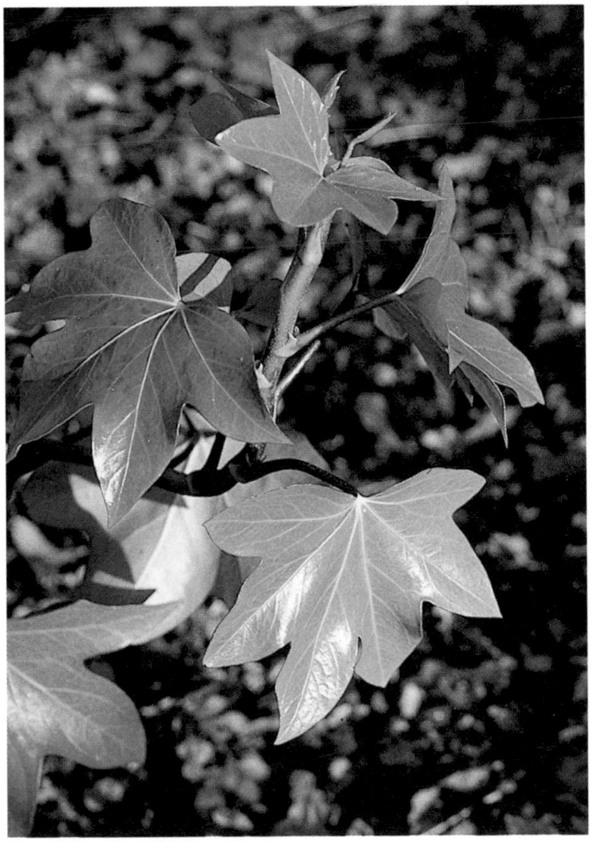

X *Fatshedera lizei*, a hybrid between plants of different genera

Just as some people are taller, thinner, longer legged, blonder or darker or than others, so some plants may have larger flowers, more attractive leaves, more compact growth or differ in other ways from other plants belonging to the same species. Such differences make certain plants more desirable to gardeners than others. Unlike people, plants can usually be cloned quite easily by propagating them vegetatively. Vegetative propagation includes any method that produces a new plant that has not grown from a seed, such as division, taking cuttings or layering. Created like this, the new plant is genetically identical to the one from which it was propagated and therefore shares its characteristics, such as particularly large flowers.

Sometimes variations do become stable so that most, or at least some, of the offspring grown from a particular plant's seed will share whatever special characteristic it has. A whole group of very similar but not genetically identical plants will then arise. If this happens in the wild, such plants may be given the status of a variety or form within the species to which they belong. If it happens in cultivation, or if the special characteristic possessed by the plants is of interest to gardeners but not to botanists, then the plants may not be given any botanical status.

Selected plants which have characteristics that gardeners value but are of no botanical significance, are known as cultivars (derived from the words cultivated varieties) and can be given cultivar names. There is an international code regulating such names and so any one cultivar can have only one valid cultivar name. Several groups of plants of major importance to gardeners have international bodies that register all valid cultivar names. A cultivar name is placed within single quotation marks after the botanical name of the plant, with an initial capital letter for each word, for example *Ilex aquifolium* 'Golden Queen'. For a plant of hybrid origin, any cultivar name should follow the botanical name of the hybrid, for example *Ilex* x *altaclerensis* 'Golden King'.

Not all hybrids have been given a botanical name. Some arose accidentally in gardens and their exact parentage may not be known. Or they may be very complex hybrids – a result of hybrids having crossed with hybrids over many generations. In such cases it is common for the cultivar name to appear immediately after the genus name, for example *Rhododendron* 'Cunningham's White'. Often cultivars used to be named in Latin in the past, for example, 'Latifolia', 'Variegata'. These older names remain in use, but the rule now is that a modern language must be used. It is not permissible to translate cultivar names from their original language.

Unfortunately, many commercial breeders and sellers of plants give plants cultivar names that are coded or meaningless. They then make up attractive selling names designed to make the plants more marketable. Such selling names often differ from one country to another. This practice is entirely contrary to the more simple and highly desirable state of having only one accepted name for any one plant throughout the world. For gardeners this should mean that they do not unwittingly buy the same plant more than once under different names. However, the practice has become established and cannot be ignored. Both the valid cultivar name and the selling name ought to appear on labels when plants are sold. It is good practice in other situations also to quote both, if they are known. The convention is that selling names should be quoted in a different form from cultivar names, without quotation marks and in a different typeface, for example Blue Princess.

There are now a number of authoritative publications that list plant names. One of the most useful to British gardeners is the Royal Horticultural Society's *Plant Finder*. Plant names that appear in this book have all been checked against the 1999–2000 edition of the *Plant Finder* and should agree with names as they are given therein. Anyone wishing to buy a plant that appears in this book should also consult the *Plant Finder*, which is available online at the Royal Horticultural Society's Web site (www.rhs.org.uk) as well as on CD-ROM and in traditional book form.

PLANT BREEDER'S RIGHTS

Just as it is possible to patent an invention, and for authors and film makers to own the copyright of their creations, so it has recently become possible for breeders of new plant cultivars to register rights in the plants they have created. Anyone wishing to propagate a plant in which such rights exist must obtain permission and will normally be asked to pay a royalty to the holder of the rights. It is unlikely that any private gardener who grows one or two plants from cuttings or layers would be taken to court, but it should be realized that propagating plants in which Plant Breeder's Rights exist, without the permission of the holder of the rights, is a breach of the law.

Rhododendron **'Cilpinense', a hybrid named when cultivars were often given Latin names**

GLOSSARY

I have tried to use as few unfamiliar words as possible. A deliberately restricted range of words has been used for describing the shapes of leaves, for which a large technical vocabulary exists. Most of the words should be easily understood, but some may need explanation. **Oval** means shaped like an egg's outline, broadest towards the leaf stalk. **Lanceolate** is similar but narrower. **Elliptical** means that the broadest width is near the middle of the leaf. **Obovate** is the same shape as oval but the other way round, with the broadest part of the leaf towards the tip. Similarly, **oblanceolate** is like lanceolate but broadest towards the tip. **Pinnate** leaves are like those of an ash tree, that is composed of several pairs of leaflets, usually with a single terminal leaflet. The **leaf axil** refers to the small area, normally containing a bud, in the acute angle between a leaf stalk and the stem to which it is attached.

SECTION 1

GROWING BROAD-LEAVED EVERGREENS

GROWING BROAD-LEAVED EVERGREENS

BROAD-LEAVED EVERGREENS are a very varied group of plants. They belong to many different plant families and come from all corners of the world. For the gardener this, of course, means that they cannot all be treated in the same way. General techniques that are widely applicable are covered here. Specific requirements of individual plants are given in Section 3.

Many broad-leaved evergreens are naturally woodland plants. Anyone who is lucky enough to have established trees in their garden will find that a wide variety of broad-leaved evergreen shrubs will thrive in the shade and shelter the trees can provide.

Aucuba japonica, Elaeagnus species and hybrids, X *Fatshedera lizei, Fatsia japonica, Hedera helix*, most *Ilex* species and hybrids, *Leucothoe* species and hybrids, *Lonicera nitida*, mahonias, *Osmanthus decorus*, *Rhododendron ponticum*, *Ruscus* species and hybrids, sarcococcas, skimmias and some viburnums will all thrive in heavy shade. Camellias, most daphnes, most bamboos, other *Osmanthus* species and hybrids, *Danae racemosa, Daphniphyllum* species, *Distylium racemosum, Itea ilicifolia, Ligustrum* species, photinias, *Pieris* species, most rhododendrons, *Sycopsis sinensis* and vacciniums all enjoy light to moderate shade in woodland. It must be borne in mind, however, that only a minority of plants are at their best in very heavy shade and that tree roots can rob the soil of water and nutrients. Great attention may need to be paid to keeping shrubs under trees adequately watered, particularly during the first year or two after planting. Regular feeding may also be needed to encourage good growth and health.

Walls and buildings can to some extent substitute for trees in providing shade and shelter, but are rarely as satisfactory. They are too solid. Trees can provide dappled shade and overhead shelter, which are far better than the blocks of shadow and lateral shelter created by buildings. Winds can funnel between buildings and race around corners, so great care must be taken when planting in such locations. Many broad-leaved evergreens are tolerant of urban conditions, however, and enjoy the warmth from heated buildings in winter.

CHOOSING PLANTS

Broad-leaved evergreens are best acquired in pots or root-balled. Root-balling is only appropriate during mid-autumn to early spring and the plants need to be planted as quickly as possible, preferably either during autumn or as early as possible in spring. Pot-grown plants can be planted at almost any time, except during frosty periods in winter or very warm, dry spells in summer.

Broad-leaved evergreens tend to need more care after planting than most other plants. They must be kept watered during dry spells until they have become established, which may take more than a year. Some, particularly shallow-rooted kinds such as rhododendrons, will always need watering during dry spells. Young plants may also need extra protection against winds, which can be provided by enclosing them in wind-breaks made of sticks or canes with sacking, horticultural fleece or similar material wrapped around them. Some of the less hardy species are also more susceptible to frost damage when young and should be wrapped in fleece during cold spells until they have grown too big for wrapping them to be easy.

It is essential to choose the right plants for your garden – and broad-leaved evergreens are no exception. It is very tempting to see a beautiful plant in a large garden and decide that you must have one in your own garden. This may be fine, but all too often conditions in your garden will not be right and the plant will never thrive and never look anything but unhappy in its new situation.

Before buying any plant, ask yourself some questions. The most important one is 'Have I got room for it?' A neat little shrub in a pot at a garden centre may rapidly grow to 3m (10ft) high and wide or more. Some plants stand pruning well, others do not, and it may be that a plant that constantly has to be cut back will never look very attractive. Choose something that will fit the space you have available. Sizes are given for all the plants described in full in Section 3. Do bear in mind, however, that the ultimate size which trees, shrubs and climbers will reach varies according to growing conditions, sometimes quite considerably. Broad-leaved evergreens are mostly quite slow-growing and many tolerate trimming well, so they are less likely to cause serious problems by outgrowing their allotted space than many other plants.

Next you must ask, 'Are conditions in my garden right?' If your garden has chalky or limy soil then there is no point in trying to grow plants that need acid soils, such as rhododendrons and camellias, unless you grow them in containers filled with acid soil and water them with rainwater. If your garden is sunny and dry, plants that need shade and moisture are unlikely to thrive. The more care that goes into making a choice, the more likely it is that good results will follow. Section 3 of this book, where the individual plants are described, is divided into sub-sections to make selecting plants easier.

SOILS

A major limiting factor that can seriously restrict your choice of garden plants is soil type. The most difficult to make a garden on is almost certainly shallow soil over chalk, because a great many plants simply will not thrive in very chalky conditions. Rhododendrons, camellias and certainly all those listed as requiring acid soils in Section 3, are not worth attempting. Even some plants which will grow quite happily in moderately limy soil will not flourish on chalk. These include *Eucryphia, Magnolia, Nothofagus* and some *Quercus* species. Those gardening in such conditions should try to buy plants from nurseries in chalky districts and ask for advice on how to grow them. If it is possible, break up the chalk to a depth of at least 45cm (18in) before planting, remove large pieces of the white rock and mix in plenty of humus. Much better results will usually be obtained.

Many gardeners, though not having to contend with very chalky soil, have soils that are more or less limy. Although it is quite easy to add lime to an acid soil, it is very difficult to make a limy soil more acid. It can be done temporarily, either by importing naturally acid soil from outside the garden or by treating the existing soil with chemicals. Over time, however, lime from the surrounding soil and subsoil, dissolved in ground water, will almost always soak into the acid soil and gradually turn it limy. The only satisfactory way to grow plants requiring acid soils in areas where the soil is naturally limy is to use containers. They must be filled with acid compost. If the local tap water is limy (it usually is), rain must be collected for watering.

It is possible to get a good idea of whether soil is limy or acid by looking at what plants are grown locally. If neighbouring gardens are full of rhododendrons, then the soil must be acid. If there is an obvious lack of such lime-hating plants, then it is likely that the soil is limy. To be sure of conditions in your garden, it is best to test the soil.

There are two main ways of doing this, either with a chemical testing kit or a pH meter. The results from either method give a pH reading for the soil. This is a graduated scale in which pH7 represents neutral, neither acid nor alkaline (limy). Lower pH numbers indicate acidity, higher ones alkalinity. Chemical testing kits are quite complicated to use, involving shaking up samples of soil with water and an indicator chemical, then checking the colour of the resultant solution against a chart. It is difficult to take more than one or two readings quickly by this method.

A pH meter is far easier to use. You simply push a metal probe into the soil and see where a needle moves to on a graduated scale. The great benefit of a meter is that it can be used to take many readings quickly. It is surprising how much soil pH can vary over quite short distances within a garden. It's worth noting, however, that pH meters sold for garden use are not always very accurate and can be difficult to use well. Soil needs to be sufficiently moist and compacted to give a good reading. Dry or loose soil will give readings too close to neutral.

An ideal garden soil, in which most plants will grow at least moderately well, will give a reading of about pH6 to 6.5. Lower readings are not a serious problem, as lime can easily be added to soil if necessary. Few plants need very alkaline soil, a pH of about 6.5 to 6.8 being high enough for virtually all to thrive. Readings higher than pH6.5, on the other hand, will make it difficult to grow lime-hating plants with any success at all. A soil pH of 7 or more will make it virtually impossible. Although limy soils cannot really be successfully acidified, it can be worth applying chemicals to lower the pH of soils just on the acid side of neutral. Flowers of sulphur mixed into the soil will make it more acid, but it is not often easy to obtain this in large quantities. Many garden centres sell ferrous sulphate, a chemical containing iron and sulphur, which also does the job. The iron content is useful, because most lime-hating plants benefit from the addition of iron to the soil. As a rough guide, the application of about 4.5kg (10lb) of ferrous sulphate to an area of about 10sq m (100sq ft) will reduce pH from 7 to 6. The ferrous sulphate can be scattered on the surface of the soil and watered in with rainwater. Only use the local tap water if it is soft, that is, not alkaline. The treated soil should be left for a few days and its pH tested again before any planting is done. A pH of about 6 is low enough for virtually all lime-hating plants to thrive. The ideal pH for most rhododendrons is about pH5 to 5.5, but most will grow perfectly well where the pH is about 6 and few are likely to suffer serious problems until the pH exceeds 6.5. If the soil pH is found to be rising again some time after it has been treated, more ferrous sulphate may be applied to the surface of the soil occasionally to maintain acidity. It is best to apply sparingly and often, rather than scattering a lot at one time, for plant roots may be damaged by temporary high concentrations of the chemical.

If testing shows a soil to be alkaline, this may not necessarily be natural. It is common practice to apply lime to garden soil and this may have been done in your garden in the past. Building work can also make soil more limy. Both cement and plaster are very alkaline materials. If pH readings are considerably higher in some parts of the garden than in others, it is quite likely that the natural soil pH has been altered by artificial means. In this case, it may well be worthwhile to treat soil with a pH higher than 7 to reduce its alkalinity.

SOIL PREPARATION

Most broad-leaved evergreens, especially those that are lime-hating, like humus-rich soil. Well-rotted leaf mould is very beneficial. Home-made garden compost, composted bark, very well-rotted manure (particularly horse manure, which contains plenty of plant fibres) and similar materials are good alternatives. Many of these materials are naturally acid and tend to acidify the soil. They should be well mixed into the soil before planting and applied as a mulch around established plants from time to time.

Preparation of soil before planting makes an enormous difference to how well plants grow. It is hard to stress this point too much. Plenty of work on the soil before planting should mean that plants grow strongly and healthily and need comparatively little attention afterwards. Meanwhile, plants in poorly prepared soil often mope and make weak, sickly growth.

Soil should be dug, or at least broken up, to a minimum depth of 45cm (18in). Double-digging is highly recommended, or at least digging to one spade's depth and breaking up the soil to a further spade's depth with a fork. Heavy soils need more breaking up than light ones. Plenty of humus should be incorporated during digging and mixed well into the soil. It is essential to ensure that drainage is adequate. If soil remains waterlogged for more than a couple of days at a time, most broad-leaved evergreens will suffer. If problem drainage cannot be solved by digging and improving the soil, then the simplest solution is to create raised beds. Raising the soil level in the beds by as little as 15cm (6in) helps considerably, especially for shallow-rooting plants such as rhododendrons. Very poor drainage may necessitate the installation of land drains and a soakaway.

After the planting site has been prepared, it is best to leave it for several days to allow the soil to settle. Weed seeds may germinate in the freshly dug soil and it is easy to kill the seedlings by hoeing while the ground is still clear. When ready to plant, check the position for planting to ensure that there is adequate space for what you are going to put in. It is very easy to overplant, for it is hard to visualize that what is now just a small young shrub may soon be several metres across. As a rough guide, large shrubs should be allowed a circular space 2.4 to 3m (8 to 10ft) across, medium shrubs a space about 1.8m (6ft) across and small shrubs one about 90cm to 1.2m (3 to 4ft) across. Allowance should be made for habit; upright shrubs need less space and spreading ones more. It is best to measure distances, if only roughly. Large gaps between newly planted trees and shrubs can be filled with temporary herbaceous plantings or low ground cover. Plants such as Lesser Periwinkle (*Vinca minor*) and Dead-nettle (*Lamium maculatum*) are excellent for this purpose. As the trees and shrubs grow, the plants between them can be removed as necessary or just left to be smothered.

PLANTING

When planting, always dig a hole much bigger than the root-ball of the plant. Ensure that the soil beneath the planting site has been well broken up and work humus-rich material into it. Then, before either removing the plant from its pot or unwrapping the root-ball, place the plant in the hole and check that the depth is correct. After planting, the soil should just cover the surface of the original soil or compost that the plant was grown in, by no more than 12mm (½in).

Planting a small Holm Oak (*Quercus ilex*) in grass. Remove a circle of turf around 1.2m (4ft) in diameter and turn the soil over to a good depth using a fork and spade. A rotavator is not essential, but makes the task much easier

Break up the soil well to more than a spade's depth, then dig out a hole considerably larger than the root-ball of the plant. Break up the soil at the bottom of the hole with a fork and add humus (e.g. leaf-mould)

Mix the soil at the bottom of the hole with the humus and tread firm. Place the plant in the hole to check the depth. After making adjustments, remove the plant from its pot and put it into its final position

Fill the hole around the plant's roots with a mixture of soil and humus, then tread firm. Mix some fertilizer into the top few inches of soil and water thoroughly. Finish off with a mulch of composted bark or similar material

Once the depth has been adjusted, the plant can be removed from its pot and placed in the hole. If it is root-balled, loosen the wrapping before placing the plant in the hole and only unwrap its roots completely afterwards. Small potted plants can be turned upside down, supported by one hand on the surface of the compost, while the other hand knocks the rim of the pot upwards to loosen it. If it is awkward to remove the plant in this way, slit the side of the pot with a knife, taking care to cause as little damage to the roots as possible, and peel the pot away from the roots. If the plant is very pot-bound, with roots circling inside the base of the pot, try to loosen the roots and spread them around the base of the planting hole.

Once the plant is in the hole with any pot or wrapping removed, soil can be filled around it. Mix the soil to be used about half and half with humus-rich compost. It is also a good idea to mix in a handful of a balanced slow-release fertilizer – one without too much nitrogen is best. Bone meal is often recommended, but as it contains calcium it should not be used on lime-hating plants unless the soil is naturally very acid, when it should do no harm. The smell of bone meal sometimes encourages animals, particularly foxes, to dig in the hope of finding something to eat. This can, of course, result in serious root disturbance. If you think this might occur, leave a small pile of bone meal on the surface so that animals can investigate it without digging.

Firm down the soil around the plant by treading on it, adding more soil to fill as necessary. Then give the plant a good watering, both to ensure that it is not short of moisture and to settle the soil. Finally, a mulch of leaf-mould or similar material may be applied around the base of the plant. This is most beneficial for woodland plants, especially those that are shallow rooting, such as rhododendrons. It is essential to ensure that newly planted broad-leaved evergreens are kept well watered until they have established a good root system, which may take a year or more. This is particularly important if they are planted under trees or close to established large shrubs, which may take up a lot of water from the soil, leaving little for the young plants. If tap water is hard, or limy, it should not be used for watering lime-hating plants. It is in any case good practice to collect rainwater for watering the garden. It will save money if tap water is metered.

When planting in woodland it may be difficult to dig a large area thoroughly because of thick tree roots. Use a fork to probe the ground and find a site reasonably clear of roots, then dig as thoroughly as possible. Small tree roots should be cut through cleanly to minimize the risk of disease entering the wound. Try to avoid cutting the roots of trees such as poplars, cherries, hawthorns and willows, as suckers are likely to grow from cut roots. As long as a substantial hole can be dug to a depth of at least 38cm (15in), most reasonably vigorous shrubs and climbers should establish well. If, after loosening the soil, it is full of pieces of chopped roots, it is best to remove it and replace it with clean soil from elsewhere in the garden. Whether it is reused or not, taking loose soil out of the hole and putting it temporarily in a wheelbarrow, makes digging as deeply as possible easier.

WIND DAMAGE

Broad-leaved evergreens tend to be susceptible to damage by strong winds, particularly during cold weather. Leaf stalks may be broken by wind, or leaves may be browned, usually beginning near the tips and along the margins. In severe cases whole leaves and even branches may be killed. Light damage will make the plant look unsightly until new growth has hidden the browned foliage, but severe damage may result in the death of the plant.

Large-leaved plants tend to be more susceptible to wind damage than small-leaved ones. The only remedy is to provide shelter to break the force of the winds. Planting more wind-resistant plants as wind-breaks is the ideal method, but wooden screening or fencing can also help. Close-boarded fencing is too impermeable to wind, which will whip over the top and underneath it, if there's a gap, causing draughts and eddies which may be at least as damaging as if there was no fence. Woven panels or other kinds of fencing which the wind can partly blow through are best. A very good screen can be made by setting wooden posts into the ground at intervals of up to about 1.8m (6ft) and fixing boards about 10cm (4in) wide between them, with gaps up to about 12mm (½in) wide between the boards. Such a screen can be made even more effective by growing Common Ivy (*Hedera helix*) up it. The height of the screen should ideally be at least 1.8m (6ft), but can be lower if it is only intended to provide shelter to small shrubs. There is information on wind-resistant hedges provided in Section 2.

SNOW

Even in areas where heavy falls of snow are infrequent, it is unwise to ignore the potential harm they can do. Broad-leaved evergreens are generally very susceptible to damage caused by the accumulation of snow on their branches. Their persistent foliage holds the snow much more than the bare branches of deciduous trees and shrubs. It is difficult to protect them from such damage, except by shaking snow off them whenever it threatens to accumulate too much. Small plants may be covered with a conical framework of canes or similar supports with horticultural fleece wrapped tightly around it. The cone should be tall in relation to its diameter so that the sides slope steeply, allowing snow to slide off. If branches do get broken by the weight of accumulated snow, they should be pruned off cleanly below the break. Most broad-leaved evergreens will recover well, even if it takes some time for the slower-growing ones to regain a good shape.

A correctly pruned shoot of Holly (*Ilex aquifolium*)

PRUNING

Broad-leaved evergreens need rather more care after planting than deciduous plants, mainly because they will lose water from their leaves during winter and therefore need to be kept adequately watered and protected from drying winds. In the longer term, however, they require less attention, as they need a minimum of pruning.

The general rule is to cut away dead wood and unhealthy shoots, but otherwise to leave them alone. They may need a little trimming to encourage shapely growth (many can be clipped into formal shapes or hedges), but the best advice on pruning is: 'If in doubt, don't!' Details of how to prune particular plants are given in Section 3 when necessary. Most broad-leaved evergreens are quite slow growing and should usually keep a good shape naturally. If they grow too large, they can either be trimmed regularly to keep them under control or, with very few exceptions, they can be cut back hard every few years. Almost all will send out plenty of new shoots from old wood and soon grow into a good shape again. The usual principles of good pruning apply. Dead, unhealthy and damaged shoots are often best cut out completely, back to the junction with a healthy branch. The cut should be made cleanly, as close to the joint as possible, leaving only a very short stump. If a branch needs to be shortened, it should be cut just above the base of a leaf. There should be a bud where the leaf joins the stem, from which new growth will be made. Angle the cut slightly away from the bud, unless the leaves grow in pairs, when the cut should be straight across the stem. Do not cut too close or too far from the bud – just under 6mm ($^1/_4$in) is ideal. Cutting too close to the bud often results in the shoot dying back beyond the bud to the next one. It is better to cut a little too long than a little too short. Always use sharp tools so that the cuts are as clean as possible. For hedges and topiary, shears and mechanical hedge trimmers can be used on plants with small leaves up to about 7.5cm (3in) long. Those with larger leaves will usually look unsightly if clipped with these tools because most leaves will be cut across. Mechanical hedge trimmers tend to shred large leaves, leaving them with ragged cut ends. Ideally, hedges of large-leaved shrubs such as *Aucuba japonica*, Cherry Laurel (*Prunus laurocerasus*) and rhododendrons should be pruned to shape with secateurs. This is very time-consuming, but the end result will be much better.

Trellis around 1.8 x 1.2m (6 x 4ft) made of lengths of wood 12mm sq (½in sq), screwed to wood blocks fixed to a wall. This trellis is suitable for twining plants. Covered with wire mesh, it would be good for clematis or mutisia

SUPPORTS FOR CLIMBERS

Many evergreen climbers are self-clinging and need no more than initial encouragement to climb up walls, trees and fences. *Decumaria, Ercilla, Euonymus fortunei, Hedera, Hydrangea, Pileostegia* and *Trachelospermum* all produce aerial roots. At most, they only need to be trained in the right direction and will then cling to almost any vertical surface.

One or two canes should be pushed into the planting hole when they are planted and angled to touch the surface up which they are to climb. Longer shoots can then be fastened loosely to the cane or canes with string or plastic ties. Once the shoots have reached the wall, fence or tree, they can be left largely to their own devices and should climb with no further encouragement. It is not necessary to provide trellis or other support for these climbers. *Holboellia* and *Lonicera* climb by twining. They will not cling naturally to a wall or a close-boarded fence so other support must be provided. In the wild, they twist around the branches of shrubs and trees and will readily do the same in cultivation. They will not twine around very thick tree trunks, however, and need to be given long canes or poles to grow up until they reach smaller branches.

An ideal trellis for fixing to walls and fences, or left free-standing, can be made from batons of wood about 12 to 25mm sq (½ to 1in sq), treated with wood preservative. One lot of batons should be laid on a hard surface parallel to each other and about 15cm (6in) apart. Another lot should then be laid across them at right angles, also parallel to each other at about the same spacing. The batons can then be pinned or nailed together wherever they cross. If the trellis is to be fixed to a wall or fence, blocks of wood at least 25mm (1in) thick should be used to mount it on, so that it is held away from the surface. Screw rather than nail it to the blocks so that it can be unscrewed whenever it needs to be taken down. If the trellis is to be free-standing, it can be fixed to upright posts. The plant that is to grow up the trellis should be able to twine around the batons and not have to be fastened to it with ties.

Clematis and *Mutisia* do not have twining stems. *Clematis* leaves twist around available supports, but will not twist around anything very thick. The same is true of the tendrils of *Mutisia*. These plants are best provided with wire-mesh supports. The mesh should be quite large, especially for *Clematis*. Chicken wire or something similar is fine. It should be stretched over some kind of support, such as trellis, and held away from the surface to which it is fixed. Some of the trellis and other support for climbers sold in garden centres is of poor design and most climbers need to be fastened to it to climb successfully. *Rubus henryi* will not fasten itself readily to any support. It does not really climb at all, but scrambles like brambles, the hooked prickles catching on branches of trees and shrubs to support the long stems. It will need to be fastened to whatever surface it is to cover.

PROPAGATION

There are two distinct means of propagating plants, by seeds or vegetatively. Seeds are produced sexually, by the fertilization of ovules by pollen. Sexual reproduction encourages genetic variation, so plants grown from seed often differ to some extent from the parent plant on which the seed developed. This variation may well be important to gardeners. If a plant has been specially selected because it has characteristics that are exceptional in its species, plants grown from its seed may not share those features and may therefore be less ornamental. If the seed parent is of hybrid origin, its offspring are highly likely to differ considerably. Bear in mind that some hybrids do not bear fertile seed. Note that if seed is collected from named cultivars, the seedlings will probably not be identical with the parent and therefore cannot bear the parent's cultivar name. It's also possible that the seed may be the result of cross-pollination with a plant of a different species, making the resultant seedlings hybrids. Nevertheless, if it is available, seed is the best way to propagate in quantity. If a long hedge of a particular kind of plant is desired, for example, buying sufficient plants is likely to be expensive. Growing them from seed may take a little longer but will be very much cheaper. Some plants are difficult to propagate by any other means.

Vegetative propagation is a blanket term covering many techniques, including taking cuttings, layering and grafting. What they have in common is that no sexual process is involved. A piece of a plant is encouraged to root and grow as a separate plant. The resulting new plant will be genetically identical with its parent, sharing all its characteristics. Selected cultivars and hybrids must be propagated vegetatively if the new plants are to be identical and bear the parent's name. Plants produced by vegetative methods of propagation usually reach a good size more rapidly than seed-grown plants. It may, however, be difficult to obtain more than a limited number of new plants by vegetative methods.

Seeds

Many broad-leaved evergreens are difficult to grow from seed, even if seed can be obtained. This should not put anyone off trying, however. It can be very rewarding to watch seedlings germinate and grow. Even if the resulting plants are not wanted personally, other gardeners are often willing to exchange plants for something that is wanted. It does not take very long to sow a few pots of seed each year and very little is lost even if there is no germination at all. Usually the seeds that do germinate make up for those that do not.

Seed is best obtained as fresh as possible. The fresher the seed, the more likely it is to germinate and, very often, the more rapidly germination is likely to occur. It is ideal if seed can be collected from plants in the garden. If you want to grow something that is not in your garden, you will have to find another source.

There are many approaches to seed sowing and various recommendations can be found in gardening literature. My own approach is quite simplistic. It may not necessarily be the best, but it gives good results much of the time. I believe in sowing seed as soon as possible after it is obtained. This is close to what happens in the wild. Ripe seed should remain viable in damp compost in a pot, whereas if it is stored dry it may not survive. If seed is sown in autumn it will often not germinate until the following spring. If it is saved and not sown until spring it may either not germinate at all or remain dormant and not germinate until the following year. Different plants vary, but as a rule of thumb I believe this approach is as good as most others.

The seed of many broad-leaved evergreens may not germinate for some time after sowing, so it is essential to use compost that will remain in good condition for a long time. This means avoiding peat-based composts. A good soil-based compost is the best for most purposes. Note that most commercial soil-based composts have lime added to them, so they cannot be used for plants that need acid soils. For growing plants such as rhododendrons from seed, some other compost must be used. It can be worth making your own, but this means having to sterilize the ingredients used for making it, otherwise it may contain weed seeds, fungi and all kinds of undesirable organisms. Sterilization can be done simply by placing material in an old tin and heating it in an oven to at least 100°C (212°F) for an hour or so.

Use pots for sowing the seeds of broad-leaved evergreens, unless they can be sown in the open ground. Open-ground sowing should only be carried out when plenty of seed is available or for very large seeds. Even so, some protection against pests is likely to give better results. Sowing in pots allows better control of conditions. For example, pots are easy to move from inside a greenhouse or cold frame to outside. Pots are better than seed trays because they are deeper and allow roots to grow longer before transplanting becomes necessary.

Put some drainage material at the bottom of the pot. Traditionally, broken pieces of clay plant pots were used for drainage, but, as plastic pots have largely replaced clay ones, clean gravel is an acceptable alternative, or a good handful of composted bark. Fill the pot almost full with soil-based seed compost, which may be mixed with composted bark for plants that like a humus-rich soil. Press the compost down until it is firm, then add more and repeat until the right level is reached. This level will depend on the size of the seeds. Large seeds should be sown about 12mm (1/2in) deep, smaller ones only about 6mm (1/4in) deep. Very tiny seeds may not need covering at all. The seeds can be scattered on the surface of the compost, or larger ones may be individually pressed lightly into it, and then covered either with sand, more compost or composted bark. For plants that like dry, sunny conditions, use sand or compost. For those that like moist conditions, composted bark is better. Then water the pots until they are well soaked. If the seeds are very small, it is best to water by standing the pots in a container with some water in it and allowing the water to soak upwards into the compost.

Pots containing tiny seeds that have been left uncovered should have a sheet of glass or plastic put on top of them to prevent the surface of the compost from drying out. Alternatively, the top of the pot can be covered with cling film. All pots should then be placed in a cool, shady place, preferably in a cold frame or an unheated glasshouse, and left until germination begins. They may need to be watered from time to time.

Some seeds need to be exposed to frost before they will germinate, so if the pots are in a cold frame, it is good to leave the frame open on dry, frosty nights. Pots in a glasshouse can be moved outside during dry, frosty weather. Once the seeds begin to germinate, the pots can be moved to a lighter place and watered more often. Seedlings should be carefully transplanted into individual pots as soon as they are large enough to be handled easily. They should be held by the leaves, not by the stems, when they are transplanted. They may need to be repotted once or twice into larger pots before they are big enough to be planted into their final positions in the garden.

Suckers

Plants which send up rooted shoots from the base can be propagated very easily by separating these shoots, or suckers, from the parent plant. This can often be done by carefully digging away the soil near the base of a sucker until the point where it rises from the main plant is exposed, then cutting it off, ensuring that the part cut away has some of its own roots. The sucker can then be planted separately as a new plant. If it has only a few roots it should be shortened, pruning it back to just above where a side branch or leaf arises from it. Weak suckers are best put into pots and grown on under glass until they have developed into strong plants. To obtain several young plants from one old plant with many basal shoots, the whole plant can be lifted in late autumn or early spring and divided. Suckering broad-leaved evergreens include bamboos, some *Berberis* species and hybrids, *Danae, Gaultheria, Leucothoe, Mahonia, Nandina, Ruscus, Sarcococca* and *Vaccinium*.

Cuttings

Most, but not all, woody plants can be propagated by cuttings. The rooting of cuttings can be improved by the use of hormone rooting powder and by applying gentle heat to the compost into which they have been inserted. Anyone intending to grow many plants from cuttings should consider buying a large propagator with a cover and provision for providing bottom heat. Even plants that grow quite easily from cuttings usually benefit from the use of a propagator with bottom heat, as the cuttings will root more quickly. An unheated propagator is less useful and really no better than the cheap alternative of placing a clear plastic bag over the top of a pot full of cuttings. Otherwise, little equipment is needed for taking cuttings. The essentials are a pair of secateurs and a sharp knife.

A cutting is basically just a piece of a branch cut off a plant and put into soil or compost in the hope that it will grow roots. Some plants root extremely easily. Almost any piece of willow (*Salix*), for example, will root if pushed into damp soil. Willow cuttings can even be pushed the wrong way up into soil and will often still grow! Most plants, however, need much more careful treatment. Comparatively few broad-leaved evergreens grow very readily from cuttings and with quite a number it is not worth attempting to propagate them by this method. Among the easiest to grow are Box (*Buxus* species), Cherry Laurel (*Prunus laurocerasus*), *Aucuba japonica* and Rosemary (*Rosmarinus officinalis*). It is probably best to start by trying to grow some of these from cuttings. When success has been achieved with these, more difficult plants can be tried.

The best time to take cuttings varies from plant to plant and is indicated in individual entries in Section 3.

Winter cuttings of holly taken without a heel. These are the tips of young shoots cut off with clean, sharp secateurs

The cuttings trimmed and ready for planting, with rooting powder and a pot filled with soil-based seed compost

The ends of the cuttings are dampened before being dipped into rooting powder and then inserted into the compost. Putting three into one pot allows for one or two to fail

Most plants grow best taken from cuttings of fairly young growth, less than a year old. Older, well-ripened wood rarely roots readily.

The simplest cuttings are the top few inches of a shoot, trimmed to just below where a leaf grows from the stem, with the tip of the shoot cut off and all the lower leaves removed. Non-flowering shoots should be chosen for cuttings. About three or four leaves should be left on the cutting. The length of bare stem below the lowest leaf should be at least as long as the portion of stem that has leaves left on it. The bottom end of the stem should then be inserted either into well-tilled soil in a shady, sheltered place in the open garden or into compost in a pot. The soil or compost should then be watered well and kept constantly damp until the cutting has produced a good root system. This basic method is fine for many plants. Success can be improved with a number of refinements. Firstly, the bottom ends of cuttings can be dipped into hormone rooting powder before they are put into soil or compost. If they are very dry the ends should be dampened with clean water first, so that the powder clings to them. This should speed up the production of roots. Secondly, the cuttings can be taken with a heel of old wood. Side shoots are removed from a branch with a sharp knife, cutting a small sliver of wood from the branch to form the bottom end of each cutting. The cuttings are then treated like ordinary cuttings. *Ceanothus* and *Pyracantha* are among broad-leaved evergreens that root much better if cuttings are taken with a heel. Camellias are often propagated using leaf-bud cuttings. These are similar to cuttings taken with a heel, except that just a leaf, with its basal bud, is cut off with the heel, rather than a side shoot. Leaf-bud cuttings should be placed into compost with the whole of the heel and most of the leaf stalk buried, leaving only the leaf above the surface. Thirdly, cuttings can be covered with some kind of clear covering to keep the air around the leaves humid and to prevent the cuttings from drying out. The simplest way of doing this is to push a couple of hoops of wire into the pot containing the cuttings and put a clear plastic bag over the wires and the top of the pot. The bag can be secured by placing a rubber band over it just below the rim of the pot. A few small holes should be made in the bag to allow some circulation of air. Propagators with clear plastic covers can be bought which serve the same purpose.

Loss of water from leaves of broad-leaved evergreens can be very great. It is highest in plants with large leaves, such as many rhododendrons. Very large leaves are best cut to about a third to a half of their original length. Leaves may also be sprayed with the same spray that is used to prevent Christmas trees dropping their needles.

Finally, many cuttings root better if the compost they are in is warm. Water loss from leaves increases with higher temperatures, so ideally the compost should be warmed but not the air above the compost. Heat is therefore best supplied from below. Propagators with heating elements to provide such bottom heat are available and are very helpful for cuttings of many plants. All cuttings are best kept shaded until they have rooted well.

Layering

Some plants tend to root naturally if their branches come into contact with the soil, especially if the branches become buried – under fallen leaves, for example. The lower branches of hollies (*Ilex* species and hybrids) often root like this. Such rooted branches can be cut off with the roots, shortened if necessary, and planted as new plants.

Many broad-leaved evergreens can be propagated by encouraging them to root in this way. This propagation method is known as layering. A flexible young branch should be bent down until it touches the soil about 20 to 30cm (8 to 12in) from its tip. A wide hole is dug where it comes to the ground and partly filled with compost, well-rotted leaf-mould or composted bark. A shallow cut is made in the shoot at the point where it touches the ground, slicing upwards towards the tip of the shoot. The cut should not be too deep, not as far as the middle of the shoot. The wounded shoot is then pegged down into the hole with a small hoop of wire or a forked twig and buried. If necessary, the shoot can be held down with a brick or stone. The layer should be kept well watered and left for at least a year before it is checked for roots. Once it has rooted, it can be separated from the parent plant.

Layering is a very easy way to propagate climbers. Those that produce aerial roots, as many broad-leaved evergreen climbers do, will root very readily if pegged down into the soil. Long shoots can be pegged down

A sleeve of plastic wrapped around a prepared stem of *Osmanthus* x *fortunei* and tied at the lower end. The other end is open so that it can be filled with rooting medium such as moss and composted bark

Once enough rooting medium has been put into the sleeve and moistened, both ends are tied firmly around the stem. Leaving the ends of the string long makes untying easier later on

at several points along their length and will produce a new plant at each point. Layering of broad-leaved evergreens is best carried out in autumn or early spring. *Rubus henryi*, like other plants of its genus, will root at the tips of its long shoots if they are buried in the ground.

Air-layering is a similar method of propagation which can be used when no branch can easily be bent down to the ground. Instead of taking the branch to the soil, the soil, or a rooting medium, is brought to the branch. A strong young shoot should be selected and a few leaves removed from it towards the base of the current year's growth. A very shallow slice should be pared off the side of the shoot at the point where a leaf grew and some rooting powder applied to the wound. Take care not to weaken the shoot too much in case it should break. A piece of polythene sheeting at least 10cm (4in) wide and 20cm (8in) long should then be wrapped loosely around the wounded part of the stem and secured tightly with string below the cut. Open up the untied end of the polythene into a funnel shape and fill it with a rooting mixture of composted bark and moss. Moisten this mixture, and then close up the top end of the polythene around the shoot and tie it up. This should form something shaped rather like a Christmas cracker of polythene, filled with the rooting medium, with the shoot running through the middle. The wound on the shoot should be completely covered by the rooting medium and polythene. Wait for at least three months before opening the top end of the polythene tube to see if roots have grown. Once they have, the polythene can be removed and the shoot severed just below the roots with secateurs. The new plant can then be put into a pot and grown on until it is robust enough to be planted in the garden.

Grafting

Grafting is quite a specialized technique and is in any case not needed for the propagation of most broad-leaved evergreens. For those reasons, it will not be described here. Anyone wishing to try it should consult other specialist publications.

SECTION 2

USING BROAD-LEAVED EVERGREENS *in the* GARDEN

USING BROAD-LEAVED EVERGREENS IN THE GARDEN

CREATING A GARDEN is a three-dimensional art. In many gardens, vertical structure is created using what is known as hard landscaping, in other words, walls, buildings, fences, arches, trellis and so on. In the majority of gardens, however, it is the plants that provide the most important vertical elements. Yet if only herbaceous and deciduous plants are used, much of this structure is lost during winter. Evergreens are essential if a year-round effect is to be obtained.

It has become common to use evergreen conifers as an important element in garden design, yet much less attention has been paid in recent times to the role of broad-leaved evergreens. This was not always the case, for they were heavily used in the formal gardens that were in fashion until the eighteenth century. Clipped box, holly and other such plants, even some that are now comparative rarities in gardens, like *Phillyrea*, were the absolute essence of these formal gardens. They provided the foundation and framework upon which they were built. When the formal garden was rejected in favour of the English landscape style, broad-leaved evergreens seem also to have gone out of favour. In later years it became fashionable to grow certain kinds, such as rhododendrons and camellias, but the concept of broad-leaved evergreens as a group of plants now seems scarcely to exist in the minds of gardeners, which is a great pity.

The usefulness of evergreens is largely self-evident. They provide permanent form and foliage effects which, though not necessarily unchanging, are at least not lost for several months every year. They can provide year-round screening. Many make excellent hedges. Their foliage is attractive in itself, and also gives a background against which to show off other plants to better effect.

Flowers that open in winter may stand out poorly against a drab backdrop of bare branches but look much better contrasted with a mass of dark green foliage. *Hamamelis* and *Chimonanthus* are good examples of this. Although it has been common in

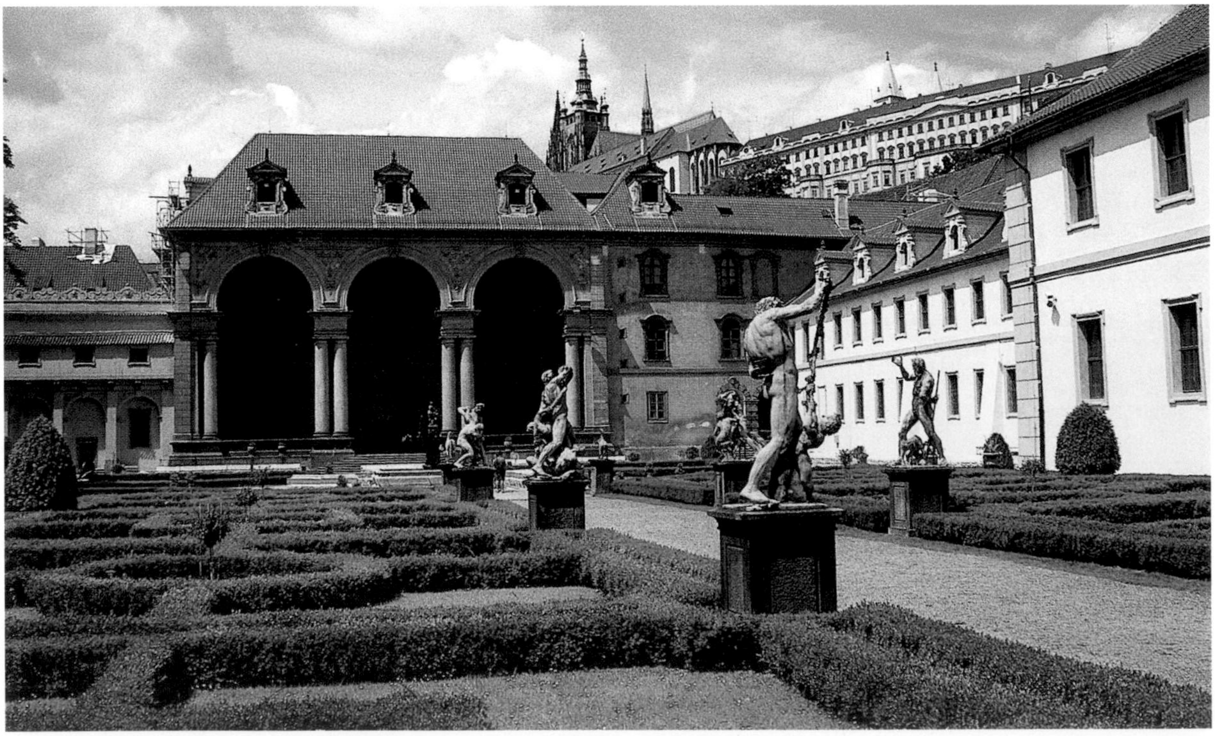

Box hedges and statuary in a formal palace garden in Prague, the Czech Republic

Cotoneaster lacteus **can make a very ornamental hedge**

recent times to use coniferous evergreens for these purposes, broad-leaved evergreens can give a much wider range of foliage effects and generally have a warmer feel. This is probably because they are more typical of tropical and subtropical regions, while coniferous forests are widespread in cold climatic zones. Bamboos, palms, camellias and *Fatsia* are examples of broad-leaved evergreens which can give a subtropical impression, yet some of all these kinds of plants are sufficiently hardy to be grown outdoors in cooler climates such as that of Britain. Broad-leaved evergreens can provide permanent masses of foliage in a wide range of textures and colours. From the very small leaves of box and *Lonicera nitida* through all kinds of intermediates to the large leaves of Cherry Laurel, many rhododendrons, *Viburnum rhytidophyllum* and *Aucuba japonica*, foliage texture for almost any desired effect can be selected. Many broad-leaved evergreens have varieties with coloured or variegated foliage, some, like hollies (*Ilex aquifolium* and *I.* x *altaclerensis*), ivies (*Hedera*) and *Pittosporum tenuifolium*, in many different variations. Whenever year-round foliage is required in a garden, there is usually a broad-leaved evergreen that is a first-rate choice for the purpose.

Another major advantage of broad-leaved evergreens over conifers is that most of them not only carry their foliage throughout the year but also have other ornamental qualities. Many bear very attractive or highly fragrant flowers, unlike conifers. Others produce colourful fruits. Rhododendrons and camellias are among the most beautiful of all flowering plants, while the blue flowers of ceanothus are virtually unique among hardy (or almost hardy) shrubs for the open garden. A large bush of eucryphia covered with white blossom is an unforgettable spectacle, especially because the flowers open in August when few other shrubs are in bloom. The flowers of sarcococcas are scarcely showy, but their sweet scent is a delight during winter. Daphnes and osmanthus also bear strongly fragrant flowers. Cotoneasters and firethorns (*Pyracantha*) are not really outstanding as flowering shrubs, but their flowers are

A large hedge of Cherry Laurel (*Prunus laurocerasus*) looks good and gives effective screening all year round, but it requires a good deal of pruning every year

followed by a profusion of colourful berries. The fruits of *Gaultheria mucronata* in their various colours are also highly ornamental. Hollies bear insignificant flowers, but a large bush with a good crop of berries brightens the dark days of autumn and winter.

Broad-leaved evergreens can bring a kaleidoscope of colours to the garden, adding seasonal interest of flowers or fruits to their permanent foliage value. Even if they were not evergreen, many would still be desirable garden plants.

One of the essentials of garden design is the definition of spaces and boundaries. For making hedges and screens, broad-leaved evergreens excel over almost all conifers with the exception of Yew (*Taxus baccata*). A major problem with most conifers is that, if they are allowed to grow too large and need to be cut back hard, they frequently produce little or no new growth from old wood. Yew is very much an exception. The commonly planted X *Cupressocyparis leylandii* is one of the worst in this respect. Trimming it needs only to be neglected for a year or two and the hedge will have grown too large. It cannot be cut back heavily without leaving bare patches where little or no regrowth will occur. It will probably need replacing completely.

By contrast, many broad-leaved evergreens can be cut down to ground level if necessary and will send up plenty of leafy young shoots. For really effective barriers, there are broad-leaved evergreens with thorns or prickly leaves, such as firethorns (*Pyracantha*) and holly. Plants for flowering or fruiting hedges are also available. Firethorn is an example of an excellent hedging plant that will produce both flowers and colourful berries. Indeed, it is one of the best of all plants for hedging because it is tough and stands clipping well. Because it tends to produce side shoots more or less at right angles to the main branches, it makes a dense hedge well furnished to ground level. Its thorns make it especially good for deterring both animals and intruders.

The toughest broad-leaved evergreens for resisting cold winds are the Common Holly (*Ilex aquifolium*) and the Highclere Holly (*Ilex* x *altaclerensis*), *Elaeagnus* x *ebbingei, Rhododendron ponticum, Rhododendron catawbiense* and a number of hybrid rhododendrons, including 'Cunningham's White' and 'Fastuosum Flore Pleno'. It should be noted that cultivars with variegated foliage are usually less tough than green-leaved plants. The hollies and *Elaeagnus* can be clipped and will make either formal or informal hedges or can

A hawthorn hedge with ivy growing through it

The dense foliage of *Viburnum davidii* can make good ground cover

be left unclipped as screens. The hardiest bamboos, particularly *Fargesia murieliae*, are also very good for wind-breaks. The taller bamboos make excellent informal hedges and screens. They are very effective planted next to buildings, walls and solid fences to soften the appearance of hard, vertical surfaces. Bamboos move with the slightest breeze and cast lovely patterns of shadow when sun falls on them. They can look particularly striking planted close to water. Traditionally, no Chinese gardener felt a garden to be complete without bamboo and it is easy to understand why. Some of them, such as the *Fargesia* species, are extremely hardy and can be grown successfully in very cold areas, so there is little reason for any garden to be without them.

In sites subject to very strong, cold winds almost all broad-leaved evergreens are likely to suffer, so it is best to use very hardy deciduous shrubs to make wind-breaks. An excellent, very hardy, impenetrable hedge can be made by planting seedlings of hawthorn (*Crataegus monogyna*, often sold for hedging as quickthorn) in a double or triple row about 15cm (6in) apart. About one to three years after planting, when they have grown to at least 60cm (2ft) tall, small young plants of Common Ivy (*Hedera helix*) may be planted at the base of the hawthorn hedge. As the ivy grows into the hawthorn it will make the hedge denser and also evergreen. Such a hedge can be clipped to the required height and will be an excellent barrier and wind-break.

To make planting the ivy easier, it is useful to set plastic plant pots into the ground at intervals of about 30 to 45cm (12 to 18in) when the hawthorn is planted. The pots should be fairly easy to remove after a year or two when the hawthorn has grown large enough. Ivy can then be planted into the holes. The size of the pots is not critical; clearly they do not need to be very big but should not be too small. This avoids disturbing the roots of the hawthorn. In areas where ivy occurs naturally, seedlings will probably appear at the base of hedges naturally, but deliberate planting is quicker and ensures more even distribution of ivy in the hedge.

Close to the sea, winds are less likely to be very cold but they will probably carry salt. Many broad-leaved evergreens are highly susceptible to damage by salt-laden winds. Quite a number, however, are salt-tolerant, particularly those from the Mediterranean region,

New Zealand and California. Good plants for screening against salty winds are *Elaeagnus* species and hybrids, most escallonias, *Euonymus japonicus*, garryas, *Griselinia littoralis*, most hollies, *Myrica cerifera*, most olearias, phillyreas, most pittosporums, pyracanthas, *Quercus ilex*, *Rhamnus alaternus* and *Viburnum tinus*. All of these will make good hedges. Cistuses and hebes, though generally not very tall and therefore of limited use for screening, are also very tolerant of coastal exposure.

The permanent foliage of evergreens shades the ground beneath them throughout the year and tends to discourage the growth of weeds. Well-established plants will smother most weeds quite effectively. For this reason, broad-leaved evergreens are often used as ground cover. This subject is not covered fully in this book, which excludes most low-growing plants, but low shrubs such as *Viburnum davidii* and a number of climbers, including ivies (*Hedera*) and *Euonymus fortunei*, are often grown as ground cover. Larger broad-leaved evergreens are good plants for wild gardens because of their weed-suppressing qualities. Very few weeds will grow beneath most of the larger rhododendrons, for instance.

Bamboo growing in a corner of a Chinese courtyard. It softens the otherwise hard and austere lines of the paved courtyard and buildings

Many broad-leaved evergreens are exotic in appearance and can give a tropical feel to a garden. Good examples are bamboos, the Chusan Palm (*Trachycarpus fortunei*), *Fatsia japonica* and camellias. If such plants are grouped together, perhaps enclosed and sheltered by hedges or screens of tougher large-leaved evergreens like Cherry Laurel or hardy rhododendrons, complete tropical-style gardens can be created. These are often very successful in urban areas where warmth and shelter from buildings can help to provide good growing conditions. Similarly, gardens that are at their best in winter can be made by grouping together plants such as early-flowering camellias, sarcococcas, *Aucuba, Daphne bholua*, garryas, mahonias, skimmias and *Sycopsis*.

In warmer areas, especially near coasts, it is easy to create gardens in Mediterranean style using broad-leaved evergreens. Native Mediterranean plants can form the backbone of such gardens. There is a wide choice of these, including *Cistus*, *Phillyrea*, *Viburnum tinus*, *Myrtus communis*, Bay (*Laurus nobilis*) and Rosemary (*Rosmarinus officinalis*). Plants that assort well with these include many from New Zealand, such as hebes, olearias, pittosporums and *Griselinia littoralis*, as well as some Californian plants like *Carpenteria* and *Ceanothus*, and the Mexican *Choisya*. Shelter from sea winds can be provided by hedges or screens of *Elaeagnus* x *ebbingei*, escallonias or *Euonymus japonicus*. Most of these plants like plenty of sun and a light, sandy soil.

By contrast, there are many broad-leaved evergreens that enjoy cool, moist, partly shady conditions. These are mainly woodland plants in the wild and will flourish very happily among mature trees in gardens. Some will tolerate heavy shade, among them *Aucuba japonica*, hollies (*Ilex*), mahonias, *Osmanthus decorus*, *Ruscus*, *Skimmia*, many viburnums and, of course, ivies (*Hedera*).

In open woodland on acid soils, especially in areas with fairly high rainfall, beautiful gardens featuring many rhododendrons can be made. While the majority of rhododendrons flower in spring and early summer, there are also very early- and very late-flowering species and hybrids. By choosing carefully, it is possible to have rhododendrons flowering in the garden for at least six months of the year. Colour and

Rhododendrons thriving in a woodland garden

interest can be brought to the garden for the rest of the year using plants such as cotoneasters, *Aucuba*, skimmias and *Gaultheria mucronata* for colourful fruits in autumn and winter and sarcococcas, *Daphne bholua*, mahonias and sycopsis for attractive and scented flowers during winter. In woodland on limy soils rhododendrons are ruled out, but there are many lime-tolerant plants that can replace them, including viburnums, *Osmanthus* and *Arbutus*.

Broad-leaved evergreens do not, of course, have to be used on their own, but can be mixed with conifers, deciduous trees and shrubs, and herbaceous plants. If the garden is being planned from scratch, it is a good idea to decide where evergreens should be used when designing the basic structure. Remember to consider how the garden will look in winter throughout all planning stages. If modifying an established garden, make decisions while actually looking at the garden during the winter. The correct placing of blocks of evergreens can transform a garden which looks bare and bleak in winter to having a much greener and warmer appearance.

Many gardens are square or rectangular, or at least have predominantly straight boundaries which become very visible during the winter months. These hard, straight lines can be obscured by clumps of bamboo or taller evergreen shrubs. Bamboos are good in small gardens as the taller ones reach a considerable height without spreading too far sideways. Clumps will expand gradually in diameter but their spread can be reduced without sacrificing height.

Plantings of deciduous shrubs and herbaceous plants can be planned around the basic framework of evergreens and will provide stronger seasonal changes, which are inevitable in any garden and can be a great attraction. The balance between various types of evergreens, deciduous trees and shrubs and herbaceous plants must depend on individual preferences, of course, and the type of garden that it is intended to create. Many gardeners, however, aspire to having a garden that looks good and has plenty of interest throughout the whole of the year. A liberal use of broad-leaved evergreens goes a long way towards achieving this ideal.

Lists of broad-leaved evergreens for various effects and purposes follow. In most cases, more detail can be found under the individual entries in Section 3.

CATEGORIES OF BROAD-LEAVED EVERGREENS

FOR HEDGES AND SCREENS (INLAND)

Aucuba japonica, Bamboos (for informal hedges and screens only), Berberis (several species and hybrids, mostly prickly), Buxus, Elaeagnus, Euonymus japonicus, Ilex (prickly), Ligustrum, Lonicera nitida, Osmanthus heterophyllus and O. x burkwoodii, Phillyrea, Prunus, Pyracantha (thorny), Rhododendron (especially the tougher species and hybrids), Quercus ilex, Viburnum tinus

FOR HEDGES AND SCREENS (NEAR COASTS)

Very resistant to salt-laden winds:
Bamboo (Fargesia), Brachyglottis, Elaeagnus x ebbingei, Escallonia, Euonymus japonicus, Hebe, Olearia x haastii, Phillyrea, Quercus ilex

Slightly less resistant to salt-laden winds:
Aucuba japonica, Arbutus, Cassinia, Choisya, Cistus, Cotoneaster, Erica, Eucalyptus, Garrya, Griselinia, Ilex, Myrica, Olearia (apart from O. x haastii), Ozothamnus, Pittosporum, Pyracantha, Rhamnus, Rosmarinus, Viburnum tinus

FOR MEDITERRANEAN-STYLE GARDENS

Arbutus, Bamboo, Brachyglottis, Bupleurum, Camellia, Carpenteria, Cassinia, Ceanothus, Choisya, Cistus, Clematis, Escallonia, Eucryphia, X Fatshedera, Fatsia, Garrya, Griselinia, Hebe, Hedera, Laurus, Ligustrum, Lonicera implexa, Magnolia, Mutisia, Myrtus, Olearia, Ozothamnus, Phillyrea, Pittosporum, Quercus, Rhamnus, Rosmarinus, Trachelospermum, Trachycarpus, Viburnum tinus

FOR TROPICAL-STYLE GARDENS

Bamboo, Camellia, Choisya, Clematis armandii, Daphniphyllum, Decumaria, Eucalyptus, Eucryphia, X Fatshedera, Fatsia, Holboellia, Hydrangea, Magnolia, Mutisia, Myrtus, Nandina, Osmanthus, Pileostegia, Rhaphiolepis, Trachelospermum, Trachycarpus, Trochodendron

FOR WOODLAND GARDENS

Arbutus, Aucuba, Buxus, Daphne, Daphniphyllum, Decumaria, Distylium, Elaeagnus, Euonymus, X Fatshedera, Fatsia, Gaultheria, Hedera, Holboellia, Hydrangea, Ilex, Itea, Leucothoe, Mahonia, Osmanthus, Photinia, Pieris, Pileostegia, Prunus, Quercus, Rhododendron, Sarcococca, Skimmia, Sycopsis, Trochodendron, Vaccinium, Viburnum

WITH LARGE LEAVES

Aucuba, Daphniphyllum, X Fatshedera, Fatsia, Hedera canariensis, Hedera colchica, Magnolia, Mahonia, Osmanthus armatus, Osmanthus yunnanensis, Prunus laurocerasus, Rhododendron (several), Trachycarpus, Viburnum rhytidophyllum

WITH VARIEGATED OR COLOURED FOLIAGE

(some species or varieties):

Aucuba, Bamboo, Brachyglottis, Buxus, Camellia, Cassinia, Choisya, Cistus, Daphne, Elaeagnus, Eucalyptus, Euonymus, X Fatshedera, Fatsia, Griselinia, Hebe, Hedera, Ilex, Laurus, Leucothoe, Ligustrum, Lonicera, Myrtus, Mahonia, Nandina, Olearia, Osmanthus, Ozothamnus, Photinia, Pieris, Pittosporum, Prunus, Pyracantha, Rhamnus, Rhododendron, Vaccinium, Viburnum

WITH FRAGRANT FLOWERS

Daphne, Decumaria, Elaeagnus, Lonicera (some), Magnolia, Mahonia (some), Olearia (some), Osmanthus, Phillyrea angustifolia, Pittosporum, Pyracantha, Rhaphiolepis, Rhododendron (some), Sarcococca, Skimmia (some), Trachelospermum

WITH WHITE, WHITISH OR CREAM FLOWERS

Arbutus (some), Camellia (some), Carpenteria, Cassinia, Choisya, Cistus (some), Clematis (some), Cotoneaster, Daphne (some), Erica (some), Escallonia (some), Eucalyptus, Eucryphia, X Fatshedera, Fatsia, Gaultheria (some), Hebe (some), Hydrangea, Kalmia (some), Leucothoe, Ligustrum, Lonicera (some), Magnolia, Myrtus, Nandina, Olearia (some), Osmanthus, Ozothamnus, Photinia, Pieris (some), Pileostegia, Pittosporum tobira, Prunus, Pyracantha, Rhaphiolepis, Rhododendron (some), Rosmarinus (some), Sarcococca, Skimmia (some), Trachelospermum, Viburnum (some)

WITH PINK FLOWERS

Arbutus unedo f. rubra, Camellia (some), Cistus (some), Daphne (some), Erica (some), Escallonia (some), Gaultheria (some), Hebe (some), Kalmia (some), Lonicera (some), Mutisia (some), Olearia phlogopappa 'Comber's Pink', Pieris (some), Rhododendron (some), Rosmarinus (some), Vaccinium (some), Viburnum (some)

WITH RED FLOWERS

Camellia (some), Distylium, Escallonia (some), Kalmia (some), Rhododendron (some)

WITH MAUVE OR PURPLE FLOWERS

Cistus (some), Ercilla, Garrya x issaquahensis, Hebe (some), Holboellia, Lonicera giraldii, Rhododendron (some)

WITH BLUE FLOWERS

Ceanothus, Hebe (some), Olearia phlogopappa 'Comber's Blue', Rhododendron (some), Rosmarinus (some)

WITH YELLOW OR ORANGE FLOWERS

Berberis, Brachyglottis, Lonicera (some), X Mahoberberis, Mahonia, Mutisia decurrens, Rhododendron (some), Skimmia laureola, Sycopsis, Trachycarpus

WITH GREEN OR GREY FLOWERS

Daphne (some), Decumaria, Erica scoparia, Garrya elliptica, Holboellia, Itea, Trochodendron

FLOWERING IN WINTER

Camellia (some), Clematis cirrhosa, Daphne bholua, Erica lusitanica, Mahonia (some), Pieris (some), Rhododendron (some), Sarcococca, Sycopsis, Viburnum tinus

FLOWERING IN SPRING

Berberis, Camellia (some), Ceanothus (some), Choisya, Cistus (some), Clematis (some), Cotoneaster (some), Daphne (some), Decumaria, Distylium, Ercilla, Erica (some), Gaultheria, Holboellia, Leucothoe, X Mahoberberis, Mahonia (some), Osmanthus (some), Photinia, Pieris (some), Prunus laurocerasus, Pyracantha, Rhododendron (some), Rosmarinus, Skimmia, Trochodendron, Viburnum (some)

FLOWERING IN SUMMER

Brachyglottis, Bupleurum, Carpenteria, Cassinia, Ceanothus (some), Cistus (some), Cotoneaster (some), Daphne (some), Erica terminalis, Escallonia, Eucalyptus pauciflora subsp. niphophila, Eucryphia, Hebe (some), Hydrangea, Itea, Kalmia, Ligustrum, Lonicera, Magnolia, Mutisia, Myrtus, Nandina, Olearia, Ozothamnus, Pittosporum tobira, Prunus lusitanica, Rhaphiolepis, Rhododendron (some), Trachelospermum, Trachycarpus, Viburnum (some)

FLOWERING IN AUTUMN

Arbutus, Camellia sasanqua, Choisya, Daphne (some), Eucalyptus gunnii, X Fatshedera, Fatsia, Hebe (some), Mahonia (some), Mutisia, Osmanthus (some), Pileostegia, Viburnum tinus

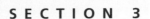

SECTION 3

DIRECTORY *of* BROAD-LEAVED EVERGREENS

WITHIN EACH SECTION, genera are listed alphabetically. The cross appearing before the name of a genus of hybrid origin is ignored, so for example, X *Fatshedera* is listed alphabetically under F. Under each genus, species are listed alphabetically, species of hybrid origin are listed after all natural species, and cultivars without a Latin species name appear last. Thus, under the genus heading Viburnum, *V. atrocyaneum* to *V. utile* are followed by *V.* x *burkwoodii* and *V.* x *globosum* and then by *V.* 'Pragense'.

At the end of each genus entry, plants not described in full but thought worthy of inclusion are mentioned briefly. If a species has more than one subspecies, variety, form or cultivar, then these are listed under the heading 'Varieties'. Cultivars of the typical plant are listed before botanical subspecies, varieties or forms, with cultivars belonging to any of these botanical groups listed with the group to which they belong. For example, under Varieties of *Myrtus communis* appear 'Flore Pleno', 'Variegata' and then subsp. *tarentina* followed by its cultivar 'Microphylla Variegata'.

Some plants have been known by more than one name. Where this occurs, the common synonym appears in brackets after the name that is now accepted as correct. There is more background information on the naming of plants in the Introduction.

ARBUTUS

A small genus of trees or large shrubs related to rhododendrons and heaths but lime-tolerant. Most species will not survive severe frost, but one or two are sufficiently hardy to be grown throughout much of the British Isles.

A. unedo, the Strawberry Tree

A large shrub or small tree with glossy leaves and brown bark which peels when old, leaving an attractive, smooth surface exposed. Good in coastal regions, withstanding gales well, but liable to damage by severe frosts.

Size: up to about 4.5m (15ft) in height, more in favourable conditions, and about half as wide as high. Usually slow-growing.

Leaves: broadly lanceolate to elliptical, dark green, glossy, somewhat leathery, often toothed.

Flowers: clusters of white, drooping, pitcher-shaped flowers in October to November.

Fruits: more or less round with a rough surface, growing to 2.5cm (1in) or more in diameter and ripening to dark red. Edible, but not very tasty; the name *unedo* is said to mean 'I eat one', with the implication being one and only one. The fruits take a year to ripen, so that, unusually, flowers and ripe fruits occur together.

Cultivation: a good tree for coastal areas, best given shelter inland. Tolerant of full sun or moderate shade. Prefers light to medium loam but is not very fussy. Although moderately lime-tolerant, it will not flourish on very limy or chalky soils.

Arbutus unedo

Propagation: by seed sown in free-draining but moisture-retentive compost in February or March.

Varieties: 'Compacta' is smaller growing than the type; 'Quercifolia' has leaves entire at the base but coarsely toothed towards the tip; f. *rubra* has pink flowers and fruits freely.

Origin: Mediterranean region, Portugal, south-west France and south-west Ireland.

A. x andrachnoides, the Hybrid Strawberry Tree, is very similar to the above, but with redder bark and rather later flowering. It is a hybrid between the above and *A. andrachne* from the eastern Mediterranean region.

BUXUS

See entry under SHRUBS for most soils, mainly for foliage effect.

CAMELLIA

See entry under SHRUBS requiring acid soils.

COTONEASTER

See entry under SHRUBS for most soils, with showy fruits.

EUCALYPTUS

A large genus of fast-growing trees, most of them from Australia. They are also known as gum trees because of the sticky resin that often exudes from their trunks and branches. Even the hardiest of them are likely to suffer in a severe winter in climates such as that of Britain. They are particularly susceptible to damage by strong, cold winds, but if killed to ground level they readily shoot again from the roots. This is an adaptation which enables them to regrow after forest fires in their native land.

In most species, leaves on young shoots are different from those on old branches. The juvenile foliage is often more attractive than the adult, and hard pruning encourages the growth of juvenile shoots. Eucalyptus trees have a very distinctive appearance and can give an exotic feeling to a planting scheme, but for this reason they require careful siting in British gardens if they are not to look out of place. They form an open crown and cast little shade. Numerous stamens are the most conspicuous feature of the flowers. The fruits are small, greenish and inconspicuous.

Eucalyptus gunnii: **bark of a young tree**

E. gunnii, the Cider Gum

One of the hardiest species, growing into a large tree where conditions are suitable. The juvenile foliage is a beautiful silvery-blue colour; much more attractive than the dull sage-green adult leaves. If cut back to ground level annually it will make a large bush with only juvenile foliage. On established trees the smooth, reddish-brown older bark flakes off in patches, revealing greyish-green new bark beneath.

Size: 18m (60ft) and more if unpruned and not damaged by cold weather.

Leaves: juvenile leaves are rounded and silvery blue; adult leaves are sickle-shaped and sage-green.

Flowers: not borne on juvenile branches; yellowish-white, opening in autumn.

Cultivation: best in warm areas, intolerant of cold winds. Will grow in most soils except thin soil over chalk. Growth is normally very fast. To maintain the growth of juvenile foliage, cut back to ground level annually in winter, otherwise prune only as necessary.

Propagation: by seed sown in late winter or early spring in sandy compost. Warmth is needed for germination.

Origin: Tasmania.

E. pauciflora subsp. niphophila (E. niphophila), the Snow Gum

From high altitudes in Australia, where it tolerates snow and frost. A small tree, growing more slowly than most gums. Its greyish-green bark peels in strips leaving pale patches.

Size: up to about 9m (30ft).

Leaves: juvenile leaves sickle-shaped, dull bluish-green; adult leaves greyish-green.

Flowers: yellowish-white in August.

Cultivation: happiest in rather dry soil in a sunny position, but fairly adaptable.

Propagation: by seed sown as for *E. gunnii*.

Origin: southern Australia.

E. pauciflora is also reasonably hardy, growing to medium size, with a whitish trunk and sickle-shaped adult leaves up to about 20cm (8in) long. Other species are worth trying, especially in warm districts.

Eucalyptus pauciflora* subsp. *niphophila

EUCRYPHIA

See entry under SHRUBS for most soils, with showy or strongly scented flowers.

GRISELINIA

See entry under SHRUBS for most soils, mainly for foliage effect.

ILEX

See entry under SHRUBS for most soils, with showy fruits.

LAURUS

See entry under SHRUBS for most soils, mainly for foliage effect.

LIGUSTRUM

See entry under SHRUBS for most soils, with showy or strongly scented flowers.

MAGNOLIA

See entry under SHRUBS for most soils, with showy or strongly scented flowers.

MAYTENUS

See entry under SHRUBS for most soils, mainly for foliage effect.

NOTHOFAGUS

The southern beeches are related to true beech (*Fagus*) but usually have much smaller leaves. They originate from South America and Australasia and most *Nothofagus* species are slightly tender. Not all of them are evergreen. They are often fast growers but withstand wind poorly and generally fail to thrive on chalky soils. Neither the flowers nor the fruits are especially showy.

N. dombeyi

A vigorous, medium to large tree with rather small, dark green leaves, which may fall in cold winters.

Size: 15 to 18m (50 to 60ft) or more.

Leaves: oval, doubly toothed, about 2.5cm (1in) long or rather larger; dark, shining green.

Cultivation: adaptable but dislikes excess lime or chalk, and strong cold winds, especially when young.

Propagation: by layering.

Origin: Chile and Argentina.

N. solanderi var. cliffortioides (N. cliffortioides), the Mountain Beech

An elegant, fast-growing tree of small to medium size.

Size: 9 to 15m (30 to 50ft) .

Leaves: oval, smaller than those of *N. dombeyi*.

Cultivation: as for *N. dombeyi*.

Propagation: by layering.

Origin: New Zealand.

N. betuloides and **N. solanderi** are also reasonably hardy and attractive trees of medium to large size.

OSMANTHUS

See entry under SHRUBS for most soils, with showy or strongly scented flowers.

PHILLYREA

See entry under SHRUBS for most soils, mainly for foliage effect.

PHOTINIA

See entry under SHRUBS for most soils, with showy fruits.

PITTOSPORUM

See entry under SHRUBS for most soils, mainly for foliage effect.

PRUNUS

See entry under SHRUBS for most soils, mainly for foliage effect.

QUERCUS

Oaks are familiar trees, but this is a very large and widespread genus including species of widely varying growth habits and general appearance. Many are large deciduous trees but some are shrubby, and quite a large number of species are evergreen. Unfortunately only a few evergreen oaks are at all common in cultivation. One of them, the Holm Oak, is perhaps the finest of all medium to large evergreen trees suitable for cultivation in temperate regions.

Q. coccifera, the Kermes Oak

A very slow-growing, dense shrub, usually of medium size, larger in favoured areas, especially near the coast. In the wild it can grow into a small tree.

Size: rarely more than about 2.4m (8ft) high in cultivation, often less, but can sometimes attain double this height.

Leaves: variable, but usually like small holly leaves about 2.5cm (1in) long, sometimes with untoothed margins, dark green, glossy.

Cultivation: likes a well-drained, loamy soil with plenty of humus, in sun or shade. Flourishes near coasts but is best given some shelter inland.

Propagation: by sowing acorns in early spring, preferably under glass. The acorns of this species ripen in their second year. In cultivation in cool climates, such as in Britain, they often fail to mature.

Origin: the Mediterranean region and Portugal.

Quercus ilex: **mature foliage**

Q. glauca
A small tree or more often a large shrub requiring an acid soil.

Size: up to about 6m (20ft) high, but often less.

Leaves: leathery, glossy, obovate, about 10cm (4in) long, sparsely toothed towards the tip.

Cultivation: likes a moist woodland soil containing plenty of humus in a sunny but sheltered position.

Propagation: by seed, if it can be obtained, sown in early spring under glass.

Origin: China, Korea and Japan.

Q. ilex, the Holm Oak
A rather slow-growing but eventually large tree forming a broad, rounded head of branches. Although it originates from the Mediterranean area, it is hardy, except in very cold inland areas. It tolerates salt-laden winds well and is happy in coastal sites. On old trees the bark is grey and heavily fissured with cracks forming rough squares.

Size: up to about 27m (90ft).

Leaves: Variable. On young trees they are often broadly elliptical with spiny teeth, rather like small holly leaves (the specific name *ilex* means holly); on mature trees leaves are more narrowly elliptical and with few or no teeth; leathery, dark green above and usually covered with greyish-white felted hairs beneath.

Flowers: the male flowers form long yellow catkins, appearing in June.

Fruits: small, green acorns more than half enclosed in scaly cups.

Cultivation: prefers well-drained soil – unhappy in heavy clay. Tolerates full sun or heavy shade and is adapted to coastal exposure. It responds well to clipping and can be used successfully for formal hedging and topiary.

Propagation: by seed. Collect acorns in autumn, when ripe, and sow them about 5cm (2in) deep in well-prepared open ground or in deep pots of sandy compost during February or March. They can be slow to germinate. Oaks resent root disturbance and should be moved with great care, preferably during late autumn to early winter or early spring. Ideally they should be grown from seed in their final site, thus avoiding transplanting. Sow more acorns than required and thin the seedlings as necessary.

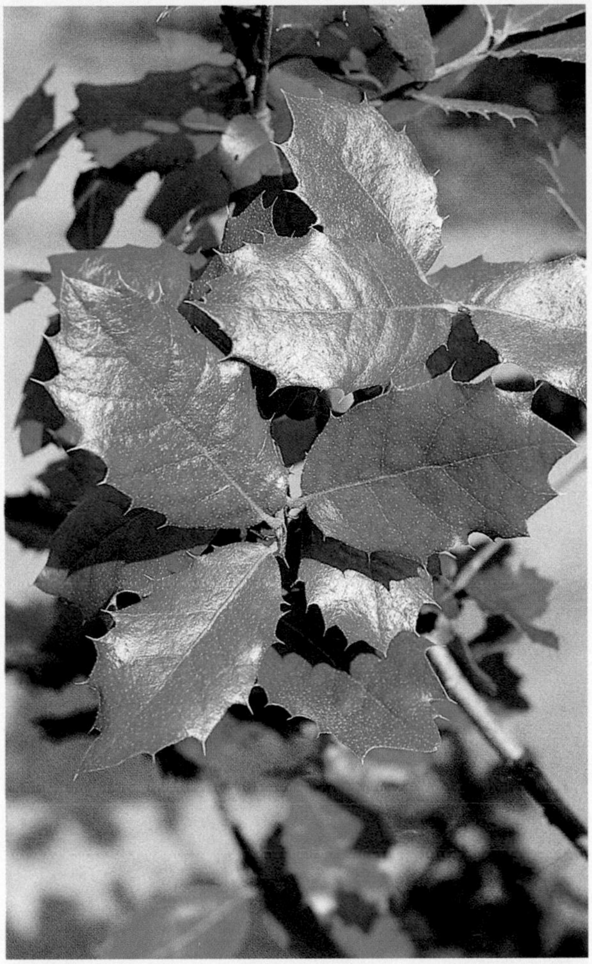
***Quercus ilex:* leaves of a young plant**

Origin: the Mediterranean region.

Q. phillyreoides
A large shrub or, more rarely, a small tree closely related to *Q. ilex*.

Size: usually not more than about 2.4 m (8ft) high, but can slowly grow into a small tree up to about 6m (20ft).

Leaves: leathery, glossy, obovate or more or less elliptical, about 5 to 7.5cm (2 to 3in) long.

Trachycarpus fortunei

Cultivation: likes a well-drained loamy soil containing plenty of humus and a sunny or slightly shaded, sheltered, position. Tolerates some lime in the soil.

Propagation: as for *Q. glauca*.

Origin: China and Japan.

Quercus acuta from Japan slowly grows into a small tree. It dislikes limy soil. There are a number of other evergreen oaks, but they are generally very scarce in cultivation and some are not very hardy.

RHODODENDRON

See entry under SHRUBS requiring acid soils.

SYCOPSIS

See entry under SHRUBS for most soils, with showy or strongly scented flowers.

TRACHYCARPUS

A genus of palms which includes the hardiest palm trees. They are invaluable for giving a subtropical feel to gardens, but can easily look out of place unless carefully sited. They are fan palms, with long-stalked leaves with a rounded, fanlike outline, deeply divided into many pointed fingers. Strong winds damage the large leaves, so shelter is essential if these trees are to look their best. Palms are dioecious, that is, flowers are either male or female and are borne on separate trees.

T. fortunei, the Chusan Palm

A fan palm growing a single erect trunk covered with the fibrous remains of old leaf bases.

Size: up to about 11m (35ft), but this will vary according to growing conditions.

Leaves: carried at the top of the trunk on long, stout stalks, dark green, stiff, about 1 to 1.5m (3 to 5ft) across. They persist for several years before dying and turning brown, but remain attached to the trunk almost indefinitely. It is best to cut the dead leaves off near the base of the leaf-stalk, leaving the brown, fibrous base of the stalk on the trunk, where it forms natural insulation against frost.

Flowers: yellow, numerous in large panicles borne among the leaves in early summer, curving downwards.

Fruits: borne only on female trees, like small, round, bluish-black dates.

Cultivation: likes a well-drained but moisture-retentive soil: a light loam with plenty of leaf-mould, compost or other humus-rich material incorporated is ideal. Growth is fastest in warm areas with high rainfall. Tolerant of full sun or light shade. Needs shelter from wind. Hardy at least throughout the southern half of England, except in very cold localities, and even in favoured areas further north.

Propagation: by seed (if it can be obtained) sown about 2.5cm (1in) deep in pots indoors or in a greenhouse and kept at a temperature of about 25°C (75°F). Sometimes suckers appear at the base of the trunk and can be separated and grown on as new plants.

Origin: central China.

T. wagnerianus has smaller leaves of stiffer appearance. A few other species are also now available in cultivation. They all look very similar, but some species may be slightly more hardy even than the Chusan Palm.

TROCHODENDRON

See entry under SHRUBS for most soils, mainly for foliage effect.

VIBURNUM

See entry under SHRUBS for most soils, with showy or strongly scented flowers.

BAMBOOS

Bamboos are really only grasses with woody stems. They form a large sub-family of somewhere near 1,000 species within the very large grass family (Gramineae or Poaceae). Although absent in the wild from Europe, they occur throughout almost all the rest of the world. They are most numerous in Asia and America, with about half of all bamboos occurring in China and about another quarter in South America. Most bamboos grow naturally in tropical or subtropical regions and are not hardy outdoors in cooler northern countries like Britain, but a significant minority occur where winters are usually cold.

They are invaluable in gardens for their elegant, erect habit which contrasts with other woody plants, and can be used to make excellent screens or as individual specimens. They look good beside water or associated with rhododendrons, camellias and other dark-leaved evergreens and give an oriental look to a garden. There are many genera of bamboos and there has been much confusion over their naming in the past, which is still not entirely resolved. One reason for this is that flowers are important for establishing relationships between plants and many bamboos flower only very occasionally, sometimes only once every 50 or 60 years. In cultivation, flowering can be even less frequent. This is no bad thing from the gardener's point of view, as some, though by no means all, bamboos die after flowering.

The height of bamboos in cultivation is very strongly influenced by growing conditions, so the following estimates of size are very much approximations. The canes grow to more or less their full height in a single season and scarcely elongate at all thereafter. In a warm, wet summer they will grow taller than in a cool, dry one. Bamboos generally like plenty of moisture during the growing season, but this does not mean that they should be planted in boggy ground. A warning needs to be given that some bamboos produce underground runners and spread rather like couch grass. They can be very invasive and should only be planted where their spread can be accommodated. None of the species described below is seriously invasive.

Chusquea culeou

A graceful, tall bamboo of distinctive appearance, unusual in having solid canes. It is very hardy. Leaves grow on short branches clustered at each joint in the cane, giving the appearance of a feather duster or bottle brush.

Size: usually about 2.4 to 3m (8 to 10ft) tall, but can reach at least twice this height. Forms dense clumps, slowly spreading in diameter.

Canes: olive-green when young, becoming yellowish with age, about 2.5cm (1in) or more in diameter, solid.

Leaves: small and narrow, about 5 to 10cm (2 to 4in) long, borne on short, slender branches clustered at each joint on the canes.

Cultivation: prefers a moist, humus-rich soil in sun or semi-shade. Good in open woodland.

Propagation: by division of old clumps in spring.

Origin: Chile.

Fargesia murieliae (Arundinaria murieliae, Sinarundinaria murieliae), the Umbrella Bamboo

One of the most commonly planted bamboos in Britain and undoubtedly one of the best. It originates from high altitudes in Hubei province, central China, and is very hardy, making it a good choice for the British climate. A slender, elegant species forming arching clumps. This is one of the species that flowers only occasionally and then usually dies.

Size: usually about 2.4 to 3 m (8 to 10ft) high, but sometimes rather more.

Canes: bright green when young, maturing to yellow, slender, only about 6 to 12mm (1/4 to 1/2in) in diameter.

Leaves: borne on long, very slender branchlets clustered at the joints of the canes, about 7.5cm (3in) long, lanceolate.

Cultivation: prefers a good, moist loam in a position sheltered from cold winds, either in sun or light shade. It is, however, quite tough and can be planted as a wind-break.

Chusquea culeou

Propagation: by division of established clumps in spring.

Origin: central China.

Fargesia nitida (Arundinaria nitida, Sinarundinaria nitida), the Fountain or Arrow Bamboo

Very similar to the above and sometimes confused with it, but has purplish canes and is generally even more slender, with narrower leaves. It grows at altitude in the mountains of western China, where it

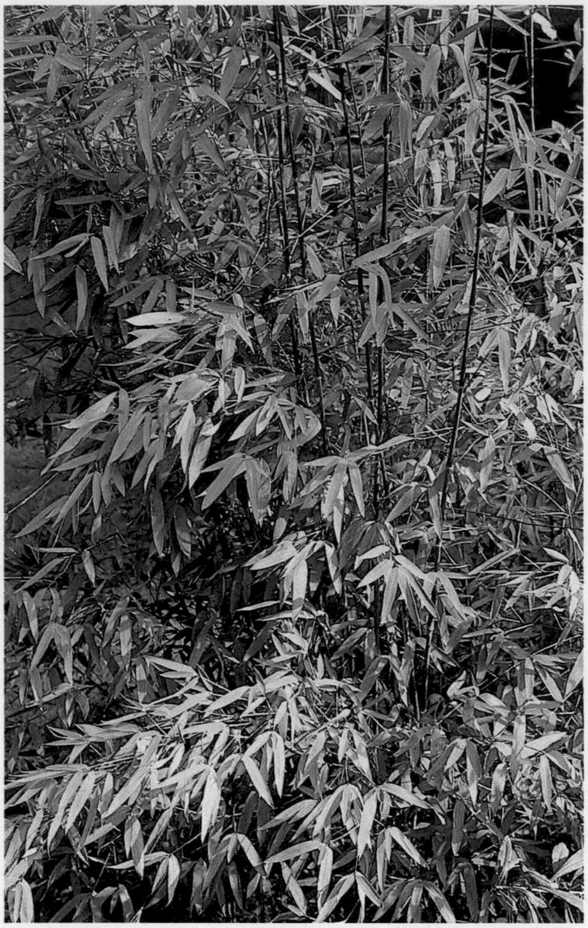

Fargesia nitida

is often exposed to severe frosts, and is very hardy. It usually dies after flowering.

Size: usually about 3 to 3.6m (10 to 12ft) high, but sometimes more.

Canes: at first green with a white bloom but soon becoming purplish, up to about 12mm (1/2in) in diameter.

Leaves: about 5 to 7.5cm (2 to 3in) long, very narrow, borne on slender branchlets clustered at the joints of the canes.

Cultivation: as for *F. murieliae*, but likes more shade and is a little less tolerant of wind.

Propagation: as for *F. murieliae*.

Origin: western China. This is the bamboo usually eaten by giant pandas.

Phyllostachys aurea
the Fishpole Bamboo

A very graceful bamboo, with interesting canes. The joints are swollen, and at the base of the cane are usually close together and angled: the whole cane often zigzags slightly.

Size: usually about 3 to 4.5m (10 to 15ft) high, sometimes a little more.

Canes: bright green when young, becoming yellow, about 2.5cm (1in) in diameter, swollen at the joints.

Leaves: usually borne on pairs of unequal branchlets from each joint of the cane, up to about 15cm (6in) long, pendulous.

Cultivation: likes rich, moist loam in a slightly sheltered position, with a little shade. Not quite as hardy as the *Fargesia* species.

Propagation: by division in spring.

Origin: eastern China.

Phyllostachys aureosulcata,
the Yellow-groove Bamboo

One of the most decorative hardy bamboos, widely cultivated in its native China. Attractive striped canes.

Size: usually about 3.6 to 4.5m (12 to 15ft) tall, but can attain twice this height.

Canes: green with a yellow stripe, often slightly zigzag, particularly near the base, about 2.5cm (1in) or a little more in diameter.

Leaves: similar to those of *P. aurea*.

Cultivation: fairly adaptable, but best planted in rich loam, in sun or a little shade.

Propagation: by division in spring.

Varieties: 'Aureocaulis' usually has entirely yellow canes; 'Spectabilis' has yellow ones striped with green, a very fine cultivar; f. *alata* ('Pekinensis') has entirely green canes.

Origin: China.

Phyllostachys bambusoides, the Giant Timber Bamboo

This is one of the largest bamboo species in its native China, widely cultivated for commercial purposes, as well as for ornament. In cooler conditions it will not attain heights of 18m (60ft) or more, with canes up to 15cm (6in) in diameter, as it may in subtropical and warm temperate climates. That said, it is well worth growing as it is very hardy and highly decorative.

Size: usually about 3 to 4.5m (10 to 15ft) tall.

Canes: green maturing to brown, straight, up to about 5cm (2in) in diameter.

Leaves: similar to those of *P. aurea*.

Cultivation: as for *P. aureosulcata*.

Propagation: by division in spring.

Varieties: 'Castillonis' has bright yellow canes with green stripes and is not as large and vigorous as the type; 'Tanakae' has canes mottled with brown. Several other cultivars exist.

Origin: China.

Phyllostachys edulis (P. mitis)

In warm climates this is a very tall bamboo, up to 24m (80ft). It will not attain anywhere near this height in cooler conditions, yet it is a strong grower and can reach a good size. Though a native of southern China, it is surprisingly hardy but unsuitable for very cold areas and can be damaged by moderately hard frost.

Size: usually up to about 4.5m (15ft) tall.

Canes: green when young, maturing to dull yellow.

Leaves: up to about 10cm (4in) long.

Cultivation: the more warmth and moisture during the growing season, the taller this bamboo will grow. It likes a moist, rich loam in full sun or a little shade, preferably with shelter. Not hardy in cold areas.

Propagation: by division in spring.

Origin: China.

Phyllostachys flexuosa

A slender bamboo of moderate height with canes that often zigzag slightly.

Size: up to about 3m (10ft) tall.

Canes: usually less than 2.5cm (1in) in diameter, green.

Leaves: up to about 13cm (5in) long.

Cultivation: a very hardy bamboo from northern China, excellent for screening. Prefers a fertile loam with plenty of moisture during the growing season, but is reasonably adaptable. Happy in full sun or light shade.

Propagation: by division in spring.

Origin: China.

Phyllostachys nigra, the Black Bamboo

When grown well, this is one of the most ornamental of all bamboos. Its black canes contrast particularly well with a pale background, such as a white wall. It is very hardy, but a little shelter will help it to look its best.

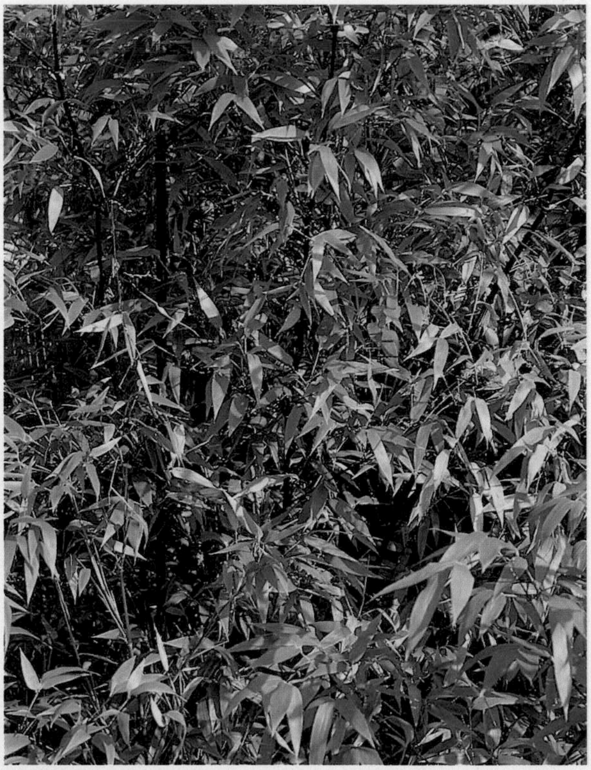

Phyllostachys nigra

Size: about 3m (10ft) tall.

Canes: at first green, becoming mottled with dark brown or black and finally entirely black, slender.

Leaves: up to about 13cm (5in) long, narrow.

Cultivation: will tolerate most soils, but a fertile loam with plenty of moisture during the growing season will produce the best results. Likes full sun or light shade, with a little shelter. In cold situations the canes may not colour well.

Propagation: by division in spring.

Varieties: 'Boryana' has canes that are green with some dark brown blotches; var. *henonis* has entirely green canes and is a little more vigorous; f. *punctata* has canes heavily blotched with black.

Origin: China, long cultivated in Japan.

Phyllostachys viridiglaucescens

A very elegant bamboo which is hardy and does well in cooler conditions, making it an excellent choice for British gardens.

Size: about 3.6 to 6m (12 to 20ft) tall or a little more in favourable conditions.

Canes: green, dusted with white meal and with purple joints when young, up to about 4cm (1½in) in diameter.

Leaves: about 10 to 13cm (4 or 5in) long, narrow.

Cultivation: grows best in a moist, rich loam in sun or light shade, with shelter from cold winds, but is quite adaptable and very hardy.

Propagation: by division in spring.

Origin: eastern China.

Pleioblastus auricomus (Arundinaria viridistriata)

A small bamboo with variegated leaves which can be extremely decorative. It is one of the most brightly coloured variegated bamboos.

Size: usually up to about 90cm (3ft) tall, but can attain 1.5 to 1.8m (5 or 6ft), especially if grown in full sun with plenty of moisture in the soil.

Pleioblastus auricomus

Canes: green and very thin, rarely as much as 6mm (1/4in) in diameter.

Leaves: up to 20cm (8in) long and about 2.5cm (1in) wide, yellow striped with green.

Cultivation: easy in most reasonable soils, in full sun or light shade. Grows taller in a rich, moist loam in full sun. Very hardy. When established, it may be clipped to ground level in autumn or winter to encourage the growth of young canes with bright, new foliage. It has often flowered in cultivation but does not die as a result.

Propagation: by division in spring.

Origin: Japan, where it has long been cultivated. It is unknown in the wild.

Pleioblastus simonii

A vigorous and hardy bamboo with a very upright habit, producing many branchlets at each joint of its canes so that it has a very leafy appearance. This makes it suitable as an informal hedge or for screening purposes, but it is less elegant in appearance than many other bamboos. The canes are often almost completely hidden by the leaves.

Size: up to 4.5m (15ft) tall or sometimes even more. It forms clumps, but has a tendency to send out underground runners to a distance of about 30 to 60cm (1 to 2ft).

Canes: rather dull, dark green, up to about 2.5cm (1in) in diameter, and dusted with white meal when young.

Leaves: sometimes almost 30cm (1ft) long but less than 2.5cm (1in) wide, two different shades of green beneath.

Cultivation: hardy and easy, but will grow taller in good loamy soil with plenty of warmth and moisture during the growing season. Happy in full sun or partial shade. Late growth can sometimes be partly browned by early frosts, making the plant look untidy in winter, but this causes no serious long-term effects.

Propagation: can often be propagated by digging up shoots which appear at a little distance from the main clump of canes and separating them from the parent plant. Established clumps may be divided in spring.

Pleioblastus simonii

Varieties: f. *variegatus* has some leaves striped with pale yellow or cream, but this character is not very consistent.

Origin: Japan.

Pseudosasa japonica is quite commonly grown in gardens, but can be a little invasive. It is very hardy and adaptable. There has been a considerable increase in the number of bamboos available from specialist nurseries during the past few years and many of them are well deserving of a place in the garden, but some are not very hardy.

SHRUBS FOR MOST SOILS

SHRUBS MAINLY FOR FOLIAGE EFFECT

AUCUBA

A small genus of large evergreen shrubs from eastern Asia. Only one species is in cultivation.

A. japonica, the Spotted Laurel

A large, rounded shrub usually about as wide as high. The foliage is dense and bushes are usually well clothed with leaves right down to the ground. It tolerates pollution and poor soils and will grow in dense shade. Male and female flowers are normally borne on separate plants, though at least one cultivar has flowers of both sexes. It has long been grown in gardens in the Far East and the earliest introductions to Europe were of cultivars with yellow spots and blotches on the leaves. These were all female and bore no berries until male plants, with unspotted green leaves, were introduced several decades later and fertilized the female flowers.

Size: up to about 3.5m (12ft) tall and as much across.

Leaves: large, up to about 20cm (8in) long, oval or elliptical, with a few coarse teeth, leathery, dark green.

Flowers: small, brownish and not very conspicuous, opening in early spring.

Fruits: clusters of large berries which remain green until well into winter and then ripen to red.

Cultivation: easy in almost any soil or position, but will look much better if given a little shelter from cold winds and planted in fertile soil. It is excellent in shady places, even in dense shade under trees.

Propagation: roots quickly if lower branches are layered, or cuttings may be taken in late autumn or early winter and inserted into humus-rich soil or compost, either in a sheltered position outdoors or in a glasshouse or cold frame. Seeds that are sown as soon as the berries ripen, about 6mm (1/4in) deep in moisture-retentive compost, will usually also give good germination, but the resultant seedlings will be variable and not necessarily identical with the seed parent.

Varieties: 'Crotonifolia' is a female cultivar with large leaves heavily spotted and blotched with gold; 'Fructu

Aucuba japonica **'Rozannie'**

Aucuba japonica **'Variegata'**

Albo' is also female, bearing yellowish-white fruit, with leaves sparsely spotted with pale green and yellow; 'Picturata' is a male variegated cultivar; 'Rozannie' is an excellent cultivar with plain green leaves, bearing male and female flowers on the same plant and fruiting very reliably; 'Variegata' ('Maculata'), the original introduction, is a female cultivar with leaves speckled yellow. There are a number of other cultivars available, and all have something to recommend them.

Origin: Japan, Korea, China.

BERBERIS

See entry under SHRUBS for most soils, with showy or strongly scented flowers.

BRACHYGLOTTIS

See entry under SHRUBS for most soils, with showy or strongly scented flowers.

BUXUS

Evergreen shrubs or small trees, usually slow-growing but adaptable to a wide variety of soils and happy in sun or shade. The flowers and fruits are small and of no decorative value. They are familiar hedging and topiary plants, but large old box hedges seem to have a tendency to go out of shape.

B. balearica, the Balearic Box

A large shrub or small, erect tree with larger leaves than Common Box.

Size: in Britain, rarely more than about 2.4m (8ft) tall, but in the wild Balearic Box can attain two or three times this height.

Leaves: oval, similar to those of Common Box but larger, usually 2.5 to 4cm (1 to 1½in) long, and bright green.

Cultivation: will not flourish in cold areas and is best grown in a sheltered, sunny position. Prefers light, somewhat limy, soil.

Propagation: by cuttings taken in August or September and inserted into moist compost in a shady place. Layering may also be used.

Origin: the Mediterranean region.

B. microphylla, the Dwarf Box

A small shrub growing into a dense, rounded shape unless clipped, as it often is. This is the box often used for very low hedges around formal flower beds.

Size: up to about 1m (3ft) tall and as wide as high. Slow-growing.

Leaves: oval to elliptical, only about 1.2cm (½in) long.

Cultivation: tolerates a wide variety of soils and full sun to moderate shade.

Propagation: by cuttings taken in August or September, or in winter, pushed into ordinary compost or prepared beds outdoors and kept shaded. Plants may also be partly buried with compost, to encourage rooting from lower branches, and left for a couple of years before being dug up and split into several new plants.

Varieties: 'Compacta' is a very small clone with tiny leaves; 'Green Pillow' is slightly less dwarf than 'Compacta', with larger, bright green, leaves; var. *japonica* is a much larger variety reaching 1.5 to 1.8m (5 or 6ft) or more. There are several other named cultivars available, most of them dwarf, of different habits and leaf colour.

Origin: Japan.

B. sempervirens, the Common Box

A familiar large shrub or small tree with dense, dark green foliage. Either a British native or at least naturalized centuries ago. It has many varieties and has been much used for hedges and topiary.

Size: up to about 5m (18ft) tall, but usually less. Slow-growing.

Leaves: oval, with recurved margins, dark green, glossy and leathery, 1.5 to 3cm (¾ to 1¼in) long.

***Buxus sempervirens* 'Elegantissima'**

Cultivation: easy in most soils and situations, but can be damaged by very strong cold winds.

Propagation: by cuttings, as for *B. microphylla*.

Varieties: 'Aureovariegata' is a medium to large shrub with leaves striped and splashed with pale yellow; 'Elegantissima' is a small to medium shrub slowly growing into a compact dome, with leaves margined with creamy-white; 'Latifolia Maculata' is small to medium in size, dense and compact, with leaves blotched yellow; 'Notata' has upper leaves of shoots tipped yellow. A number of other varieties of varying habit and leaf colour are also available.

Origin: southern Europe, north Africa, western Asia.

Buxus bodinieri, B. wallichiana and a few other species are in cultivation but are likely only to appeal to those with a particular enthusiasm for growing box.

CASSINIA

See entry under SHRUBS for most soils, with showy or strongly scented flowers.

DAPHNIPHYLLUM

A genus of about 30 trees and shrubs, mostly from subtropical south-east Asia. A few species from China and Japan are hardy in cooler regions like Britain. Although the flowers are inconspicuous, they have very striking foliage reminiscent of some rhododendrons. As they are lime-tolerant, they are useful where rhododendrons cannot be grown. Best in semi-shade in a moist soil with plenty of humus in it, but they tend to be slow growing even in ideal conditions.

D. himalense var. macropodum (D. macropodum)

A large shrub well clothed with quite big, leathery leaves with purple-red leaf stalks. Excellent background for winter-flowering shrubs such as *Hamamelis*.

Size: up to 3 or 4m (10 or 12ft) tall, possibly eventually more in ideal conditions, rather slow-growing. Usually about as wide as high.

Leaves: leathery, elliptical to oblanceolate, 14 to 25cm (6 to 10in) long, light green above, glaucous beneath, with purple-red leaf stalks.

Cultivation: a woodland plant in the wild, it prefers a sheltered position in semi-shade with a humus-rich, moisture-retentive soil. Lime-tolerant.

Propagation: by cuttings of nearly ripe wood in summer, preferably in a closed propagator with bottom heat, or by layering.

Origin: China, Korea and Japan.

D. humile is similar to the above but much smaller, rarely exceeding 1.2 or 1.5m (4 or 5ft), slow-growing and usually at least as wide as high. It comes from Japan.

ELAEAGNUS

Evergreen and deciduous shrubs and small trees, mainly occurring in east and south-east Asia, in both subtropical and temperate regions. A minority of species is found in western Asia, Europe and North America. There are several dozen evergreen species, but many of them are from subtropical regions and not frost-hardy. They generally have small flowers of little ornamental value, but with a pleasant scent. They are fast growers and resistant to wind and make excellent hedges and screens in exposed areas, even near coasts.

E. macrophylla

A shrub of medium to large size with rounded leaves covered with silvery scales when young.

Size: usually up to about 1.8m (6ft) tall, but sometimes as much as 3m (10ft) or rather more. Often as wide as high.

Leaves: oval or broadly oval to nearly round, about 5 to 8cm (2 to 3in) long, and almost leathery. They are covered on both surfaces with silvery scales when young, the scales on the upper surface falling as the leaves mature.

Flowers: very small, white, opening in late autumn, fragrant.

Cultivation: easy in most soils except for very chalky ones, and it prefers an open position or only slight shade.

Propagation: by cuttings inserted into sandy compost in autumn, preferably in a cold frame or unheated glasshouse; by layering; by seeds sown in light compost in late winter or early spring.

Origin: eastern China, Korea and Japan.

Elaeagnus pungens **'Maculata'**

E. pungens

A large, vigorous shrub, sometimes spiny. It has long been cultivated in the Far East. Several variegated cultivars exist, most smaller and less vigorous than the type.

Size: usually up to about 3m (10ft) tall, but sometimes rather more, and about as wide as high.

Leaves: elliptical to broadly elliptical, 5 to 10cm (2 to 4in) long, leathery, at first scaly above but becoming green and shiny, white and brown scales persisting on the lower surface.

Flowers: small, whitish, fragrant, opening in autumn or early winter.

Cultivation: easy in most soils, prefers a sunny position.

Propagation: as for *E. macrophylla*.

Varieties: 'Dicksonii' has leaves broadly-margined with yellow and is erect and rather slow growing; 'Maculata' is of moderate growth with leaves with a central splash of golden-yellow; 'Variegata', large and vigorous, has leaves margined with pale yellow. There are a couple of other variegated cultivars.

Origin: China and Japan.

E. x ebbingei

A very vigorous, large, tough shrub, excellent for screens, even in coastal areas. A hybrid between the two species described above.

Size: 3 to 4.5m (10 to 15ft) or more high, usually slightly less wide.

Leaves: similar to those of *E. macrophylla*.

Flowers: small, fragrant, opening in autumn, borne only by mature plants on old wood so that they are hidden by the leaves.

Cultivation: easy in most soils and situations, fast growing, tolerates wind well.

Propagation: by cuttings, as for *E. macrophylla*, or by layering.

Varieties: 'Coastal Gold' is a strong-growing cultivar with leaves that are broadly and irregularly edged with yellow, and makes a very good choice for coastal areas; 'Gilt Edge' is a slower-growing, often smaller cultivar which rarely exceeds 3m (10ft) in height and about as much across, and has its leaves edged with yellow; 'Limelight', which is about as large and vigorous as the type, has leaves with a central blotch of yellow. There are a few other cultivars now becoming available.

Origin: a garden hybrid between *E. macrophylla* and *E. pungens*.

E. x reflexa

A much scarcer plant in gardens than *E.* x *ebbingei*. It is likewise large and vigorous, but tending to a rather untidy growth habit, as it produces long and fairly straggling branches. It usually bears a few scattered spines.

Size: 4.5m (15ft) or more high and as much wide.

Leaves: similar to those of *E. pungens*.

Cultivation: easy in most soils and positions.

Propagation: by cuttings, as for *E. macrophylla*, or by layers.

Origin: a garden hybrid between *E. glabra* and *E. pungens*.

EUONYMUS

A large genus of shrubs and trees, most of which are deciduous, but also including several evergreen species, some of which are climbers. Unfortunately the fruits, which are the principal feature of the deciduous species, are generally rather small and much less effective in the evergreens. The flowers are small and greenish and of very little decorative value. Evergreen *Euonymus* species are useful in coastal areas but most of them are liable to suffer frost damage in cold localities.

E. fortunei

See entry under CLIMBERS.

Euonymus kiautschovicus **in flower.** ***Euonymus*** **flowers are generally not showy**

E. japonicus (E. ovatus),
the Japanese Spindle

A dense, fairly upright shrub of moderate vigour. Grows well in coastal areas and in towns and can make a good hedge, but not sufficiently hardy to thrive in very cold regions.

Size: usually up to about 1.8 to 2.4m (6 to 8ft) tall and slightly less across, but it can eventually reach twice that height – especially in favourable warm localities.

Leaves: obovate or elliptical, about 2.5 to 5cm (1 to 2in) long, dark green, leathery, glossy.

Fruits: small, pink, rarely very effective.

Cultivation: happy in most soils in either full sun or shade. It performs best, though, if given some shelter in colder areas.

Propagation: by cuttings of well-ripened recent growth inserted into sandy compost in autumn or winter, under glass.

Varieties: 'Albomarginatus' has its leaves edged with white; 'Aureus' has leaves with a golden centre, but they tend to revert to plain green; 'Latifolius Albomarginatus' is probably the best variegated form – its leaves have a broad white margin; 'Microphyllus' is a small, dense, slow-growing cultivar which somewhat resembles box; 'Microphyllus Albovariegatus' is a white-variegated form of the preceding; 'Microphyllus Pulchellus' is again similar, but has leaves with yellow variegation; 'Ovatus Aureus' is a slow-growing cultivar with foliage variegated creamy-yellow, which needs sun to colour well; and 'Robustus' is a hardier cultivar than the type with roundish leaves. There are several other cultivars available, some of which have variegated foliage.

Origin: Japan.

E. kiautschovicus

A medium to large, spreading shrub similar to *E. japonicus* but hardier and less dense. In especially cold winters it may lose its leaves, but it is usually fully evergreen.

Size: usually up to about 1.8 to 2.4m (6 to 8ft) tall, but can attain more in favourable conditions. Often wider than high.

Leaves: elliptical to obovate, 5 to 7.5cm (2 to 3in) long, dark green, almost leathery.

Fruits: small, pink, ripening during winter.

Cultivation: not very fussy as to soil, tolerates sun or moderate shade.

Propagation: as for *E. japonicus*.

Origin: China.

E. myrianthus

Eventually a large shrub, but rather slow-growing. It has more distinctive foliage than the two *Euonymus* species described above and generally larger, more showy fruits.

Size: up to about 3m (10ft) high, but slow-growing.

X *Fatshedera lizei* 'Variegata'

Leaves: as much as 12.5cm (5in) long, elliptical to oblanceolate, with bluntly-toothed margins, dark green, leathery.

Fruits: Orange and yellow, about 1.2cm (1/2in) in diameter, in clusters, ripening in late autumn.

Cultivation: easy in most soils, but prefers a moist woodland soil with plenty of humus, in sun or moderate shade.

Propagation: as for *E. japonicus*.

Origin: western China.

X FATSHEDERA

An interesting bigeneric hybrid, tolerant of shade, pollution, coastal exposure and almost all soils. Often seen as a houseplant, but hardy outdoors in most areas.

X F. lizei

A shrub of modest size with a somewhat sprawling habit, excellent for shady areas, where it will make good ground cover.

Size: up to about 1.2 to 1.5m (4 to 5ft) tall and at least as wide as high.

Leaves: very like large ivy leaves, about 10 to 15cm (4 to 6in) long and wide, sometimes bigger.

Flowers: small and white, borne in round heads, opening in autumn.

Cultivation: easy in most situations and soils, especially useful for very shady places.

Propagation: by cuttings taken in winter and inserted into an open compost, preferably in a cold frame or unheated glasshouse, or by layering; branches which touch the soil may root naturally from nodes.

Varieties: a few variegated cultivars exist, including 'Annemieke' ('Lemon and Lime'), 'Aurea' and 'Variegata'.

Origin: a garden hybrid between *Fatsia japonica* and Irish Ivy (*Hedera hibernica*).

Fatsia japonica

FATSIA

A Far Eastern genus of just one or two species, belonging to the large family of Araliads (Araliaceae), which includes both ivy and ginseng.

F. japonica (Aralia sieboldii)

A medium to large shrub of exotic appearance which grows well in shade but is not very hardy and is readily damaged by cold winds. It produces thick stems with few branches which tend to sprawl.

Size: up to about 3m (10ft) high and more across.

Leaves: large, often 30cm (12in) or more across, more or less circular in outline but divided, with usually nine pointed segments, dark, shining green and somewhat leathery.

Flowers: well-established plants will produce large, rounded heads of small, whitish flowers in November.

Cultivation: the ideal site is a sheltered one in woodland with a deep soil layer, rich in organic matter such as leaf-mould, but this shrub will generally succeed in most free-draining cultivated soils, preferably in semi-shade. It does best if given adequate protection from cold winds.

Propagation: by cuttings under glass in late winter or early spring, preferably with bottom heat, or by layering.

Varieties: 'Variegata' has a whitish blotch at the tip of each segment of the leaf.

Origin: Japan.

GRISELINIA

A small genus of trees and shrubs from New Zealand and South America. Most are tender. Only one species is generally cultivated outdoors in Britain.

G. littoralis

A large, erect shrub or small tree with attractive, pale green, shiny foliage. It is liable to frost damage in cold areas inland, but is excellent near coasts as it is highly resistant to salt-laden winds. The flowers are inconspicuous.

Size: 3m (10ft) or more high, about 1.8m (6ft) wide. In mild localities, particularly near sheltered coasts such as those in south-west England, it may grow considerably taller.

Leaves: oval, with smooth margins, about 7.5 to 10cm (3 to 4in) long, leathery, pale green, glossy.

Cultivation: succeeds in all reasonable soils but dislikes clay; tolerates sun or shade. Not reliably hardy in colder areas but excellent for hedging or screening near coasts owing to its ability to withstand salt-laden winds.

Propagation: by cuttings in sandy soil or compost in late autumn or winter, preferably under glass.

Varieties: 'Bantry Bay', 'Dixon's Cream' and 'Variegata' all have variegated foliage.

Origin: New Zealand.

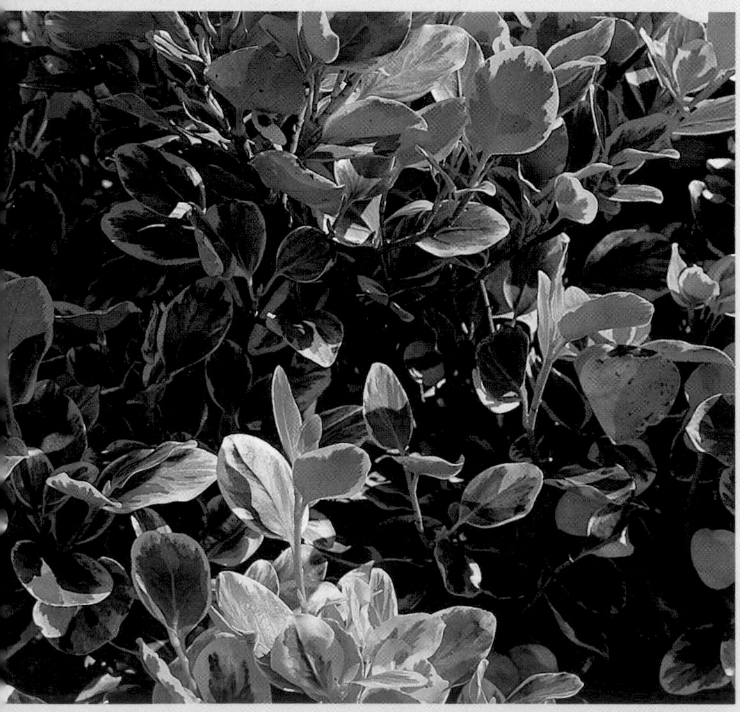

***Griselinia littoralis* 'Variegata'**

ILEX

See entry under SHRUBS for most soils, with showy fruits.

LAURUS

A small genus of evergreen trees and shrubs. The flowers are small and yellowish, the fruit a small black berry. Neither is very ornamental.

Laurus nobilis

L. nobilis, the Bay Tree

A large, erect shrub or, under favourable conditions, a small to medium tree. This is the true Laurel of the classical writers, though the Cherry Laurel (*Prunus laurocerasus*) usually usurps the name now. Its leaves are highly aromatic when crushed and are the bay leaves used in cooking.

Size: up to about 20m (65ft) high, but usually much less in cultivation in Britain.

Leaves: elliptical, with wavy edges, stiff, dark green, about 7.5 to 10cm (3 to 4in) long.

Cultivation: not very fussy about soil, as long as drainage is good. Prefers a warm situation in either full sun or partial shade. Thrives in coastal regions, but can suffer frost damage inland, especially when young. Bay can be clipped and will make a good hedge in mild areas.

Propagation: by cuttings inserted into sandy soil or compost in autumn or early winter, under glass.

Varieties: 'Aurea' has yellow leaves; f. *angustifolia* is a hardier form with narrow, pale green leaves.

Origin: the Mediterranean region.

LONICERA

The honeysuckles form a large genus of shrubs and climbers from Europe, Asia, north Africa and North America. About half the 200 or so species occur in eastern Asia. Most are deciduous but there are a few evergreens. Honeysuckles are usually thought of as climbers, but the majority are shrubby.

L. nitida

A shrub of medium size with tiny, dark green leaves. It has been much used for hedging in the past, but has thin branches with little strength and tends to become untidy as it ages. The flowers are very small and pale yellow, but most cultivated forms rarely flower at all.

Size: up to about 1.8m (6ft) tall or a little more, often more or less as wide as high.

Leaves: dark, shiny green, usually less than 12mm (1/2in) long, broadly oval or broadly elliptical to almost round, densely clothing young shoots.

Cultivation: best in a sunny position in fertile medium loam containing plenty of humus; it rarely looks good if grown in poor soil or too much shade. Responds well to clipping and has often been used for hedging, but can become untidy as it matures with gaps where there is little foliage, especially if it is not regularly clipped twice a year.

Propagation: by cuttings taken in July and August and inserted into sandy compost in a shaded frame; by layering; if seeds can be obtained they should be sown in late winter in pots of free draining compost.

Varieties: 'Baggesen's Gold', is a very commonly available cultivar with attractive yellow foliage; 'Fertilis' is an erect-growing cultivar which produces fragrant flowers reasonably freely, followed by small, purplish-black berries; 'Silver Beauty' has

Lonicera nitida **'Baggesen's Gold'**

leaves which are marked with silver-white. A few other cultivars are also available.

Origin: China.

See also CLIMBERS.

MAYTENUS

A genus of about 200 evergreen trees and shrubs, mostly from Africa and not hardy in cooler climates like that of northern Europe. One species is an exception to this but is not commonly planted, so its hardiness has not been well tested in different localities.

M. boaria (M. chilensis)

A large shrub or small to medium tree, looking similar to willow. The flowers are small and greenish-white, opening in spring, but of little decorative effect. Male and female flowers are usually borne on separate trees, so fruits, which are small and greenish-orange, will only be set on female trees if a male tree is near.

Size: up to about 18m (60ft) high in Britain but often much less, quite slow-growing.

Leaves: fairly narrowly elliptical with toothed margins, about 5cm (2in) long, shiny, mid-green.

Cultivation: tolerant of a wide range of soils, as long as they are reasonably free-draining. Prefers an open, sunny site and grows well in coastal areas.

Propagation: one reason for its scarcity in gardens may be that it is not easy to propagate. Suckers are sometimes produced and can be carefully separated and grown on; cuttings taken in summer and layering may also produce worthwhile results.

Varieties: 'Worplesdon Fastigiate' does not appear to be significantly narrower in growth than the type but is a female clone and will fruit if planted with a male tree.

Origin: Chile and other countries of South America.

PHILLYREA

A small genus of shrubs and small trees related to *Osmanthus.* The flowers are not showy but are fragrant. Leaves are borne in pairs. Both of the following species are very tolerant of coastal conditions. They stand clipping well and were much used for topiary during the seventeenth century.

P. angustifolia

A dense, rounded shrub of medium to large size with quite narrow leaves.

Size: up to about 2.4 to 3m (8 to 10ft) tall and rather less across.

Phillyrea angustifolia

Leaves: lanceolate to narrowly elliptical or more or less linear, about 5 to 7.5cm (2 to 3in) long, stiff.

Flowers: small, pale greenish-yellow, not conspicuous, but fragrant, opening in May and June.

Cultivation: easy in almost any soil as long as it is reasonably free-draining. Happy in full sun or light shade. Very tolerant of coastal conditions and good for hedging or screening.

Propagation: by cuttings taken in autumn or winter, inserted into sandy soil or compost, preferably in a frame or cool glasshouse.

Varieties: f. *rosmarinifolia* has very narrow leaves and is smaller and more compact.

Origin: the Mediterranean region.

P. latifolia (including P. media)

A dense large shrub or small tree with smooth or slightly rough greyish bark. The leaves are variable, but always broader than those of the above species. It is reminiscent of a small Holm Oak and is a good substitute for it where space is limited.

Size: up to about 9m (30ft) high in cultivation, but usually not more than about 6m (20ft) away from warm coastal areas. Makes a broad, round-headed tree.

Leaves: oval, or lanceolate to elliptical, glossy, dark green, sometimes with toothed margins, about 5cm (2in) long.

Flowers: greenish-white, small, not conspicuous and only slightly fragrant, opening in May and June.

Cultivation: easy in most soils in either full sun or partial shade, tolerates pollution and coastal conditions, good for hedging and screening.

Propagation: as for *P. angustifolia.*

Origin: the Mediterranean region and Portugal.

PHOTINIA

See entry under SHRUBS for most soils, with showy fruits.

***Pittosporum tenuifolium* 'James Stirling'**

***Pittosporum tenuifolium* 'Silver Queen'**

PITTOSPORUM

A large genus of about 300 species of evergreen shrubs and trees, distributed across Australasia, the islands of the south-west Pacific, south-east Asia and east Asia, mainly in tropical and subtropical zones. Only a few species are sufficiently hardy to be grown outdoors in cooler climates such as that of Britain. Of those that are, most originate from New Zealand and tend to grow well in coastal areas. The flowers are usually more or less insignificant, but are sometimes fragrant.

P. crassifolium, the Karo

One of the hardiest species, surviving most winters unharmed in inland areas of southern England. It grows into a large, dense shrub or even a small tree and is useful for screening or shelter in coastal areas.

Size: up to about 6m (20ft) tall in mild areas.

Leaves: oval or obovate, blunt with inrolled margins, 5 to 7.5cm (2 to 3in) long, leathery, dark green above, white felted beneath.

Flowers: rather small, deep purple, opening in spring.

Cultivation: will thrive in most soils, even chalky ones, as long as they are well-drained. Prefers a sunny situation. Excellent near coasts, but susceptible to frost damage in cold winters inland.

Propagation: by summer cuttings of half-ripened wood inserted into sandy compost under glass in shade.

Origin: New Zealand.

P. dallii

Sufficiently hardy to survive all but extremely cold winters. It grows into a large, spreading shrub or occasionally makes a small, rounded tree. Its flowers are white and fragrant but these only rarely develop on plants in cultivation in cooler climates such as that of Britain.

Size: up to about 6m (20ft) tall and often almost as wide as high.

Leaves: elliptical to more or less lanceolate, with toothed or occasionally untoothed margins, leathery, dull green, about 7.5cm (3in) long.

Cultivation: as for *P. crassifolium*.

Propagation: as for *P. crassifolium*.

Origin: New Zealand.

P. divaricatum

A shrub of small to medium size, very different in appearance from other cultivated species, with tangled, wiry branches and small leaves.

Size: up to about 1.8m (6ft) high.

Leaves: About 1.2 to 1.5cm (1/2 to 3/4in) long, variable in shape, on young plants usually narrow and deeply toothed or divided, on mature plants obovate to elliptical and often untoothed, sometimes lobed or deeply toothed.

Flowers: small, maroon, opening in May.

Cultivation: as for *P. crassifolium*.

Propagation: as for *P. crassifolium*.

Origin: New Zealand.

P. tenuifolium

An attractive large shrub or small tree with pale green, wavy-edged leaves borne on blackish branchlets. The flowers are small but fragrant.

Size: up to as much as 9m (30ft) high, erect.

Leaves: about 5cm (2in) long, shiny, pale green, lanceolate to elliptical, with wavy edges.

Cultivation: as for *P. crassifolium*.

Propagation: as for *P. crassifolium*.

Varieties: 'Abbotsbury Gold' has leaves with golden-yellow variegation; 'James Stirling' has bronze to greyish-green foliage; 'Purpureum' has leaves which age to bronze-purple but is less hardy than the type; 'Silver Queen' has leaves variegated with creamy-white and is smaller than the type; 'Warnham Gold' has greenish-yellow to golden-yellow foliage. There are a few dozen other good cultivars available.

Origin: New Zealand.

P. tobira 'Nanum'

The type of this species is too tender for cultivation outdoors in any but the mildest areas, but this selected smaller cultivar is hardier and worth trying in most of southern England or further north near coasts, if it can be given shelter. Its flowers are far more decorative than any other reasonably hardy *Pittosporum*.

Size: up to about 1.5 to 1.8m (5 or 6ft) high and more or less as wide, fairly slow-growing.

Pittosporum tobira

Leaves: dark green, leathery, oval to elliptical, about 7.5cm (3in) long, usually densely crowded near the ends of the branches.

Flowers: in terminal heads about 5 to 7.5cm (2 to 3in) across, creamy-white ageing to yellow, very fragrant, opening in late spring to summer.

Cultivation: not very fussy about soil, best in a fairly open but sheltered situation, but will tolerate slight shade.

Propagation: as for *P. crassifolium*, or by layering.

Origin: China.

PRUNUS

A large and familiar genus, mainly of deciduous trees, including cherries, plums, peaches and apricots. A few species are evergreen, including two of the most commonly cultivated of all hardy ornamental evergreen shrubs.

P. laurocerasus, the Cherry Laurel

A large and vigorous shrub or small tree with big, shiny leaves. This is the common laurel often used for hedging. The leaves contain cyanide and are poisonous.

Size: up to 6m (20ft) or more, and often almost as wide as high.

Leaves: usually more or less obovate, leathery, glossy, mid- to dark green, up to 20cm (8in) long.

Flowers: erect spikes of whitish flowers open in March or April, but are not particularly showy. Plants grown in shade tend to carry little flower.

Fruits: Dark reddish-purple fruits like small cherries ripen in late summer or autumn and are usually quickly eaten by birds.

Cultivation: easy in most soils except for very chalky ones. Often used for hedging and can make a fine hedge, but very vigorous and difficult to keep to a height much less than about 2.4m (8ft). Some of the smaller-growing cultivars are more appropriate for lower hedges. The large leaves are shredded by mechanical hedge trimmers, so pruning Cherry Laurel hedges with secateurs is recommended, preferably in April and perhaps again in late summer. Cherry Laurel will make a fine small tree if pruned to a single main trunk and encouraged to make upright growth. In very cold areas it can suffer damage in winter.

Prunus laurocerasus

Propagation: cuttings taken in winter and placed in shaded outdoor beds usually root well.

Varieties: there are at least two dozen cultivars of Cherry Laurel currently available, including some with variegated foliage, such as 'Castlewellan', 'Green Marble', 'Taff's Golden Gleam' and 'Variegata'. Others are of lower growth than the type, including 'Otto Luyken' and 'Zabeliana', and others still have distinctive foliage, including 'Camelliifolia', with twisted leaves, 'Latifolia', a very large-leaved cultivar, and 'Rotundifolia', a good bushy cultivar for hedging, with leaves half as wide as long.

Origin: south-east Europe and Asia Minor.

P. lusitanica, the Portugal Laurel

Closely related to the Cherry Laurel, but in many ways superior, though the leaves are smaller. Portugal Laurel is hardier and better able to tolerate chalky soils, even shallow ones, than the Cherry Laurel. Its flowers also have more decorative value, and it more readily grows into a slightly taller tree. Although Portugal Laurel is more rarely used for hedging in Britain, it makes at least as good a hedge as the Cherry Laurel.

Size: usually attaining about 8m (25ft) in height, but sometimes considerably more, and forming a large, more or less conical shrub or a small to medium tree.

Leaves: about 7 or 8cm (3in) long, oval to elliptical with a slightly attenuated tip and finely toothed margins, dark glossy green above, leaf stalks and young branches reddish.

Flowers: small, white, in long pendulous spikes, opening in June.

Fruits: small, red at first becoming dark purple.

Cultivation: easy on almost any soil, even on shallow chalky ones. Usually slower-growing than the Cherry Laurel. With careful pruning, it can make a very fine large hedge or screen or, with time, a beautiful specimen tree.

Propagation: as for *P. laurocerasus*.

Varieties: 'Myrtifolia' has smaller leaves than the type and grows into a dense conical shape; 'Variegata' has foliage variegated with white, sometimes tinged with pink; subsp. *azorica* has larger, thicker leaves than the type, characteristically a bright green colour, reddish when very young.

Origin: south-west Europe.

QUERCUS

See entry under TREES.

Prunus lusitanica

Rhamnus alaternus

RHAMNUS

A large genus of mainly deciduous shrubs and trees with inconspicuous flowers but attractive fruits.

R. alaternus, the Mediterranean Buckthorn

A large, fast-growing, erect shrub with glossy foliage. The attractive fruits are not always seen in cultivation.

Size: up to about 3m (10ft) high, sometimes more.

Leaves: more or less oval, but rather variable, about 2.5 to 5cm (1 to 2in) long, glossy, leathery, dark green.

Fruits: small round berries, red at first, becoming black. Often sparse or lacking in cultivation in Britain.

Cultivation: thrives in a wide range of soils, tolerates pollution and is excellent near the sea. Happy in sun or moderate shade. Damaged by frost in very cold areas.

Propagation: by cuttings inserted into free-draining compost in shade under glass in autumn or winter.

Varieties: 'Argenteovariegata' has leaves marbled with grey and with a creamy-white margin, but is less vigorous and a little less hardy than the type.

Origin: the Mediterranean region and Portugal.

TROCHODENDRON

A genus with its own family (Trochodendraceae), containing only one species.

T. aralioides

A large, spreading shrub or small tree, slow-growing in cultivation in Britain. Its odd green flowers are quietly attractive.

Size: up to as much as 9m (30ft) high, but often less.

Leaves: rather variable in size and shape, generally broadly oval to obovate but sometimes narrower, about 5 to 10cm (2 to 4in) long, leathery, shiny, pale green.

Flowers: borne in branched heads in spring and early summer, round, about 12mm (1/2in) in diameter, and green in colour.

Cultivation: prefers a moist loam with high humus content, in sun or shade. It is not happy in shallow chalky soils.

Propagation: by cuttings of half-ripe shoots in summer, inserted into sandy compost in a propagator with bottom heat.

Origin: China (Taiwan), Korea and Japan.

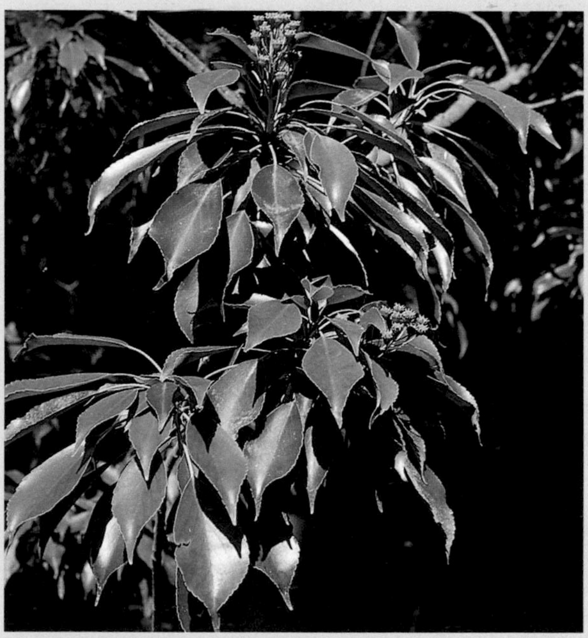

Trochodendron aralioides

SHRUBS WITH SHOWY OR STRONGLY SCENTED FLOWERS

ARBUTUS

See entry under TREES.

BERBERIS

A genus of several hundred deciduous and evergreen, usually spiny, shrubs, mainly from the Himalayan region and the Far East, but also occurring in other parts of Asia, Europe, north Africa and the Americas. The evergreen species are almost all from the Himalayan region, China and South America.

They are generally easy to grow and quite tough, tolerating most soils, even rather poor ones. They have attractive flowers, more or less invariably of a shade of yellow but, while a few cover themselves with a mass of bloom, most tend to hide their flowers under their leaves and are not outstanding as flowering shrubs. Flowering is often poor if berberis are grown in too much shade. The fruits are usually black or bluish-black and rarely stand out well against the dark foliage, but can be quietly attractive. Many evergreen berberis are well clothed with foliage to ground level and make good ground cover or informal hedges and screens. Some can be clipped into formal hedges. Being prickly, they are fairly good at deterring animals and unwanted intruders. Berberis are often propagated by seed, but cross-pollinate very readily and many seed-grown plants are hybrids. For this reason, many berberis in cultivation are not true to name.

B. calliantha

A small, dense, prickly shrub with leaves like small holly leaves. The young stems are red.

Size: up to about 1.2m (4ft) high and usually at least as much wide.

Leaves: about 2.5 to 5cm (1 to 2in) long, broadly elliptical with prickly margins, glossy dark green above, whitish beneath.

Flowers: large for the genus, solitary or in clusters of two or three, opening in spring, pale yellow, hanging below the branches and rarely making a good show.

Cultivation: easy in most soils, tolerates sun or moderate shade. Usually well clothed with leaves down to the ground, it can make attractive ground cover or a low, formal or informal hedge.

Propagation: by seed sown in early winter and exposed to frost; by layering.

Origin: southern Tibet.

B. candidula

A small, very dense, spiny shrub forming a mound of arching branches clothed with shiny dark green foliage.

Size: up to about 90cm (3ft) high and often twice as wide.

Leaves: elliptical, about 12mm (1/2in) or a little more in length, stiff and leathery, glossy dark green above and whitish underneath, with a few short prickles on the margins.

Flowers: solitary, pale yellow, opening in spring, rather small and often hidden among the foliage.

Cultivation: easy, tolerant of a wide range of soils and sun or shade. Good ground cover but rather dull.

Propagation: as for *B. calliantha.*

Origin: western China.

B. coxii

A medium-sized species with striking foliage.

Size: up to about 1.5m (5ft) tall.

Leaves: about 2.5 to 5cm (1 to 2in) long, elliptical, with prickly margins, dark green above and whitish underneath.

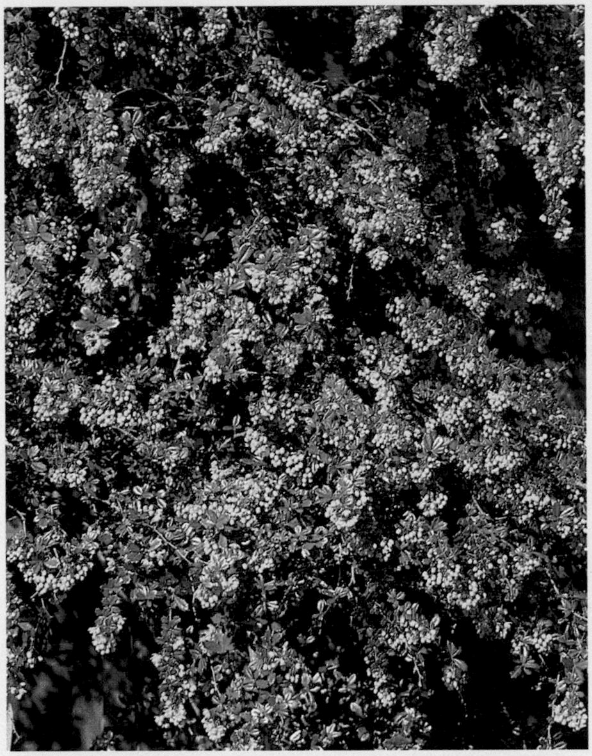

Berberis darwinii

Flowers: yellow, in small hanging clusters in spring.

Cultivation: tolerant of most soil types, prefers sun or light shade.

Propagation: by seed, as for *B. calliantha*; by cuttings of well-ripened young shoots in autumn or winter, inserted into sandy compost under glass; by layering.

Origin: northern Burma.

B. darwinii

One of the finest plants in the genus and a highly ornamental, large flowering shrub. It responds well to clipping and can be made into a formal hedge, though it may become rather bare at the base with age. It is excellent as an informal hedge.

Size: up to about 3m (10ft) tall and about 1.8m (6ft) across, quite fast growing.

Leaves: like small holly leaves, about 2.5cm (1in) long, glossy dark green.

Flowers: orange, borne in hanging clusters in March, April or May, often more or less covering the plant.

Cultivation: easy in most soils, likes sun or light shade. As a hedge, prune or clip immediately after flowering has finished.

Propagation: as for *B. coxii*.

Origin: Argentina and Chile.

B. gagnepainii

A small to medium shrub of dense growth, excellent as an informal hedge but can also be clipped to make a low formal hedge.

Size: usually up to about 1.5m (5ft) tall and about 90cm (3ft) wide.

Leaves: narrowly oval, 2.5cm (1in) or more long, with prickly margins, dark green or greyish-green above, paler beneath, densely clothing the branches.

Flowers: yellow, in clusters of three to five in spring.

Cultivation: easy in most soils in sun or light shade. For hedging, prune or clip after flowering.

Propagation: as for *B. coxii*.

Origin: western China.

Berberis julianae

B. julianae

A large shrub densely clothed with leaves to ground level. One of the best berberis for hedging.

Size: up to about 3m (10ft) tall and 1.8m (6ft) wide, fairly quick growing.

Leaves: lanceolate to elliptical, about 2.5 to 7.5cm (1 to 3in) long, with prickly margins, dark green above, paler beneath.

Flowers: pale yellow, slightly scented, in hanging clusters of ten or more, opening in spring.

Cultivation: easy in most soils, in sun or moderate shade. Makes an excellent, dense, prickly hedge, well clothed with leaves to ground level. Best as an informal hedge but can be pruned or clipped after flowering to make a formal hedge.

Propagation: as for *B. coxii*.

Origin: western China.

B. linearifolia

A somewhat untidy shrub with a tendency to sucker, but with the most strongly coloured flowers of any of the berberis. It needs careful siting to avoid colour clashes with neighbouring plants. The narrow, non-prickly leaves are very different from those of most of its relatives.

Size: about 1.8m (6ft) tall and rather less than that across, but increasing in width with age as suckers arise near the base of the plant.

Leaves: about 2.5 to 5cm (1 to 2in) long, linear, dark green with smooth edges.

Berberis* x *stenophylla

Flowers: reddish-orange, produced in early spring, making a fine display.

Cultivation: easy in most soils, best in sun or light shade. The growth is upright and rather straggly, so this is not a good hedging plant, except as a very informal hedge.

Propagation: by removing suckers from the base of the plant, or by seed, cuttings or layering (as for *B. coxii*).

Varieties: 'Orange King' is a selected cultivar with larger flowers of a very strong colour.

Origin: Argentina, Chile.

B. manipurana

A vigorous large shrub with bold foliage.

Size: up to about 3m (10ft) tall.

Leaves: elliptical to broadly elliptical, about 7.5cm (3in) long, with a few marginal prickles, dark green, shiny.

Flowers: yellow, in hanging clusters of up to about 20, opening in spring.

Cultivation: easy in most soils, in sun or light shade.

Propagation: as for *B. coxii*.

Origin: north-east India.

B. pruinosa

A vigorous medium shrub with sea-green foliage.

Size: usually 1.5 to 1.8m (5 to 6ft) tall.

Leaves: more or less elliptical, about 5cm (2in) long, coarsely toothed, stiffly leathery, dark glossy green above, whitish beneath.

Flowers: yellow, in clusters of about a dozen, opening in spring.

Cultivation: easy in most soils, in sun or partial shade.

Propagation: as for *B. coxii*.

Origin: south-east Tibet, south-west China.

B. sargentiana

A very fine medium to large, dense shrub with decorative foliage and reddish branches.

Size: usually up to about 1.8 to 2.1m (6 to 7ft) tall or a little more.

Leaves: elliptical, up to 10 to 12.5cm (4 to 5in) long, with finely prickly margins, reddish when young, dark green and leathery when mature.

Flowers: pale yellow with some red streaks, borne in small clusters of about half a dozen, opening in April or May.

Cultivation: easy in most soils, either in sun or moderate shade.

Propagation: as for *B. coxii*.

Origin: western China.

B. verruculosa

A small to medium shrub with arching branches, forming a dense mound.

Size: slowly attaining as much as 1.5 to 1.8m (5 to 6ft) high, or even a little more after many years, and as much across.

Leaves: rather small, usually not more than 2.5cm (1in) long, elliptical to obovate, glossy dark green above and whitish beneath.

Flowers: golden-yellow, but usually solitary and not making much of a show.

Cultivation: easy in most soils, either in sun or moderate shade.

Propagation: as for *B. coxii*.

Origin: western China.

B. x lologensis

An extremely attractive natural hybrid producing a fine display of flowers in spring. It is a vigorous grower, rapidly attaining several feet in height, and can make a good informal hedge.

Size: up to about 1.8 to 2.4m (6 to 8ft) tall, of fairly erect habit.

Leaves: variable, in a range of shapes intermediate between those of leaves of the parent plants, sometimes with prickly and non-prickly leaves on the same plant.

Flowers: apricot-yellow in hanging clusters in spring.

Cultivation: easy in most soils, in sun or light shade.

Propagation: as it is a hybrid it will not come true from seed; by cuttings, as for *B. coxii*; by layering; sometimes basal suckers can be separated from the parent plant.

Varieties: 'Apricot Queen' is a fine selected cultivar. A couple of other cultivars, also good, are sometimes offered by nurseries.

Origin: a natural hybrid between *B. darwinii* and *B. linearifolia*, found in Argentina.

B. x stenophylla

A large and somewhat untidy shrub, spreading into a wide clump by basal suckers. Can form a very effective, dense, spiny informal hedge where sufficient space exists, but not recommended for small gardens. Very attractive in flower.

Size: up to about 3m (10ft) tall, basal shoots at first erect and then arching, suckering at the base to form an ever-widening clump.

Leaves: small, less than 2.5cm (1in) long, narrowly elliptical or lanceolate, dark green, spine tipped.

Flowers: golden-yellow, scented, borne in clusters in April and May, making a good show.

Cultivation: easy in almost any soil, best in sun or light shade.

Propagation: easily propagated by digging out and separating basal suckers.

Varieties: 'Autumnalis' is a smaller cultivar which usually flowers twice a year, in spring and autumn; 'Coccinea' is a small cultivar with red flower buds opening orange; 'Irwinii' is another small cultivar with deep yellow flowers; 'Lemon Queen' ('Cream Showers') has pale flowers; 'Pink Pearl', a variable shrub, has leaves sometimes dark green and sometimes variegated with pink and cream, and flowers of different colours on the same bush, from pale yellow to orange or pink or a mixture of these colours. Several other cultivars, mainly small or dwarf, also exist.

Origin: a hybrid between *B. darwinii* and *B. empetrifolia*.

B. chrysosphaera, **B. congestiflora**, **B. glaucocarpa**, **B. hypokerina**, **B. lempergiana**, **B. replicata** and **B. veitchii** are other evergreen species sometimes available from nurseries that are well worth a place in the garden. There are also a number of other evergreen berberis species, mostly scarce in cultivation, that may occasionally be encountered. Most are easily grown and attractive, if not always outstanding.

BRACHYGLOTTIS

(formerly included in **Senecio**)

Small or medium shrubs, most of them with grey leaves and bearing yellow flowers in summer, similar to those of Ragwort. They were formerly included in the same genus as Ragwort, *Senecio*. They are generally not very hardy but are excellent in coastal areas, suffering little or no damage from salt-laden winds. They make good informal hedges and will withstand some clipping.

B. elaeagnifolia

A stiff, dense shrub of medium size with flowers of little decorative value.

Size: up to about 1.5 to 1.8m (5 to 6ft) tall.

Leaves: 7.5 to 15cm (3 to 6in) long, oval, leathery, glossy above, thickly felted with buff hairs beneath.

Flowers: in clusters at the ends of branches, small, not very showy.

Cultivation: likes a dryish, free-draining soil and plenty of sun. Stands coastal exposure very well, but needs to be given shelter inland and may suffer badly in cold winters.

***Brachyglottis* 'Sunshine'**

Propagation: by cuttings of half-ripened wood in late summer, inserted into sandy compost under glass.

Origin: New Zealand.

B. monroi

A small, dense shrub often wider than it is high with showy flowers.

Size: up to 90cm (3ft) tall and usually more across.

Leaves: elliptical or oval, about 5 to 7.5cm (2 to 3in) long, densely white-felted all over when young, the upper surface gradually losing these hairs and becoming greenish.

Flowers: yellow, opening in summer, similar to Ragwort flowers, borne in dense clusters at the ends of the branches.

Cultivation: likes well-drained soil in full sun. Not very hardy but does well in coastal areas.

Propagation: as for *B. elaeagnifolia.*

Origin: New Zealand.

B. rotundifolia (Senecio reinholdii)

A dense, rounded shrub of medium size. Its flowers are not very showy.

Size: up to about 1.5 to 1.8m (5 to 6ft) tall and about as much across.

Leaves: thick, rounded and leathery, about 7.5 to 12.5cm (3 to 5in) long, glossy green above and felted underneath.

Flowers: yellow, tiny, not very showy.

Cultivation: as for *B. elaeagnifolia*. It is exceptionally resistant to salt-laden winds.

Propagation: as for *B. elaeagnifolia.*

Origin: New Zealand.

B. (Dunedin Group) 'Sunshine'

A dense, broad, rounded shrub with grey foliage and showy yellow flowers. It is hardier than most plants of this genus.

Size: about 90cm (3ft) tall; almost twice as much across.

Leaves: oval to lanceolate, about 5 to 7.5cm (2 to 3in) long, greyish-green above and white beneath.

Flowers: bears clusters of yellow flowers, similar in appearance to those of Ragwort, borne at the ends of the branches in summer.

Cultivation: prefers well-drained soil in a sunny position. Best given some shelter inland and not hardy enough for very cold areas.

Propagation: as for *B. elaeagnifolia.*

Origin: a hybrid derived from two or more species of the genus.

BUPLEURUM

A genus of herbaceous and shrubby plants of the same family as Cow Parsley.

B. fruticosum, the Shrubby Hare's-ear

An unusual shrub, excellent in coastal areas, where it withstands salty winds well.

Size: up to about 1.8m (6ft) tall, and fairly erect in habit.

Leaves: deep bluish-green, shiny, elliptical to obovate, smooth, untoothed.

Flowers: round, flattish heads of yellow flowers open over a long period in summer.

Cultivation: easy in a light soil, even a chalky one, in full sun. Not absolutely hardy and needs some shelter in cold areas inland, but withstands coastal exposure very well.

Bupleurum fruticosum **in seed**

Carpenteria californica

Propagation: by seed collected as soon as ripe and sown immediately in a light compost under glass; by cuttings taken in September and inserted into sandy compost under glass.

Origin: the Mediterranean region.

CARPENTERIA

A genus of only one species.

C. californica

A very attractive flowering shrub of medium size, unfortunately not very hardy. It is best grown against a sunny wall in cooler areas, though it usually recovers well if it suffers damage in winter.

Size: usually up to about 1.8 to 2.4m (6 to 8ft) tall and almost as much across, but can grow larger in mild areas.

Leaves: lanceolate, about 5cm (2in) long, dark green above, greyish-felted beneath.

Flowers: white, five-petalled with a central boss of yellow stamens, up to about 7.5cm (3in) across, opening in June or July.

Cultivation: needs plenty of sun and warmth and a light soil.

Propagation: by cuttings of half-ripened shoots taken in August and inserted into sandy compost under glass; by seed, sown in March in sandy compost under glass.

Varieties: 'Ladham's Variety' is a selected large-flowered cultivar. A couple of other selected cultivars exist.

Origin: California.

CASSINIA

Shrubs of the daisy family with foliage and habit reminiscent of heather. None are fully hardy but a few are good plants for coastal areas.

C. leptophylla

An erect shrub with tiny leaves.

Size: up to about 1.8m (6ft).

Leaves: tiny, dark green, with white or yellowish down beneath, giving an overall greyish appearance.

Cassinia leptophylla subsp. *vauvilliersii*

Ceanothus 'Puget Blue'

Flowers: heads of small white flowers are borne on the ends of branches in late summer.

Cultivation: likes light soil in a warm, sunny position; tolerates chalky soils. Not reliably hardy in cold localities, but happy near coasts.

Propagation: by cuttings taken in summer.

Varieties: subsp. *fulvida*, the Golden Heather, grows to only about half the height and has golden hairy leaves; subsp. *vauvilliersii* is similar to subsp. *fulvida* but taller and less golden; subsp. *vauvilliersii* var. *albida*, the Silver Heather, has stems and leaves covered with silvery-white hairs.

Origin: New Zealand.

CEANOTHUS

A large genus of evergreen, semi-evergreen and deciduous shrubs, often called Californian lilacs. Many have attractive, glossy foliage and plentiful flowers, but unfortunately none is very hardy. Only the hardiest are described below. Late frosts will often destroy the flower buds of the spring-flowering kinds even if the rest of the plant is little damaged. They cannot really be recommended for cold areas but, because most have lovely blue flowers unrivalled in any other moderately hardy shrub, many gardeners will feel that they are worth taking some trouble to grow. They need a warm site with plenty of sun and are usually best planted against a wall, although in warm coastal areas they will do well in open situations. They generally do not flourish on very chalky soils.

C. thyrsiflorus

A large shrub with bright blue flowers and attractive glossy foliage.

Size: can attain 9m (30ft) in height in favoured localities, but 4.5 to 6m (15 to 20ft) is more usual.

Leaves: small, more or less oval, about 2.5cm (1in) in length, dark, glossy green with toothed margins.

Flowers: individually small, in dense, rounded clusters, often smothering the shrub, bright blue with a hint of lilac, opening in May or June.

Cultivation: easy in a light to medium loam in a warm, sunny position, against a wall except in mild areas. Dead flower heads are best pruned off after flowering.

Propagation: by cuttings inserted into sandy compost under glass in September.

Varieties: var. *repens* is a low-growing, spreading variety, reaching about 0.9m to 1.2m (3 to 4ft) high and several times as wide.

Origin: California.

C. x veitchianus

A large hybrid Californian lilac which is outstanding for its hardiness, depth of flower colour and freedom of flowering.

Size: up to about 3m (10ft) tall.

Leaves: similar to those of *C. thyrsiflorus* but a little larger and broader.

Flowers: masses of small, blue flowers in rounded clusters in May and June.

Cultivation: as for *C. thyrsiflorus*.

Propagation: as for *C. thyrsiflorus*.

Origin: a garden hybrid between *C. rigidus* and *C. thyrsiflorus*.

C. 'Autumnal Blue'

Unusual among evergreen Californian lilacs in that it flowers in late summer and autumn.

Size: up to about 3m (10ft) or a little more in height and almost as wide.

Leaves: similar to those of *C. thyrsiflorus* but usually a little larger.

Flowers: masses of rich blue flowers which open from July onwards.

Cultivation: as for *C. thyrsiflorus*, but any pruning should be done in spring.

Propagation: by cuttings taken in winter and inserted into sandy compost under glass, preferably with bottom heat.

Origin: a garden hybrid of uncertain parentage.

C. 'Delight' is very fine, with rich blue flowers in spring; **C. 'Puget Blue'**, which is sometimes listed as a selected form of *C. impressus*, has deep blue flowers in spring to early summer and is very free-flowering; **C. 'Southmead'** is a dense shrub of medium size with dark, glossy foliage and bright blue flowers in late spring. There are many other Californian lilacs, but those listed here are among the hardiest and best for most gardens.

CHOISYA

Shrubs belonging to the same family as Rue, with leaves that smell almost as strongly when bruised.

C. ternata, the Mexican Orange Blossom

A rounded shrub of medium to large size which is surprisingly hardy considering its country of origin. The white flowers are sweetly scented and usually open over a long period.

Size: up to about 1.8m (6ft) tall, or more in favoured, mild areas, and as wide as it is high.

Choisya ternata

Leaves: up to about 10cm (4in) long, divided into three elliptical to oblanceolate leaflets, the central one slightly larger than the others, shiny, mid- to dark green, aromatic when rubbed or crushed.

Flowers: white, five-petalled, about 2.5cm (1in) across, in fairly dense clusters at the ends of the branches, opening in spring and summer and sometimes again in autumn.

Cultivation: easy in most soils in sun or shade. Best sheltered from cold winds, but hardy enough to survive most winters undamaged. Early flower buds may be destroyed by late frosts, but more will appear later.

Propagation: by cuttings of half-ripened wood taken in late summer and inserted into sandy compost under glass.

Varieties: 'Lich' (Sundance), a cultivar with golden foliage that rarely flowers, is less robust and hardy than the type, and usually smaller in size.

Origin: Mexico.

C. 'Aztec Pearl' is a smaller shrub of hybrid origin with narrower leaflets.

CISTUS

A fairly large genus mainly from the Mediterranean region, known as sun roses in English. Most are small shrubs but a few are of medium to large size. They all require a warm, sunny position in free-draining soil and none is very hardy. They are extremely wind-resistant, however, and thrive in warmer coastal areas. They are also tolerant of chalky soils. All sun roses flower over quite a long period, usually during May, June and July, bearing delicate flowers with five crumpled petals and a central mass of yellow stamens. The individual flowers last only a day, but sufficient are produced to make a fine display, especially on hot, sunny days. Sun roses are quite easily grown from seed, but they tend to hybridize readily, so that if different kinds are grown together the seed collected from them will often produce hybrid offspring.

C. albidus, the Grey-leaved Sun Rose

A small, rounded bush with greyish-white foliage and quite large, purplish-pink flowers.

Size: up to about 60 to 90cm (2 to 3ft) tall and as much across.

***Choisya ternata* 'Lich'**

Cistus albidus

Leaves: more or less elliptical, 2.5 to 5cm (1 to 2in) long, densely covered with greyish-white hairs.

Flowers: about 5cm (2in) across, purplish-pink.

Cultivation: easy in a sunny position in mild areas, preferably in a light soil.

Propagation: by seed sown in sandy compost under glass in March; by cuttings taken in September and inserted into sandy compost under glass.

Origin: the western Mediterranean area.

C. clusii

A delicate shrub with very narrow leaves and rather small, white flowers.

Size: up to about 90cm (3ft) tall.

Leaves: linear, dark green above, whitish-hairy beneath, up to about 2.5cm (1in) long.

Flowers: white, about 2.5cm (1in) in diameter.

Cultivation: needs plenty of sun and heat; can only be recommended for southern Britain, especially coasts.

Propagation: as for *C. albidus*.

Origin: Spain, Italy, north-west Africa.

C. creticus (C. villosus)

A small, usually rounded, shrub, with young stems clothed with reddish hairs. It is very like *C. albidus*, but the leaves are greener and the flowers are usually slightly less purplish.

Size: up to about 90cm (3ft) tall.

Leaves: oval to elliptical, varying in size but usually about 2.5cm (1in) long, green or greyish-green.

Flowers: purplish-pink, about 5cm (2in) across.

Cultivation: as for *C. albidus*.

Propagation: as for *C. albidus*.

Origin: the Mediterranean region.

C. ladanifer, the Gum Sun Rose

An aromatic and sticky shrub, of medium or sometimes large size, one of the largest of the sun roses. The large flowers have attractive blotches at the base of each petal. Often confused with *C.* x *cyprius*.

Size: up to about 1.2 to 1.5m (4 or 5ft) tall, more in favoured areas.

Leaves: narrowly lanceolate, about 5 to 7.5cm (2 to 3in) long, deep green above, paler and hairy beneath.

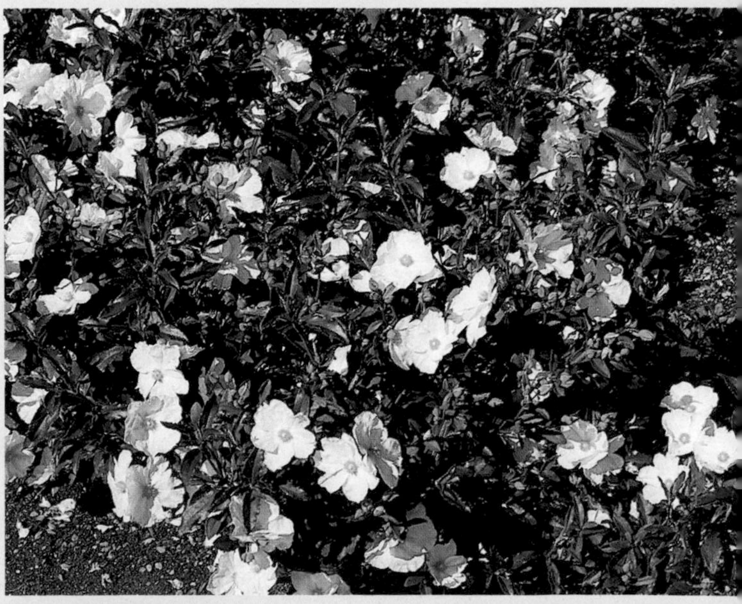

Cistus ladanifer var. *sulcatus*

Flowers: up to 10cm (4in) across, white with a maroon blotch at the base of each petal.

Cultivation: not very hardy, but good in warm coastal areas. Needs plenty of sun and well-drained soil.

Propagation: as for *C. albidus*.

Varieties: 'Pat' is a very large-flowered, comparatively hardy cultivar; var. *albiflorus* has completely white, unblotched flowers; var. *sulcatus* (*C. palhinhae*) is lower growing, also with pure white flowers.

Origin: the western Mediterranean region.

C. laurifolius

One of the largest and hardiest of the sun roses, the best species to try in colder parts of Britain.

Size: usually up to about 1.8m (6ft) high, but can grow taller in favoured localities; of fairly erect habit.

Leaves: oval to lanceolate, about 5cm (2in) long, dark green above, white and hairy beneath.

Flowers: white, about 5cm (2in) or a little more across.

Cistus salviifolius

Cultivation: easy in full sun in a light soil, quite vigorous and fairly hardy.

Propagation: as for *C. albidus*.

Origin: south-western parts of Europe.

C. monspeliensis, the Narrow-leaved or Montpelier Sun Rose

A small sun rose with narrow, green leaves and white flowers.

Size: up to about 60cm (2ft) tall.

Leaves: linear to narrowly lanceolate, about 2.5cm (1in) long, dark green above, greyish beneath.

Flowers: white, about 2.5cm (1in) in diameter.

Cultivation: as for *C. albidus*.

Propagation: as for *C. albidus*.

Origin: the Mediterranean region.

C. populifolius

One of the hardiest species, of medium size, with moderately large white flowers.

Size: up to about 1.5m (5ft) tall, and fairly erect in habit.

Leaves: oval with a slightly heart-shaped base, deep green above, paler and hairy beneath, up to about 10cm (4in) long.

Flowers: white, about 5cm (2in) across.

Cultivation: as for *C. laurifolius*.

Propagation: as for *C. albidus*.

Origin: south-western parts of Europe and north-west Africa.

C. salviifolius, the Sage-leaved Sun Rose

A low, spreading shrub with greyish-green leaves and quite large, white flowers.

Cistus x *purpureus*

Size: up to about 90cm (3ft) tall, often rather less, and usually wider than high.

Leaves: oval to elliptical, greyish-green, about 2.5cm (1in) long.

Flowers: white, nearly 5cm (2in) across.

Cultivation: as for *C. albidus*.

Propagation: as for *C. albidus*.

Varieties: 'Prostratus' is a very low-growing, spreading cultivar.

Origin: the Mediterranean region.

C. x cyprius

A vigorous and comparatively hardy hybrid of medium to large size.

Size: up to about 1.8 m (6ft) tall or a little more.

Leaves: intermediate between those of its parents, lanceolate, deep green above.

Flowers: white with a dark red blotch at the base of each petal, about 7.5cm (3in) across.

Cultivation: as for *C. laurifolius*.

Propagation: as for *C. albidus*.

Varieties: 'Albiflorus' has pure white flowers.

Origin: a hybrid between *C. ladanifer* and *C. laurifolius*.

C. x hybridus (C. x corbariensis)

A fairly hardy sun rose of moderate size, with white flowers.

Size: up to about 90cm (3ft) high.

Leaves: oval, green, and about 2.5 to 7.5cm (1 to 3in) long.

Flowers: white, about 5cm (2in) across.

Cultivation: as for *C. laurifolius*.

Propagation: as for *C. albidus*.

Origin: a hybrid between *C. populifolius* and *C. salviifolius*.

C. 'Silver Pink'

Another very hardy hybrid of uncertain origin. The name describes the flower colour.

Size: up to about 90cm (3ft) tall.

Leaves: oval, about 2.5 to 5cm (1 to 2in) long, green.

Flowers: bright pink, about 5cm (2in) across.

Cultivation: as for *C. laurifolius*.

Propagation: as for *C. albidus*.

Origin: a chance seedling, possibly a hybrid between *C. incanus* and *C. laurifolius*.

C. x dansereaui, **C. x pulverulentus 'Sunset'** and **C. x purpureus** are among a number of other *Cistus* hybrids and cultivars that are highly ornamental and very worthy of cultivation, especially in mild coastal areas where they will thrive.

COTONEASTER

See entry under SHRUBS for most soils, with showy fruits.

DAPHNE

A medium-sized genus of mainly small, deciduous and evergreen shrubs which occur in Europe, north Africa and Asia. The flowers are tubular with usually four spreading lobes and almost always have a strong, sweet fragrance. Some bear conspicuous berries after the flowers. Most daphnes tend to bear their leaves clustered towards the ends of the branches, sometimes almost in whorls close to the tips. They are tolerant of both acid and alkaline soils. All parts of most daphnes are poisonous to man, though their berries are often eaten by birds.

D. acutiloba

One of the larger daphnes, with white flowers in July, often followed by red fruits. It tends not to be long lived and there are some doubts about its hardiness. It is a woodland plant in the wild and therefore might be expected to benefit from some shelter.

Size: usually up to about 1.2 to 1.5m (4 to 5ft) tall, fairly erect and open in habit.

Leaves: lanceolate, about 5 to 7.5cm (2 to 3in) long, bright green, somewhat leathery.

Flowers: white, in clusters of about five to seven, usually not very fragrant, opening in June or July.

Fruits: red berries, which ripen in late summer or early autumn.

Daphne acutiloba

Cultivation: grows best in a humus-rich, fertile soil in sun or light shade. Doubtfully hardy in cold areas and therefore best given some protection, especially shelter from cold winds.

Propagation: usually self-pollinates and fruits freely. Birds may eat the fruits, but if some can be collected when ripe or nearly ripe seeds can be extracted from the soft pulp. These seeds can be sown immediately and usually germinate within two months. The seedlings should then be kept under glass through the winter and grown on the next year. Seed can also be kept until the spring and appears still to germinate well. Cuttings of half-ripened wood taken in July or August also often give good results.

Origin: western China.

Daphne bholua

D. bholua

An extremely fine winter-flowering shrub which is unfortunately not easy to propagate and so remains rather scarce in cultivation. It is variable and is sometimes completely deciduous: in hard winters even the more evergreen forms may lose at least some of their leaves. The hardiest forms are probably those that are deciduous, but the evergreen cultivars usually available in Britain are reasonably hardy. It does not fruit well in cultivation.

Size: in the wild it may reach as much as 3.6m (12ft) or even rather more in height, but in cultivation it usually does not exceed 3m (10ft).

Leaves: narrowly elliptical to oblanceolate, about 5 to 10cm (2 to 4in) long, dark green, somewhat leathery.

Flowers: white, usually suffused with pink or purple, at least on the outside, opening from as early as November until as late as March, very fragrant.

Cultivation: the evergreen forms are woodland plants in the wild and are best planted in humus-rich soil with plenty of moisture, but free-draining, in light to moderate shade. Even very chalky soils are tolerated well. It is often erect and rather openly branched and, like many daphnes, benefits from having the tips of branches trimmed off from time to time to encourage a more bushy habit.

Propagation: If fresh seed can be obtained it usually germinates well, but old seed soon becomes less viable. Softwood cuttings taken with a heel in late spring or early summer often root well but may be slow to grow away. Layering, including air layering, might be expected to be rather more successful. Grafting on to stock of more common daphnes is a frequently used means of propagating this plant.

Varieties: 'Damon Ridge' is a hardy, evergreen cultivar; 'Jacqueline Postill' is evergreen to semi-evergreen with pink flowers in January and February.

Origin: the Himalayan region, from Nepal eastwards.

D. laureola, the Spurge Laurel

An uncommon native species, not one of the best daphnes, because its flowers are rather dull and greenish, usually with poor scent. It flowers early in the year and tolerates considerable shade, so has some value in the garden.

Size: up to about 1.5m (5ft) tall, fairly erect, usually quite bushy.

Leaves: obovate to oblanceolate, about 2.5 to 5cm (1 to 2in) long, dark green, leathery.

Flowers: green or yellowish-green, in clusters of up to about ten in leaf axils near the tips of branches, usually poorly scented but sometimes pleasantly fragrant towards evening, opening in February to April.

Fruits: small black berries.

Cultivation: easy in most soils, particularly happy in an alkaline woodland soil. Tolerates sun and heavy shade but is best in light to moderate shade.

Propagation: easily grown from seed. Collect the berries when they ripen and remove the seeds from the fleshy pulp. Sow them immediately and leave them over winter, allowing exposure to cold. They should germinate the following spring. Old seed germinates slowly and erratically. Cuttings of half-ripe wood taken in July and August usually root well.

Varieties: subsp. *philippi* from the Pyrenees is low growing and compact, usually not more than about 38cm (15in) high.

Origin: Europe, including Britain, and north Africa.

D. odora

A fine shrub with very fragrant flowers in late winter and early spring. However, it very rarely produces fruits in cultivation.

Size: up to about 1.5 to 1.8m (5 to 6ft) tall, rather openly branched, more or less erect when young but often spreading with age.

Leaves: clustered towards the tips of the shoots, glossy green, leathery, oblanceolate, about 5 to 7.5cm (2 to 3in) long.

Flowers: in dense terminal clusters, reddish-purple in bud, white or pinkish inside, very sweetly fragrant, usually opening in February or March.

Cultivation: not reliably hardy in Britain, good against a north- or west-facing wall. Tends not to flower well in heavy shade. A humus-rich soil is best. It does not like very chalky soils.

Daphne odora 'Aureomarginata'

Propagation: most easily propagated by cuttings, either of the tips of shoots, taken in January or February, or of half-ripe shoots taken in July or August. Both kinds root most readily in a closed propagator with bottom heat.

Varieties: 'Aureomarginata', a cultivar with leaves edged with pale yellow or cream, is hardier than the type and can be grown outside satisfactorily at least in southern England. There are several other selected cultivars available.

Origin: long cultivated in the Far East, probably a native of China.

D. pontica

Somewhat resembling the Spurge Laurel, this is another daphne that is not among the most beautiful, but it is hardy and fairly easy to grow and produces fragrant flowers early in the year.

Size: may attain as much as 1.5m (5ft) in height, but usually not exceeding 90cm (3ft). It is often twice as wide as high.

Leaves: clustered towards the ends of the branches, deep shiny green and leathery, obovate, about 5 to 10cm (2 to 4in) long.

Flowers: yellowish-green, in pairs or threes in the upper leaf axils, usually fragrant, with a long, slender tube and narrow lobes.

Fruits: small black berries, usually freely produced.

Cultivation: easy in similar conditions to *D. laureola*, except that it has less preference for alkaline soil.

Propagation: as for *D. laureola*.

Origin: Bulgaria, Turkey and the Caucasus.

D. tangutica (including **D. retusa**)

A robust, hardy daphne flowering in spring and usually producing plentiful bright red fruits, which birds find very palatable.

Size: up to about 1.8m (6ft) tall but often less, more or less erect and rather openly branched.

Leaves: oblanceolate to elliptical, about 5cm (2in) long, deep green.

Flowers: purplish-red outside, white and sometimes tinged with reddish-purple within, very fragrant, with the blooms opening during April and May.

Fruits: red berries, usually freely produced but rapidly eaten by birds.

Cultivation: easy in a humus-rich soil in full sun or partial shade. Sometimes said to need an acid soil, but good specimens have been grown on chalk.

Propagation: fresh seeds sown in autumn and exposed to cold winter conditions usually germinate well the following spring. Cuttings of both soft wood taken in June or July, and half-ripe wood taken in late July or August, usually root easily.

Varieties: *D. retusa* used to be considered a separate species from *D. tangutica*. In the wild a range of intermediates occurs which does not allow two separate species to be maintained, but in cultivation the two are noticeably different. The description above refers to *D. tangutica* in the narrow sense. What is now often referred to as *D. tangutica* Retusa Group is a smaller, more compact and rounded shrub of slower growth, usually growing to about 60cm (2ft) high and at least as wide.

Origin: west China.

Daphne retusa

D. x hybrida

A rare hybrid which apparently originated in France in 1820, valuable for its long period of flowering. It appears to be sterile, producing no fruits.

Size: up to about 1.5m (5ft) tall and at least half as much across.

Leaves: usually about 5cm (2in) long or a little more, oblanceolate, dark green and glossy.

Flowers: in small clusters at the ends of branches, deep reddish-purple outside, paler inside, very fragrant, opening more or less throughout the year, though usually mainly in spring and autumn and with little or no flower in July and August.

Cultivation: of doubtful hardiness, so it is best in a sheltered site, treated like *D. odora*.

Propagation: since seed cannot be used, the best method is by cuttings of half-ripe wood taken in July and August.

Origin: believed to be a hybrid between *D. odora* and *D. collina*.

DISTYLIUM

A small genus of evergreen trees and shrubs related to the witch hazels (*Hamamelis*), mainly from tropical to subtropical areas in east and south-east Asia. Only one or two species are hardy enough to be grown outdoors in the cooler climates of northern Europe.

D. racemosum

A slow-growing evergreen shrub or small tree with shiny, leathery leaves, producing moderately showy flowers in spring.

Size: rarely growing to more than about 3m (10ft) in cultivation, but occasionally attains tree size. Usually wide spreading.

Leaves: about 5cm (2in) long, elliptical to obovate, leathery, dark green, shiny.

Flowers: in small clusters, with no petals but conspicuous red stamens, opening in April.

Cultivation: best in woodland conditions, with a humus-rich soil with plenty of moisture and partial shade. Best sheltered from cold winds.

Propagation: by cuttings of half-ripened wood taken in July and inserted into sandy compost in a closed propagator with bottom heat.

Origin: Japan, Korea and China.

ELAEAGNUS

See entry under SHRUBS for most soils, mainly for foliage effect.

ESCALLONIA

A medium-sized genus of evergreen shrubs, mainly from South America. They are among the more attractive flowering evergreens, but unfortunately are generally not very hardy and will rarely thrive in cold areas inland unless they are given some protection from severe frosts. Even if they do not suffer any serious frost damage, they may tend to be semi-evergreen in colder areas. They are excellent near coasts, however, where they make good hedges and screens. Most of the escallonias commonly grown are hybrids, which are often hardier than the species. Any necessary pruning, or clipping when used for hedging, should be done immediately after flowering. Escallonia flowers have five petals and are fairly small, varying from white through pink to red. The seed-capsules are not showy.

E. rubra

A variable, medium to large shrub, excellent in coastal areas, where it withstands gales very well. It makes a fine hedge or wind-break.

Size: up to about 3m (10ft) tall or a little more and rather less in width.

Leaves: rather small, about 2.5cm (1in) long, glossy dark green above, obovate, with toothed margins, aromatic.

Flowers: red, in clusters along the branches, about 12mm (1/2in) in diameter, opening in July.

Escallonia 'Apple Blossom'

Cultivation: easy in any light soil, in sun or light shade. Best grown against a wall in colder areas.

Propagation: by cuttings of ripened wood inserted into sandy compost under glass in late summer or early winter.

Varieties: 'Crimson Spire' is an erect, vigorous cultivar growing to about 2.1m (7ft) tall, with bright crimson flowers; 'Ingramii' is tall and vigorous, up to about 4m (13ft) high, with deep pink flowers; 'Woodside' is a small, spreading shrub with crimson flowers; var. *macrantha* is rather larger than the type, up to about 4m (13ft) tall, vigorous, with rosy-red flowers in June.

Origin: Chile.

E. 'Apple Blossom', **E. 'Donard Radiance'**, **E. 'Edinensis'**, **E. 'Langleyensis'**, **E. 'Peach Blossom'** and **E. 'Pride of Donard'** are all excellent cultivars of hybrid origin, most of them growing to between about 1.8 to 2.4m (6 to 8ft) tall.

EUCRYPHIA

A small genus of deciduous and evergreen shrubs and trees from South America and Australasia. Few are very hardy and none is suitable for very cold districts unless they can be given shelter. They like to have their roots shaded and are generally not very lime-tolerant. Where they can be grown well, they are extremely beautiful summer-flowering shrubs or small trees, smothering themselves with white flowers which have four petals and a conspicuous central mass of yellow stamens.

E. lucida

The hardiest of the evergreen species, growing into a large, dense shrub or eventually a small tree, especially in mild areas. It bears fragrant flowers in early summer.

Size: up to about 4.5m (15ft) tall, more in mild areas.

Leaves: elliptical, undivided, about 5 to 7.5cm (2 to 3in) long, glossy dark green above, glaucous beneath.

Eucryphia x *nymansensis*

Eucryphia x *nymansensis* 'Nymansay' flowers

Flowers: fragrant, white, somewhat pendulous, about 5cm (2in) across, opening in June and July.

Cultivation: requires a moist, humus-rich soil, preferably neutral or slightly acid, in a sheltered position, with some shade for the roots.

Propagation: by layering, or by seed sown in spring in a humus-rich compost under glass.

Origin: Tasmania.

E. x intermedia

A fast-growing, reasonably hardy hybrid.

Size: usually up to about 4.5m (15ft) high, but sometimes growing into a small tree, especially in warmer parts of Britain.

Leaves: variable, with both simple and compound leaves with three leaflets occurring on the same plant, usually about 5 to 7.5cm (2 to 3in) long, dark, glossy green above, glaucous beneath.

Flowers: about 5cm (2in) across, white, opening in August and September.

Cultivation: as for *E. lucida*.

Propagation: by layering.

Varieties: 'Rostrevor' is a very floriferous selected cultivar.

Origin: A hybrid between the deciduous or semi-evergreen *E. glutinosa* and *E. lucida*.

E. x nymansensis

A variable, fairly vigorous hybrid with large flowers.

Size: large, eventually a small or medium tree as much as 9 to 12m (30 to 40ft) tall.

Leaves: variable, both simple and compound leaves appear on the same plant, generally similar to those of *E.* x *intermedia*, but with very short stalks.

Flowers: white, 5 to 7.5cm (2 to 3in) across, usually opening in August and September.

Cultivation: as for *E. lucida*, but more lime-tolerant.

Propagation: by layering.

Varieties: 'Mount Usher', with flowers that are often semi-double and many leaves heart-shaped, is usually a large shrub but can grow into a small tree; 'Nymansay' is vigorous and floriferous, often growing into a small or even a medium tree.

Origin: a hybrid between *E. cordifolia* and *E. glutinosa*.

E. milliganii is a very attractive, small-leaved species from Tasmania, flowering freely even as a small shrub. It is not very hardy, but worth growing against a warm wall and usually takes many years to exceed 3.6m (12ft).

X FATSHEDERA

See entry under SHRUBS for most soils, mainly for foliage effect.

FATSIA

See entry under SHRUBS for most soils, mainly for foliage effect.

GARRYA

A small genus of evergreen shrubs, mainly from the southern United States and Mexico. None is absolutely hardy, but a few are sufficiently so to be grown successfully at least in milder areas of northern Europe such as the south of England. They are quite vigorous, tolerant of coastal exposure and pollution and most types of soil, as long as they are free-draining. Male and female flowers are borne on separate plants, the males usually being more attractive. Although they could not be considered first-rate, they are borne in winter when any flowers are welcome in the garden.

G. elliptica

The most commonly grown plant of this genus, this is a large shrub with dark green foliage, bearing long, dangling catkins for several weeks in winter.

Size: up to about 3.6 to 4.5m (12 to 15ft) tall and almost as wide, vigorous and usually fast growing.

Leaves: oval to elliptical, about 5 to 7.5cm (2 to 3in) long, shiny dark green above, greyish beneath, with undulating margins.

Flowers: long, hanging grey catkins are borne on male plants in January to March. Female catkins are much less showy.

Fruits: female plants bear long clusters of purplish-brown fruits in spring.

Cultivation: easy in most well-drained soils, good in coastal areas and tolerant of air pollution. Happy in sun or moderate shade, but will not flower freely in heavy shade. Not absolutely hardy, so best grown against a wall in colder areas. Garryas resent root disturbance, so established plants move badly.

Propagation: by cuttings taken in August or September, inserted into sandy compost in pots under glass.

Varieties: 'James Roof' is a selected, strong-growing male cultivar with very long catkins.

Origin: west coast of the United States.

G. x issaquahensis

A hybrid, similar in general appearance to *G. elliptica*, but with catkins of a different colour.

Size: usually up to about 3.6m (12ft) tall and almost as much across.

Leaves: very similar to those of *G. elliptica*.

Garrya elliptica

Flowers: catkins with vinous red bracts are borne throughout winter, opening to reveal yellowish flowers in early spring.

Cultivation: quite vigorous and easy in most soils in sun or moderate shade, best grown against a wall in colder areas.

Propagation: as for *G. elliptica*.

Varieties: 'Glasnevin Wine' is the most commonly available cultivar, with very attractive catkins.

Origin: a garden hybrid between *G. elliptica* and *G. fremontii*.

HEBE

(formerly included in **Veronica**)

A large genus of mainly dwarf and small, evergreen shrubs, almost all from New Zealand. Few are fully hardy: generally speaking, the smaller ones with very small leaves are hardier than the bigger ones with larger leaves. Only the hardiest can be recommended for general planting in colder inland areas, but many are good in coastal regions, surviving in very exposed situations. Several have a long flowering period in summer and autumn and are highly ornamental.

There are a large number of hebes in cultivation, and more hybrids are continually being produced. Only a small selection are described here. They are intended to be a representative sample, and are not by any means the only hebes worth considering. It must always be borne in mind that hebes are on the borderline of hardiness and are likely to suffer damage in hard winters.

H. cupressoides

A shrub of very distinct appearance with tiny leaves.

Size: often only about 60cm (2ft) high, but can grow to 1.8m (6ft) or even a little more.

Leaves: tiny, green or greyish, covering the branches, which look very like those of a cypress tree.

Flowers: very pale lilac, small but usually produced quite abundantly in June and July on mature plants. Young plants tend to flower sparsely or not at all.

Hebe cupressoides

Cultivation: easy in most well-drained soils in a sunny situation, good near coasts, but needs some shelter inland and is not hardy enough for very cold areas.

Propagation: by cuttings of more or less ripened growth inserted into sandy compost under glass in late summer or early autumn, or during early winter.

Origin: New Zealand.

H. elliptica

A small or medium shrub with pale green foliage and quite large, white flowers in summer.

Size: usually about 1.2 to 1.8m (4 to 6ft) tall, but can attain much more in very mild areas.

Leaves: oval or obovate, about 5cm (2in) long, and pale green.

Flowers: large for the genus, white and fragrant, in elongated flower heads in July.

Cultivation: as for *H. cupressoides*.

Propagation: as for *H. cupressoides*.

Origin: New Zealand and the extreme south of South America.

H. leiophylla

Among the hardiest species, a small shrub with narrow leaves and long heads of flowers in summer.

Size: usually up to about 1.2m (4ft) high.

Leaves: narrowly lanceolate or elliptical, about 7.5 to 10cm (3 to 4in) long.

Flowers: in heads about 10cm (4in) long in July and August, white.

Cultivation: as for *H. cupressoides*.

Propagation: as for *H. cupressoides*.

Origin: New Zealand.

H. rakaiensis

A small shrub of compact, rounded habit with bright green foliage and white flowers in summer.

Size: up to about 90cm (3ft) high and usually rather wider.

Leaves: small, less than 2.5cm (1in) long, elliptical, bright green.

Flowers: in short, dense spikes, white, opening in June and July.

Cultivation: as for *H. cupressoides*.

Propagation: as for *H. cupressoides*.

Origin: New Zealand.

H. salicifolia

A medium or even large shrub, one of the biggest reasonably hardy species of the genus, with a long flowering period.

Size: usually up to about 1.5 to 1.8m (5 or 6ft) high, but can attain 3m (10ft) or a little more in favoured locations.

Leaves: lanceolate, about 7.5cm (3in) long, and bright green.

Flowers: in long heads, opening over a long period in summer, usually from June to August or September, white, sometimes tinged with lilac.

Cultivation: as for *H. cupressoides*.

Propagation: as for *H. cupressoides*.

Varieties: 'Snow Wreath' and 'Variegata' are both variegated cultivars.

Origin: New Zealand.

Hebe rakaiensis

H. 'Autumn Glory'

A very attractive and commonly grown hybrid. Usually a small rounded shrub, flowering over a long period.

Size: usually not more than about 1.2m (4ft) high and about the same wide.

Leaves: rounded, about 2.5 to 5cm (1 to 2in) long, rather leathery.

Flowers: in fairly short, erect heads, violet-blue, borne for many weeks from mid-summer until mid-autumn.

Cultivation: hardier than most hebes, not very fussy about soil as long as it is free-draining, prefers full sun.

Propagation: as for *H. cupressoides*.

Origin: a garden hybrid of uncertain origin.

H. 'Blue Clouds'

A comparatively hardy small shrub with abundant blue flowers over a long period.

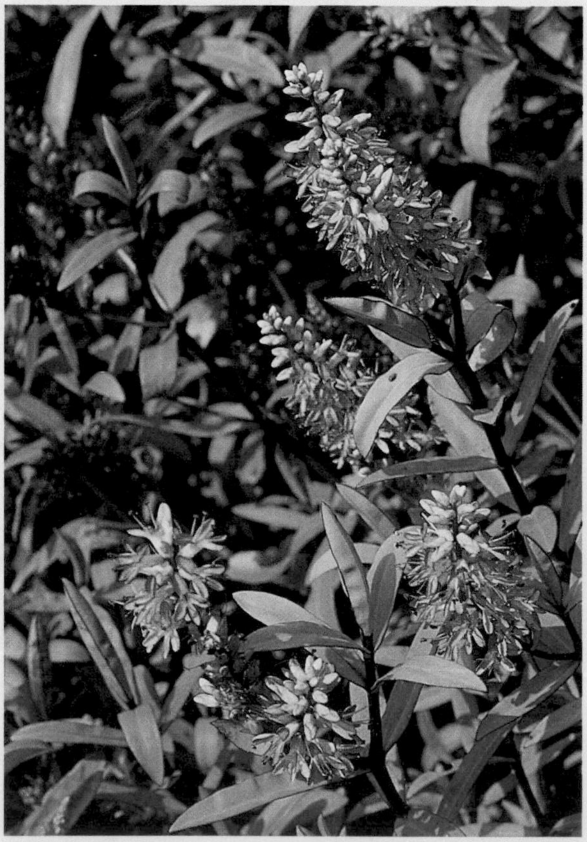

Hebe **'Blue Clouds'**

Size: up to about 90cm (3ft) tall and about as wide.

Leaves: more or less elliptical, about 2.5 to 5cm (1 to 2in) long, tinted reddish-purple when young.

Flowers: in elongated heads about 5 to 7.5cm (2 or 3in) long, blue, opening from June onwards into late summer or autumn.

Cultivation: as for *H.* 'Autumn Glory'.

Propagation: as for *H. cupressoides*.

Origin: a garden hybrid.

H. 'Great Orme'

A compact small shrub with large leaves and a long flowering period.

Size: up to about 90cm (3ft) high and at least as wide.

Leaves: lanceolate, 5 to 7.5cm (2 to 3in) long.

Flowers: in dense, elongated heads, bright pink, opening from mid-summer until well into autumn.

Cultivation: moderately hardy, and easy to grow in any light soil in full sun.

Propagation: as for *H. cupressoides*.

Origin: a garden hybrid.

H. 'Lindsayi'

A very hardy hebe growing into a small, rounded shrub, with pink flowers.

Size: up to about 90cm (3ft) high and as much across.

Leaves: rounded, about 2.5cm (1in) long.

Flowers: pink, in short heads in summer.

Cultivation: as for *H.* 'Autumn Glory'.

Propagation: as for *H. cupressoides*.

Origin: a garden hybrid between *H. amplexicaulis* and *H. pimeleoides*.

***Hebe* 'Midsummer Beauty'**

H. 'Marjorie'

Another very hardy hybrid growing into a small, neat bush with pale violet and white flowers.

Size: about 90cm (3ft) high and wide.

Leaves: large, about 5 to 7.5cm (2 to 3in) long, oval to elliptical, softly leathery.

Flowers: in heads 5 to 7.5cm (2 to 3in) long, pale violet and white, opening from mid-summer until mid-autumn.

Cultivation: as for *H.* 'Autumn Glory'.

Propagation: as for *H. cupressoides.*

Origin: A garden hybrid.

H. 'Midsummer Beauty'

A fairly hardy, attractive small shrub with leaves reddish beneath and lavender flowers for a long period in summer and autumn.

Size: up to about 1.2 to 1.5m (4 or 5ft) high and rather less across.

Leaves: large, lanceolate, about 7.5cm (3in) long, light green above, reddish beneath.

Flowers: in long heads, lavender, opening from mid-summer until well into autumn.

Cultivation: moderately hardy, and easy to grow in any light soil in full sun.

Propagation: as for *H. cupressoides.*

Origin: a garden hybrid.

ITEA

A small genus of evergreen and deciduous shrubs and trees, from eastern Asia and North America. The individual flowers are very small, but are borne in long clusters like catkins which are quite attractive. Most of the evergreen species are from subtropical regions, and only one is more or less hardy.

I. ilicifolia

A quietly beautiful shrub of medium to large size, requiring shelter and often grown against a wall.

Itea ilicifolia

Size: usually up to about 1.8m (6ft) high, but may grow to 3m (10ft) against a wall.

Leaves: broadly elliptical, about 5 to 7.5cm (2 to 3in) long, dark green, leathery, with sharply toothed, more or less spiny, margins.

Flowers: greenish-white, in pendulous flower-heads looking like catkins, up to as much as 25cm (10in) long, opening in August.

Cultivation: likes a moist, humus-rich soil and light to moderate shade, with shelter in colder areas, especially from cold winds. It is best grown against a warm wall, preferably facing west or north, though it will cope with any aspect.

Propagation: by cuttings taken in late summer and inserted into sandy compost under glass, or preferably in a propagator with bottom heat.

Origin: south-west China.

LIGUSTRUM

A moderate-sized genus of evergreen, semi-evergreen and deciduous shrubs and trees, mainly from east and south-east Asia, but also occurring in other parts of Asia, Europe and Australia. Most species are not hardy in regions with cooler climates, such as Britain. They are closely related to lilacs (*Syringa*), but always have white flowers with a strong, rather musty scent. They are mainly fast growing and tolerant of a wide range of soil conditions and of sun or shade. Several species make good hedges.

L. delavayanum

A rather variable, medium shrub with small leaves. It is not quite hardy enough to thrive in very cold regions.

Size: usually up to about 1.8 to 2.4m (6 to 8ft) high and of spreading habit.

Leaves: oval to elliptical, about 2.5cm (1in) long, somewhat leathery, smooth.

Flowers: in dense clusters, white, opening over quite a long period in summer.

Cultivation: easy in most soils, in sun or moderate shade. A good hedging plant in areas with milder winters, but needs shelter in colder areas.

Propagation: by cuttings of young shoots under glass in summer, or cuttings of ripe shoots taken in early winter put into shaded outdoor beds or an unheated glasshouse.

Origin: south-west China.

L. henryi

A compact, medium to large shrub with small leaves and small flower heads in summer.

Size: usually up to about 2.4 to 3m (8 or 10ft) high, fairly erect in habit.

Leaves: broadly oval to rounded, about 2.5cm (1in) long, smooth, shiny and somewhat leathery.

Flowers: in heads 2.5 to 7.5cm (1 to 3in) long, white, opening in July or August.

Cultivation: easy in most soils in sun or shade.

Propagation: as for *L. delavayanum.*

Origin: central and western China.

L. japonicum, the Japanese Privet

A dense, medium to large shrub with glossy, deep green foliage and large, branched flower heads in late summer. It is excellent as a hedge, better than the much more commonly used *L. ovalifolium*, which is less dense and often more or less deciduous in cold areas.

Size: usually about 1.8 to 2.4m (6 to 8ft) high, but can grow larger.

Leaves: elliptical to broadly oval, about 5 to 7.5cm (2 to 3in) long, leathery, shiny, deep green above and yellowish-green beneath.

Flowers: borne in large, branched clusters at the ends of branches in late summer, white.

Cultivation: easy in most soils in sun or shade, makes an excellent screen or hedge.

Propagation: as for *L. delavayanum.*

Varieties: 'Rotundifolium' is a slow-growing, very compact cultivar with rounded, very dark green leaves.

Origin: Japan and Korea.

***Ligustrum japonicum* 'Rotundifolium'**

Ligustrum lucidum

L. lucidum

A large shrub or small tree with large leaves and big, branched clusters of white flowers in late summer or autumn.

Size: up to as much as 9m (30ft) tall.

Leaves: oval or elliptical, about 7.5 to 12.5cm (3 to 5in) long, glossy, leathery, mid-green.

Flowers: in large, branched heads at the ends of branches, creamy-white, opening from late summer onwards into autumn.

Cultivation: easy in most soils in sun or moderate shade. Not absolutely hardy and may suffer frost damage in colder areas. To encourage this plant to grow into a shapely tree, prune to one main shoot in late winter.

Propagation: as for *L. delavayanum.*

Varieties: 'Excelsum Superbum' has leaves variegated with yellow and cream and will grow into a small tree; 'Latifolium' has large, dark green leaves; 'Tricolor' has rather narrow leaves with a white margin, tinged pink when young.

Origin: China and Korea.

Magnolia grandiflora

MAGNOLIA

A moderate-sized genus of deciduous and evergreen trees and shrubs from Asia and North America. Many of the evergreen species are from subtropical to tropical regions and so are either tender or half-hardy. Only one is really hardy enough to be grown in cooler regions, but is likely to suffer damage in very severe winters. Magnolias are magnificent plants, with large flowers and leaves, and are worth taking the trouble to grow well.

M. grandiflora

A fine, very large, evergreen shrub or a small to medium tree with big, glossy leaves and beautiful, fragrant flowers.

Size: given time and favourable conditions, it can grow to 9m (30ft) or more, but is more usually about half that height.

Leaves: thick and leathery, elliptical to obovate, up to about 20cm (8in) long, dark, glossy green above, often felted reddish-brown beneath, especially when young.

Flowers: rather like water lily flowers, about 20cm (8in) across, creamy-white, fragrant, not normally borne on young plants and rarely abundant. They usually open over a long period in summer and early autumn.

Cultivation: Requires a deep, humus-rich loam and does not like very chalky soils. In colder districts it is best grown against a warm wall, preferably facing south or west, and will always grow faster and flower better against a wall. In milder areas it will rarely suffer any frost damage in the open, given a sunny site and some shelter.

Propagation: not easy to propagate, for the amateur the best method is layering or air layering in summer or autumn.

Varieties: 'Exmouth' has very large and fragrant flowers, borne even on quite young plants; 'Goliath' has shorter and broader leaves with little felt beneath and large flowers, also produced when quite young; 'Saint Mary' is compact in habit and flowers when very young; 'Undulata' has leaves with wavy margins, green beneath, and flowers when young; 'Victoria' also flowers as a young plant and is said to be exceptionally hardy, though it has scarcely been grown in Britain for long enough to be thoroughly tested. Several other named cultivars, with varying qualities, are sometimes offered by nurseries.

Origin: south-east United States.

M. delavayi is another very fine evergreen magnolia, with extremely large leaves, up to 30cm (1ft) or even a little more in length. Unfortunately it is only hardy enough to be grown outdoors in very mild areas. In Britain, it is only likely to flourish outdoors in very warm sheltered positions in the south and west.

X MAHOBERBERIS

The genera *Mahonia* and *Berberis* are very closely related and a number of hybrids between plants from the two have occurred, usually with the seed-parent being *Mahonia*. A few of the hybrids are worthy of cultivation in gardens.

X M. aquisargentii

A rather strange, small to medium shrub with different kinds of leaves on the one plant and yellow flowers in the spring.

Size: up to about 1.5 to 1.8m (5 to 6ft) tall and rather less across, but tending to broaden with age.

Leaves: variable: long and elliptic-lanceolate or shorter and ovate-lanceolate, with short or long spines on the margins. Some leaves have three leaflets, others are simple. All are dark, shiny-green above, paler beneath.

Flowers: yellow, in clusters at the ends of branches, opening in April or May.

Fruits: small black berries follow the flowers.

Cultivation: easy in any soil, in sun or moderate shade.

Propagation: by separating basal suckers from the original plant.

Origin: a hybrid between *Mahonia aquifolium* and *Berberis sargentiana.*

MAHONIA

(formerly included in **Berberis**)

A fairly small genus, very closely related to *Berberis*, but differing in appearance because the leaves are pinnate. In some species they are very large and striking. Several species are very valuable winter-flowering shrubs. They come from the Himalayan region, China and North America, and not all are fully hardy. Like *Berberis*, they have yellow flowers.

M. aquifolium, the Oregon Grape

A small shrub spreading fairly slowly by basal suckers, useful for growing in shady areas where soil is poor.

Size: up to about 90cm (3ft) tall, sometimes more, erect in habit but producing suckers and gradually spreading into a small thicket.

Leaves: pinnate, with usually five to nine leaflets with prickly margins, about 15 to 25cm (6 to 10in) long, dark, glossy green, sometimes turning reddish in winter.

Flowers: yellow, in dense clusters at the ends of shoots, opening in early spring.

Fruits: bluish-black berries.

Cultivation: easy in any soil in any situation, tolerant of sun or heavy shade, but at its best in a moist, humus-rich soil in light to moderate shade.

Propagation: most easily propagated by separating suckers from the main plant.

Varieties: 'Apollo' is a selected cultivar with golden-yellow flowers and leaves turning brownish in winter; 'Atropurpurea' has leaves which turn reddish throughout winter and early spring. Several other selected cultivars are available.

Origin: western North America.

M. fortunei

A distinctive *Mahonia,* with narrow leaflets, flowering in autumn.

Size: up to about 1.8m (6ft) or a little more in height, rather slow-growing, erect in habit, and suckering from the base.

Leaves: pinnate, up to about 25cm (10in) long, with usually five to nine lanceolate or narrowly elliptical leaflets with spine-toothed margins, dark green.

Flowers: bright yellow, in rather small, elongated clusters at the ends of branches, opening in autumn.

Cultivation: likes a sheltered site in partial shade, preferably with a humus-rich soil, but is not very fussy. A good woodland plant.

Propagation: by separation of suckers from the main plant, or by cuttings of half-ripe wood taken during late summer and inserted into a moist but free-draining compost under glass or, preferably, in a closed propagator with bottom heat.

Origin: central China.

M. japonica (including M. bealei)

A fine winter-flowering shrub with very large and highly decorative leaves.

Size: about 1.8 to 3m (6 to 10ft) tall, fairly erect but gradually becoming more bushy and spreading.

Leaves: very large, up to about 45cm (18in) long, divided into between 9 and 17 stiff, dark green leaflets with prickly margins. Often clustered towards the ends of the stems, forming big ruffs of foliage.

Flowers: pale yellow, in long heads clustered together at the ends of branches, usually opening in late winter. Young flower buds are liable to suffer damage from frost.

Cultivation: easy in most soils in sun or shade, but best in a moist, humus-rich soil in light shade.

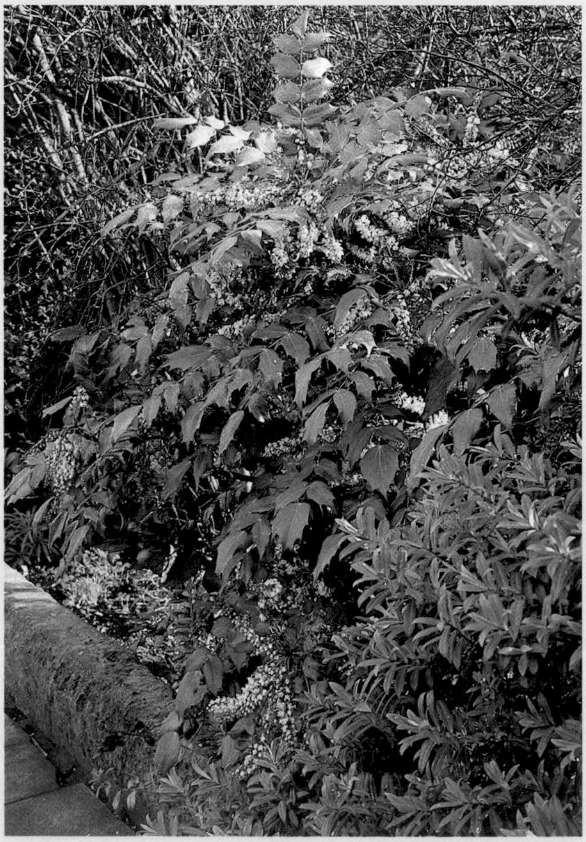

Mahonia japonica

Propagation: by cuttings of half-ripe wood taken in late summer and inserted into a moist but free-draining compost under glass or, preferably, in a closed propagator with bottom heat.

Varieties: 'Hivernant' ('Hiemalis') flowers in early winter, sometimes as early as November; *M. bealei* was formerly considered a distinct species, differing from *M. japonica* chiefly in having shorter, erect heads of flowers, but is now no longer separated. For horticultural purposes, it may be named *M. japonica* Bealei Group.

Origin: China.

M. x media

Very fine plants of hybrid origin with impressive foliage, which flower during winter. The cross has been made several times, which has resulted in several different named cultivars.

Size: A vigorous shrub up to about 2.4 to 3m (8 to 10ft) tall, erect in habit.

Leaves: up to about 60cm (2ft) long, pinnate with usually 11 to 19 spine-toothed, dark-green leaflets, tending to be clustered towards the ends of the stems, forming ruffs of foliage.

Flowers: pale to deep yellow, often fragrant, in long erect or spreading heads, opening in winter.

Cultivation: as for *M. japonica.*

Propagation: as for *M. japonica.*

Varieties: 'Buckland' has very long leaves and long, spreading heads of flowers; 'Charity' also has long leaves and deep yellow flowers in early winter; 'Lionel Fortescue', 'Underway' and 'Winter Sun' are other excellent cultivars of this group.

Origin: garden hybrids between *M. japonica* and the somewhat tender *M. lomariifolia.*

M. x wagneri, believed to be a hybrid between *M. aquifolium* and *M. pinnata*, resembles *M. aquifolium*, but is considerably taller, up to about 1.8m (6ft) in height, and flowers very freely in spring. Two fine selected cultivars of this hybrid are 'Pinnacle' and 'Undulata'.

MYRTUS

A small genus of a mainly tropical family of plants.

M. communis, the Common Myrtle

A large shrub with aromatic foliage and attractive white flowers, unfortunately not very hardy in northern European countries such as Britain, where it is only suitable for mild localities.

Size: up to 4.8m (16ft) tall, but usually not much more than 3.6m (12ft) except in very mild areas. A dense, many-branched shrub which is often as wide as high.

Leaves: oval, about 2.5cm (1in) long, untoothed, dark, shiny green, aromatic when bruised.

Flowers: white, sometimes tinged pink, with five rounded petals and a central mass of white stamens, about 2.5cm (1in) in diameter, borne singly along the branches from July to September, often in profusion.

Fruits: bluish-black berries follow the flowers.

Cultivation: needs a well-drained soil and plenty of sun. In colder inland areas it is best grown against a south- or west-facing wall. Stands coastal exposure well.

Propagation: by cuttings taken in summer and inserted into sandy compost, preferably in a closed propagator with bottom heat.

Varieties: 'Flore Pleno' has double flowers; 'Variegata' has its leaves margined with creamy-white; subsp. *tarentina* is smaller, not more than about 1.8m (6ft) high, with smaller, narrower leaves, and is a little hardier; 'Microphylla Variegata' is a variegated form of this subspecies.

Origin: the Mediterranean region and Portugal.

Myrtus communis **subsp.** ***tarentina***

NANDINA

A genus of only one species, related to *Berberis* but very different in appearance.

N. domestica, the Sacred Bamboo

A medium shrub with very decorative foliage and long, upright, unbranched stems reminiscent of bamboo. Not absolutely hardy but will survive most winters undamaged in much of Britain, especially if given a sheltered site.

Size: up to about 1.8 to 2.4m (6 to 8ft) tall, gradually forming a wide clump of erect stems.

Leaves: large, up to about 45cm (18in) long, divided into many lanceolate leaflets about 2.5 to 7.5cm (1 to 3in) long, stiff, green, often tinged red when young and during the winter.

Flowers: small, white, in large clusters at the ends of the branches during summer, not always freely borne.

Fruits: small, round, red berries ripen in autumn, but are often not produced abundantly in cultivation.

Cultivation: will thrive in any reasonable soil. Prefers full sun and some shelter.

Propagation: it is quite often possible to divide established plants or to separate rooted basal shoots from the main plant. Cuttings taken in summer and inserted into sandy compost in a propagator, with bottom heat, will usually root slowly.

Varieties: 'Firepower' is a smaller cultivar, usually not exceeding 90cm (3ft) in height, with strongly coloured foliage in shades of cream, orange and red, especially when young; 'Nana Purpurea' is similar in habit, with reddish-purple foliage throughout the year; while 'Pygmaea' is also similar in habit, but with leaves of more normal coloration. A few other cultivars, mostly small-growing, are also available.

Origin: China, Japan and India.

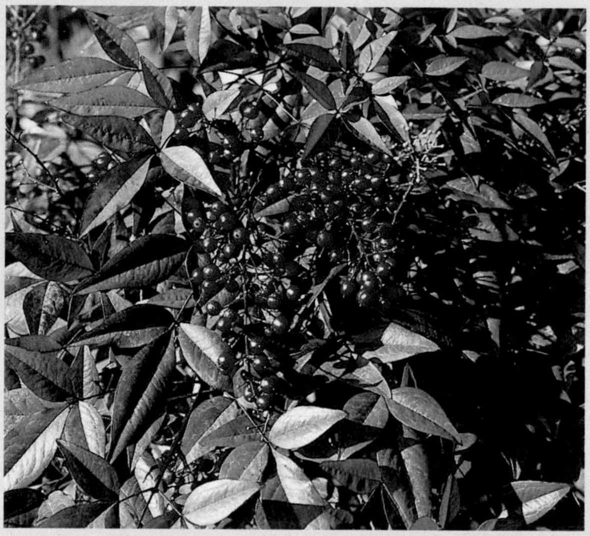

Nandina domestica

OLEARIA

The daisy bushes are a large genus of shrubs and trees from Australasia, most of them not or scarcely hardy in Britain and areas with similar cooler climates. The hardiest are from New Zealand. They are good evergreen shrubs for coastal areas, withstanding salty winds well and often also tolerating atmospheric pollution. They are generally sun-loving and easy to grow, producing clusters of usually white or cream, daisy-like flowers in summer. Some make excellent hedges.

O. ilicifolia

A very decorative medium to large shrub of dense habit with greyish leaves similar to holly leaves, and fragrant flowers in early summer. Moderately hardy.

Size: up to 1.8 to 3m (6 to 10ft) high but less across.

Leaves: elliptical, about 5 to 10cm (2 to 4in) long, thick, leathery, greyish-green above, felted off-white beneath, with large, sharp teeth on the margins.

Flowers: broad clusters of white flowers open in June.

Cultivation: easy in most well-drained soils in full sun, good on coasts but inland prone to damage in winter.

Propagation: by cuttings of firm young shoots inserted into sandy compost under glass in summer, preferably in a closed propagator.

Origin: New Zealand.

O. macrodonta, the New Zealand Holly

A large shrub, or even a small tree in very mild areas, with peeling bark and flowers in broad clusters in summer. Not quite as hardy as *O.* x *haastii*.

Size: usually up to about 3m (10ft) tall, but can attain 4.5 to 6m (15 to 20ft) in very mild areas. Slightly less wide than it is high.

Leaves: oval with spiny teeth on the margins, similar to holly leaves, about 7.5cm (3in) long, greyish-green above, white beneath.

Flowers: white with yellow centres in large clusters up to 15cm (6in) across, opening from June to August.

Cultivation: as for *O.* x *haastii*. An excellent hedge or screen, especially near the coast, where it withstands strong, salty winds very well.

Propagation: as for *O. ilicifolia*.

Origin: New Zealand.

O. nummulariifolia

A stiffly branched medium shrub of unusual appearance with yellowish foliage and small, solitary, flowers.

Size: up to about 1.5m (5ft) tall.

Leaves: small, thick, rounded, usually less than 2.5cm (1in) long, yellowish-green, and densely crowded on the branches.

Flowers: small, white, borne singly along the branches in July, fragrant.

Cultivation: as for *O. ilicifolia*.

Propagation: as for *O. ilicifolia*.

Origin: New Zealand.

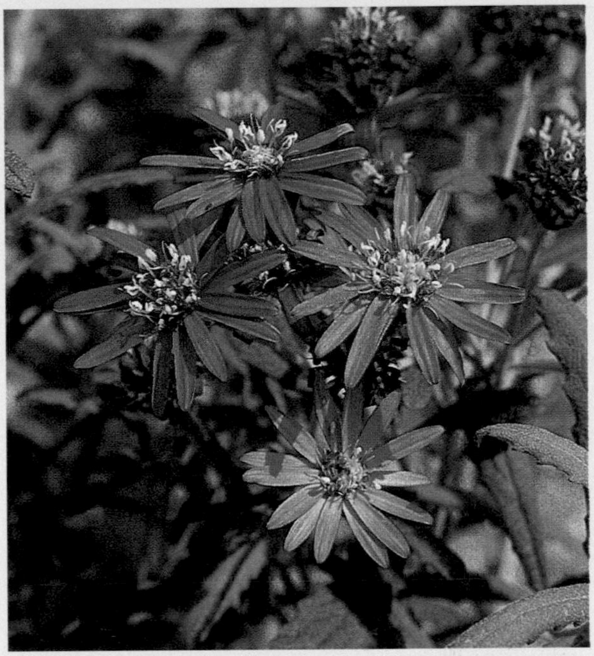

Olearia phlogopappa **'Comber's Blue'**

O. phlogopappa, the Tasmanian Daisy Bush

Not very hardy, but one of the finest of the daisy bushes in flower. Selected cultivars have pink and mauve-blue flowers. Variable, but usually of medium size, with narrow, greyish leaves.

Size: up to about 2.4m (8ft) tall, but very liable to be cut down by frost.

Leaves: more or less linear, about 2.5cm (1in) long, soft, greyish.

Flowers: usually about 12mm (1/2in) across, like small Michaelmas daisies, in clusters along the branches in May, white to pink or bluish.

Olearia macrodonta

Cultivation: easy in any well-drained soil in full sun, but only hardy in very mild areas. It needs shelter in colder areas, where it is best grown against a warm, sunny wall.

Propagation: as for *O. ilicifolia*.

Varieties: 'Comber's Blue' is a fine selected cultivar with mauvish-blue flowers; 'Comber's Pink' ('Rosea') has pink flowers.

O. x haastii

A rounded, medium shrub with small leaves and masses of fragrant white flowers in summer. One of the hardiest plants of this genus, only rarely suffering in winter and tolerant of pollution. It makes an excellent hedge.

Size: up to about 1.5 to 1.8m (5 to 6ft) or sometimes rather more in height and as much across.

Leaves: oval, up to about 2.5cm (1in) long, dark green above, felted white beneath, untoothed.

Flowers: fragrant, white with yellow centres, in clusters, covering the bush in July and August.

Osmanthus delavayi

Cultivation: easy in most soils as long as they are not too heavy, prefers a sunny site.

Propagation: as for *O. ilicifolia*.

Origin: a hybrid between *O. avicenniifolia* and *O. moschata*, originating in New Zealand.

OSMANTHUS
(including **Siphonosmanthus**)

A genus of about three dozen evergreen shrubs and small trees, mainly from Asia, with one or two from America. Most of the cultivated species are from the Far East. Many of the species are from subtropical regions and are not hardy in areas with winter frost. Others are very nearly hardy and a few are only likely to suffer damage in extremely severe winters. They belong to the same family as lilacs, privets and jasmines. Most have very sweetly fragrant flowers which are sometimes also quite showy, though in the species with larger leaves they tend to be hidden among the foliage.

O. armatus

A large, dense shrub with big, holly-like leaves and sweetly fragrant flowers in autumn.

Size: up to about 3.6m (12ft) tall and usually about as wide.

Leaves: about 7.5 to 15cm (3 to 6in) long, elliptical or oblong-lanceolate, often with spine-toothed margins but sometimes untoothed, thick and leathery.

Flowers: small, white, sweetly scented, opening in September or October.

Cultivation: naturally a woodland plant and therefore prefers a humus-rich soil with light shade, but it will tolerate most soil types and full sun or even fairly heavy shade. It will benefit from some protection from cold winds.

Propagation: by cuttings of firm young shoots inserted into sandy compost under glass, taken either in summer or in early winter, or by layering.

Origin: western China.

Osmanthus heterophyllus: a mature bush in flower

Osmanthus heterophyllus 'Goshiki'

O. decorus (Phillyrea decora)

A large shrub, often wider than it is high, bearing fragrant flowers in spring which may be followed by small, rounded, purplish-black fruits. One of the hardiest plants of this genus.

Size: up to about 3m (10ft) tall and at least as much in width.

Leaves: up to about 12.5cm (5in) long, elliptical to lanceolate, untoothed, leathery.

Flowers: small, white, fragrant, opening in April and May.

Cultivation: tough and quite easy in most soils and situations, but at its best in a humus-rich soil with a little shade and shelter.

Propagation: by cuttings of more or less ripened shoots taken in summer and inserted into sandy compost under glass, or of ripe young shoots taken in early winter; by layering.

Origin: western Asia.

O. delavayi

Deservedly one of the most commonly grown plants of this genus and a very beautiful shrub with small leaves and abundant flowers. It is almost totally hardy, but its flowers are liable to be browned by late frosts, so some shelter is of benefit.

Size: up to about 1.8m (6ft) high and often rather more across, slow-growing.

Leaves: small, oval or broadly elliptical, about 2.5cm (1in) long, with toothed margins, dark green, thick and leathery.

Flowers: small, white, fragrant, in clusters all along the branches, often covering the bush, opening in March or April.

Cultivation: best in a humus-rich soil in light shade with some shelter, but tolerant of most soils and full sun or moderate shade.

Propagation: as for *O. decorus*.

Origin: western China.

O. heterophyllus (O. ilicifolius)

A rather slow-growing but eventually large shrub, occasionally a small tree, with leaves like small holly leaves and sweetly scented flowers in autumn. It produces dense growth and withstands clipping well, so can make a good hedge.

Size: up to as much as 6m (20ft) tall but often only about half that, fairly erect.

Leaves: about 5cm (2in) long, elliptical, usually with a few spiny teeth on the margins but sometimes untoothed, especially on mature plants, dark green, glossy and leathery.

Flowers: in small clusters at the bases of the leaves, small, white, fragrant, opening in September and October.

Cultivation: fairly easy, not very fussy about soil but will make faster growth in a moist, humus-rich loam in a warm position in full sun or light shade. Some shelter from cold winds is beneficial.

Propagation: as for *O. armatus*.

Varieties: 'Aureomarginatus' has leaves margined with yellow; 'Goshiki' has leaves heavily splashed and streaked with yellow and cream; 'Gulftide' has strongly spiny leaves and is very dense in habit; 'Purpureus' has leaves and stems tinged with purple, especially when young; 'Variegatus' has leaves margined with creamy-white. A few other varieties exist.

Origin: Japan.

O. serrulatus

Usually a medium shrub in cultivation, but can become a small tree as much as 8m (25ft) or so high in the wild. It is slow-growing and compact, with large leaves edged with sharp teeth, or sometimes untoothed. Clusters of small, white, fragrant flowers are borne in the leaf axils in spring.

Size: usually up to about 1.8 to 2.4m (6 to 8ft) tall in cultivation in cool climates such as that of Britain, eventually more in warm, damp areas.

Leaves: up to about 12.5cm (5in) long, elliptical to broadly oblanceolate, dark green, leathery, margins usually sharply toothed but sometimes smooth.

Flowers: usually opening in April or May, in clusters of about half a dozen at the base of the leaves, white and fragrant.

Cultivation: Best in a moist, humus-rich loam in woodland conditions, but not too fussy and will tolerate full sun in an open situation.

Propagation: as for *O. decorus*.

Origin: China.

O. yunnanensis (O. forrestii)

A fine large shrub or small tree with large, variable leaves and small, white, fragrant flowers in late winter. The young shoots are an attractive dark reddish-bronze colour.

Size: up to about 6m (20ft) high or even more in favoured localities, moderately fast-growing.

Leaves: rather similar to those of *O. serrulatus*; elliptical to broadly lanceolate, about 12.5cm (5in) long, untoothed or with sharply toothed margins, leathery, dark green.

Flowers: small, creamy-white or pale yellowish-white, fragrant, opening in late winter to early spring.

Cultivation: fairly easy in most reasonable garden soils in any situation, but best in moderate shade in a moist, humus-rich soil and tolerant of quite heavy shade.

Propagation: as for *O. decorus*.

Origin: western China and Tibet.

Osmanthus yunnanensis

Osmanthus x fortunei

O. x burkwoodii (X Osmarea burkwoodii)

As popular and widely grown as *O. delavayi*, this is a fine, hardy shrub of dense growth, eventually a large shrub but quite slow-growing. Its flowers open later than those of *O. delavayi* and are rather less showy, but very fragrant. It can be clipped and will make a good hedge.

Size: up to about 3m (10ft) high and rather more than half as wide.

Leaves: oval to elliptical, about 2.5 to 5cm (1 to 2in) long, dark, shiny green, somewhat leathery, with very finely toothed margins.

Flowers: small, white, tubular flowers, similar to those of *O. delavayi* but more hidden by the foliage, open in April or May. They are very fragrant.

Cultivation: easy in almost any soil, including chalky soils, preferably in semi-shade. It will thrive best in fertile loam containing plenty of humus.

Propagation: as for *O. decorus*.

Origin: a garden hybrid between *O. decorus* and *O. delavayi* which originated in about 1930.

O. x fortunei

A very fine shrub of hybrid origin which deserves to be much more commonly grown. It is of dense habit and quite vigorous growth and produces highly fragrant flowers in autumn.

Size: usually up to about 2.1 to 2.4m (7 to 8ft) tall, but may sometimes reach twice that height.

Leaves: broadly elliptical or oval, about 7.5cm (3in) long, dark green, leathery, with conspicuous veins and sharply toothed margins.

Flowers: small, white, in clusters in the leaf axils and somewhat hidden by the foliage, but very fragrant, opening in September or October.

Cultivation: requires similar growing conditions to *O. heterophyllus*, one of its parents, but is rather more robust and faster growing.

Propagation: as for *O. decorus*.

Origin: a hybrid between the tender *O. fragrans* and *O. heterophyllus* which originated in the Far East (probably Japan) and was introduced to Western gardens in the mid-nineteenth century.

OZOTHAMNUS

(formerly included in **Helichrysum**)

A small genus of evergreen shrubs related to Helichrysum and often included in that genus in the past. They come from Australasia and are generally of doubtful hardiness in cooler northern climates, such as that of Britain. Only a very few species are sufficiently hardy to be included here.

O. rosmarinifolius (Helichrysum diosmifolium, H. rosmarinifolium)

A medium to large, dense shrub with white-woolly stems and small rosemary-like leaves, flowering in summer and requiring plenty of warmth and free-draining soil.

Size: up to about 1.5m (5ft) tall and as much wide, but can attain 2.7m (9ft) in favourable situations, especially against a warm wall.

Leaves: linear, up to about 5cm (2in) long, dark green above, white beneath.

Flowers: red in bud, opening creamy-white, in dense clusters at the ends of stems, carried over quite a long period from mid- to late summer.

Cultivation: requires a warm position in full sun with free-draining soil. Good in mild areas but not absolutely hardy and best against a warm wall in areas susceptible to frost.

Propagation: by cuttings of half-ripened shoots inserted into sandy compost under glass in August.

Varieties: 'Silver Jubilee' has silvery foliage and is usually rather smaller than the type, possibly also a little hardier.

Origin: Tasmania.

O. ledifolius is less often grown but probably the hardiest plant in this genus, growing to about 1.2m (4ft) high and wide, with leaves yellow underneath.

PHILLYREA

See entry under SHRUBS for most soils, mainly for foliage effect.

PHOTINIA

See entry under SHRUBS for most soils, with showy fruits.

PITTOSPORUM

See entry under SHRUBS for most soils, mainly for foliage effect.

PRUNUS

See entry under SHRUBS for most soils, mainly for foliage effect.

PYRACANTHA

See entry under SHRUBS for most soils, with showy fruits.

RHAPHIOLEPIS (RAPHIOLEPIS)

A small genus of evergreen shrubs and small trees related to *Cotoneaster* and *Photinia*, mainly from subtropical to tropical regions in east and south-east Asia and not hardy. One species is more or less reliably hardy, at least in warmer regions.

R. umbellata

An evergreen shrub, usually small, rounded and slow-growing, but in very favourable conditions it can become large. It has leathery leaves of moderate size and attractive clusters of white flowers in summer, followed by blackish fruits.

Size: usually up to about 1.2m (4ft) high and wide, rounded, rather slow-growing, but in the wild it sometimes grows into a small tree and it may become a large shrub under favourable conditions in cultivation.

Leaves: leathery, elliptical or oval to obovate, usually about 5 to 7.5cm (2 to 3in) long, dark green above, paler beneath, reddish when young.

Flowers: in rounded, upright clusters at the ends of branches, white, opening from June onwards;

individual flowers are rather like large hawthorn flowers, but more sweetly scented.

Fruits: round, up to about 1cm (1/3in) in diameter, blackish-purple with a white bloom.

Cultivation: prefers a moist, medium loam containing plenty of humus, in full sun or partial shade, preferably in a fairly warm situation. In cold areas it may need some protection from the worst weather, but in milder areas it usually only suffers damage in exceptionally severe winters.

Propagation: by cuttings of ripe wood taken in August and inserted into loamy compost under glass, or preferably in a closed propagator with gentle bottom heat; or by cuttings taken in winter and kept under glass.

Origin: Japan, Korea and China.

ROSMARINUS

A small genus of evergreen, aromatic shrubs from the Mediterranean region. Only one species is commonly grown in northern Europe, where it is hardy at least in warmer areas.

R. officinalis, Rosemary

A very variable shrub, with both upright and prostrate varieties, familiar as a culinary herb but attractive enough to be grown as an ornamental shrub.

Size: up to about 1.8m (6ft) high and wide, or sometimes a little larger.

Leaves: linear, leathery, dark green above, white beneath, about 2.5cm (1in) long.

Flowers: borne in small clusters in the leaf axils all along the branches in May, greyish-blue.

Cultivation: easy in most soils, but best in light, well-drained soil in a warm, sunny situation. May need protection in winter in cold areas. Good near coasts, tolerating salty winds well.

Propagation: by cuttings of half-ripened shoots, preferably with a heel of old wood, in late summer, inserted into sandy compost; or by cuttings taken in winter and kept under glass.

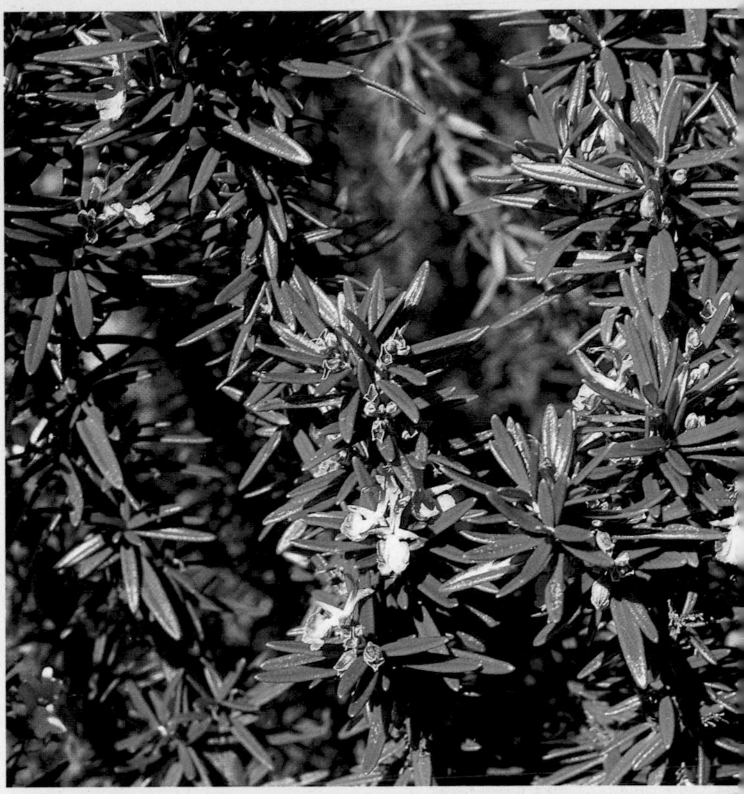

***Rosmarinus officinalis* 'Tuscan Blue'**

Varieties: there are numerous varieties, many more compact than the type, varying in growth habit and flower colour. 'Aureus' ('Aureovariegatus') has yellow variegated foliage; 'Lady in White' has white flowers in mid-summer; 'Roseus' has purplish-pink flowers; 'Miss Jessopp's Upright' ('Fastigiatus') is strong-growing and upright in habit; 'Sissinghurst Blue' is one of the finest selections,with deep blue flowers, and is also upright in habit; 'Tuscan Blue' is small with broader leaves and brighter flowers than the type, but is less hardy.

Origin: the Mediterranean region.

SARCOCOCCA

Sometimes known as Christmas Box or Sweet Box and closely related to true Box (*Buxus*). This is a genus of a score or so of evergreen shrubs from eastern and southern Asia. Most of them are from subtropical to tropical regions and therefore are not hardy in colder climates with severe winters.

Like true Box, they bear flowers that are not very showy, but they open in winter and are very fragrant. One or two plants close to the main door to a house

Sarcococca confusa

can provide a great deal of pleasure at a time of year when most gardens hold few delights. Planted in masses the scent can spread over a large area, particularly on warmer days. The few hardy species come from the Himalayan region and China and are woodland plants in the wild, tolerant of dense shade.

S. confusa

A small to medium shrub of dense habit, forming a mound of shining foliage. The flowers are borne in clusters all along the branches in winter and are followed by black berries which ripen at about the same time that the next year's flowers open.

Size: usually up to about 1.2m (4ft) high and wide, but can grow to as much as 1.8m (6ft) tall.

Leaves: elliptical, tapering to a point, about 2.5 to 5cm (1 to 2in) long, glossy green above, paler beneath.

Flowers: small, white, borne in clusters in the leaf axils all along the stems, opening in January or February, very sweetly scented.

Fruits: black berries about 1cm (1/3in) in diameter, taking about a year to ripen and sometimes still on the bush in early summer. They are only moderately attractive to birds.

Cultivation: easy in most soils including chalky soils, but best in a moist loam, in a shady or semi-shady position. Will grow well under trees.

Propagation: by cuttings of ripened wood inserted into sandy compost in shade under glass during September or October, or by detaching basal suckers.

Origin: uncertain; believed probably to have come from China.

S. hookeriana

An erect shrub which can grow quite tall but is usually small in cultivation. It has longer leaves than the other species described here and usually flowers a little later.

Size: usually up to about 0.9 to 1.2m (3 to 4ft) tall, but can attain 1.8m (6ft) or even more. Its branches are quite upright, but it suckers from the base and gradually makes a broad mound of foliage.

Leaves: up to about 10cm (4in) in length, lanceolate, dark, shiny green.

Flowers: white with a pink tinge, fragrant, usually opening in February or early March.

Fruits: similar to those of *S. confusa.*

Cultivation: easy in most soils, including chalky ones, but best in a moist, humus-rich loam, in shade or semi-shade.

Propagation: as for *S. confusa*; most varieties of this species sucker fairly freely.

Sarcococca hookeriana var. *digyna*

Sycopsis sinensis

Varieties: var. *digyna* is very similar to the type but slightly hardier; 'Purple Stem' is a selected form of var. *digyna* with reddish-purple stems; var. *humilis* is much lower growing, usually to no more than 60cm (2ft), with a more widely suckering habit.

Origin: the Himalayan region and China.

S. orientalis was introduced into cultivation in Britain more recently than the other species described here and is still more rarely cultivated; it is very similar to *S. confusa* but with longer leaves. **S. ruscifolia** is also very similar to *S. confusa* but has dark red berries.

SKIMMIA

See entry under SHRUBS for most soils, with showy fruits.

SYCOPSIS

A small genus of evergreen shrubs and small trees related to the witch hazels (*Hamamelis*). They originate from southern and eastern Asia, most of the species occurring in subtropical and tropical regions which means that they are not hardy in colder climates with harsh winters. A few of the Chinese species grow far enough north to be frost hardy, however, and one or two are in cultivation, though not often seen in gardens.

S. sinensis

A medium to large shrub or sometimes a small tree. Its flowers open early in the year and have no petals, but their yellow stamens with red anthers are attractive and reasonably conspicuous.

Size: usually up to about 6m (20ft) tall or sometimes rather more.

Leaves: oval to lanceolate, about 5 to 10cm (2 to 4in) long, leathery, dark green above, lighter beneath.

Flowers: in small elongated clusters in the leaf axils, opening in winter, usually in January or February. There are no petals, but bunches of yellow stamens with red anthers spring from reddish-brown bracts.

Viburnum cinnamomifolium

Cultivation: prefers a moist, humus-rich soil in a slightly shaded position.

Propagation: by cuttings of half-ripened wood taken in July and inserted into a sandy compost in a propagator with bottom heat.

Origin: China.

TROCHODENDRON

See entry under SHRUBS for most soils, mainly for foliage effect.

VIBURNUM

A large genus of deciduous and evergreen shrubs, occasionally small trees, distributed throughout temperate and subtropical regions of the world. A few species are European natives, but most of those in cultivation originate from eastern Asia, where the genus is particularly well represented. More than 70 species occur in China.

This is a very fine, garden-worthy genus, especially useful for those gardens on alkaline soils where rhododendrons cannot be grown. The evergreen species, the minority in the genus, include some excellent foliage plants. Some also produce attractive flowers and fruits. As a rule, viburnums fruit better when they are grown in groups so that cross-pollination can occur. Most evergreen viburnums have quite large leaves and can suffer damage from cold winds in winter unless given some shelter. They generally thrive in woodland.

V. atrocyaneum (V. wardii)

A dense, medium to large shrub with glossy, dark green foliage, tinged purple when young. Flat heads of small, white flowers open in late spring and are followed by dark blue fruits which ripen in autumn and usually persist well into the winter.

Size: up to about 3m (10ft) tall, often rather less.

Leaves: about 5 to 7.5cm (2 to 3in) long, oval or elliptical to obovate, leathery, dark green and glossy above, pale green below, purplish when young.

Flowers: individually small, borne in flat, rounded heads up to about 5cm (2in) across, white, usually opening in May or June.

Fruits: more or less pear-shaped, small, about 6mm (1/4in) long, dark blue, in heads up to 7.5cm (3in) or a little more across.

Cultivation: prefers a humus-rich soil with plenty of moisture, preferably in light to moderate shade. Damp woodland conditions are ideal, but will also flourish in mixed shrub borders.

Propagation: by cuttings of half-ripened shoots taken in July or August and inserted into sandy compost in a propagator with bottom heat; by cuttings taken in winter and kept under glass; by layering in autumn; by seed sown in late autumn and kept in a cold frame through winter.

Origin: the eastern Himalayan region, Burma, south-west China, northern Thailand.

V. cinnamomifolium

A large shrub with bold, glossy foliage and off-white flowers followed by bluish-black fruits. It resembles the much more commonly cultivated *V. davidii*, but grows much taller.

Size: usually up to about 2.4m (8ft) tall and about half as much across, but may eventually grow to 3.6m (12ft) or more.

Leaves: more or less elliptical, 7.5 to 12.5cm (3 to 5in) long, dark glossy green with three veins arising from the base of the leaf and impressed on the upper surface.

Flowers: individually very small, in flat heads about 7.5 to 12.5cm (3 to 5in) across, dull yellowish-white, opening in May or June.

Fruits: small, rounded, in large clusters, bluish-black, ripening in late summer to early autumn and usually persisting well into the winter.

Cultivation: easy in most soils, preferably in light shade, but prefers a humus-rich soil in open woodland.

Propagation: as for *V. atrocyaneum*.

Origin: south-west China.

V. davidii

A small shrub usually growing into a dome, wider than it is high. It makes good ground cover if planted in groups with the individual plants about 60 to 90cm (2 to 3ft) apart. It is often used like this in large-scale landscaping around commercial buildings. The flowers are not very showy as they are a rather dirty white, but the blue fruits can be very striking. Unfortunately they are often not produced in any quantity. Some individual plants seem to be predominantly male and rarely bare any fruits at all, while others are mainly female, bearing fruits but needing to be pollinated by a male plant. There are also other plants which scarcely ever flower, so it is worth looking at container-grown plants when they are flowering or fruiting and buying only the best. To ensure fruiting, several plants should be grown together. Some nurseries supply plants labelled male or female. One male plant should be enough to pollinate several females.

Size: usually up to about 90cm (3ft) high and rather more across.

Leaves: more or less elliptical, about 7.5 to 12.5cm (3 to 5in) long, dark green, leathery, with three conspicuous veins running from the base to near the tip.

Flowers: in flat heads in June, dull white.

Fruits: turquoise-blue, usually borne from autumn well into winter, but rarely abundant. Plants fruit best if grown in groups.

Viburnum davidii

Viburnum rhytidophyllum **in fruit**

Cultivation: easy in any soil, but ideally requiring moisture-retentive, fertile, humus-rich medium loam. Best in semi-shade, but tolerates quite heavy shade or sun. Leaves can suffer damage from strong, cold winds.

Propagation: as for *V. atrocyaneum.*

Origin: western China.

V. harryanum

A dense, medium shrub with small, rounded leaves, bearing white flowers in spring followed by black fruits.

Size: up to about 2.4m (8ft) tall, dense and bushy.

Leaves: small, less than 2.5cm (1in) long, more or less round, dark green.

Flowers: white, in small flat heads, opening in May.

Fruits: shiny black, ripening in autumn and usually lasting well into winter.

Cultivation: as for *V. cinnamomifolium.*

Propagation: as for *V. atrocyaneum.*

Origin: China.

V. henryi

A very attractive medium to large shrub of erect habit with glossy foliage, white flowers in summer and fruits which turn red and then black. It has been in cultivation for almost a century, yet is still scarce in British gardens. It deserves to be grown more often.

Size: usually up to about 3m (10ft) high, but can grow taller and may become a small tree.

Leaves: elliptical, usually about 5 to 12.5cm (2 to 5in) long, leathery, glossy dark green, sharply toothed at least towards the tip.

Flowers: fragrant, white, borne in long, broad heads from June to July.

Fruits: rather more than 6mm (1/4in) long, usually freely borne, ripening in late summer and early autumn, becoming bright red at first and later purplish-black.

Cultivation: easy in most soils and situations except dry sites. A moist, humus-rich soil in a partially shaded position is ideal.

Propagation: as for *V. atrocyaneum.*

Origin: China.

V. japonicum (V. macrophyllum)

A fine medium shrub with large leaves and fragrant white flowers in summer followed by red fruits. Unfortunately it does not flower as a young plant.

Size: usually up to about 2.4 to 3m (8 to 10ft) tall.

Leaves: up to 15cm (6in) long, more or less elliptical, leathery, glossy dark green.

Flowers: fragrant, white, in dense, rounded clusters, opening in June. Does not normally flower until it is several years old.

Fruits: ripening in autumn, red.

Cultivation: prefers a moist, humus-rich soil and light shade. The large leaves are susceptible to damage by strong, cold winds, so some shelter is desirable.

Propagation: as for *V. atrocyaneum*, but the large leaves should be cut to about half their length when preparing cuttings.

Origin: Japan.

Viburnum rhytidophyllum **in flower**

V. rhytidophyllum

A vigorous shrub with striking foliage, large heads of creamy-white flowers in late spring and fruits which turn red and then black. It is easy in most conditions, including chalky soils, and is deservedly popular. Single plants rarely fruit well as they require cross-pollination.

Size: usually grows to about 3 to 3.6m (10 to 12ft) tall, but may attain more and can become a small tree.

Leaves: usually up to about 17.5cm (7in) long, but sometimes even larger, more or less elliptical, thick and leathery with deeply impressed veins on the dark green upper surface and a greyish-white or fawn-tinged woolly under-surface.

Flowers: individually small, creamy white, in dense, domed heads up to 10cm (4in) or a little more across, opening in May.

Fruits: about 6mm (1/4in) long, turning red in autumn and then black, but not borne freely on single plants; plant a group of two or three close together to obtain a good crop of fruits.

Cultivation: easy in most soils and situations, an excellent evergreen foliage shrub for gardens where calcifuge plants cannot be grown. It will thrive in sun or quite heavy shade.

Propagation: as for *V. japonicum.*

Varieties: 'Roseum' has pink flowers; 'Variegatum' has variegated foliage.

Origin: China.

V. tinus, Laurustinus

A deservedly popular, medium to large, evergreen shrub, extremely valuable for its winter flowering. It has foliage of thinner texture than other evergreen viburnums. It is good near coasts, hardy enough for all but very cold areas and tolerant of at least moderate shade. It flowers best in light shade to full sun.

Size: usually up to about 3m (10ft) tall and rather less across, but can grow larger.

Leaves: oval, usually about 5 to 7.5cm (2 to 3in) long, mid- to dark green, thinly leathery.

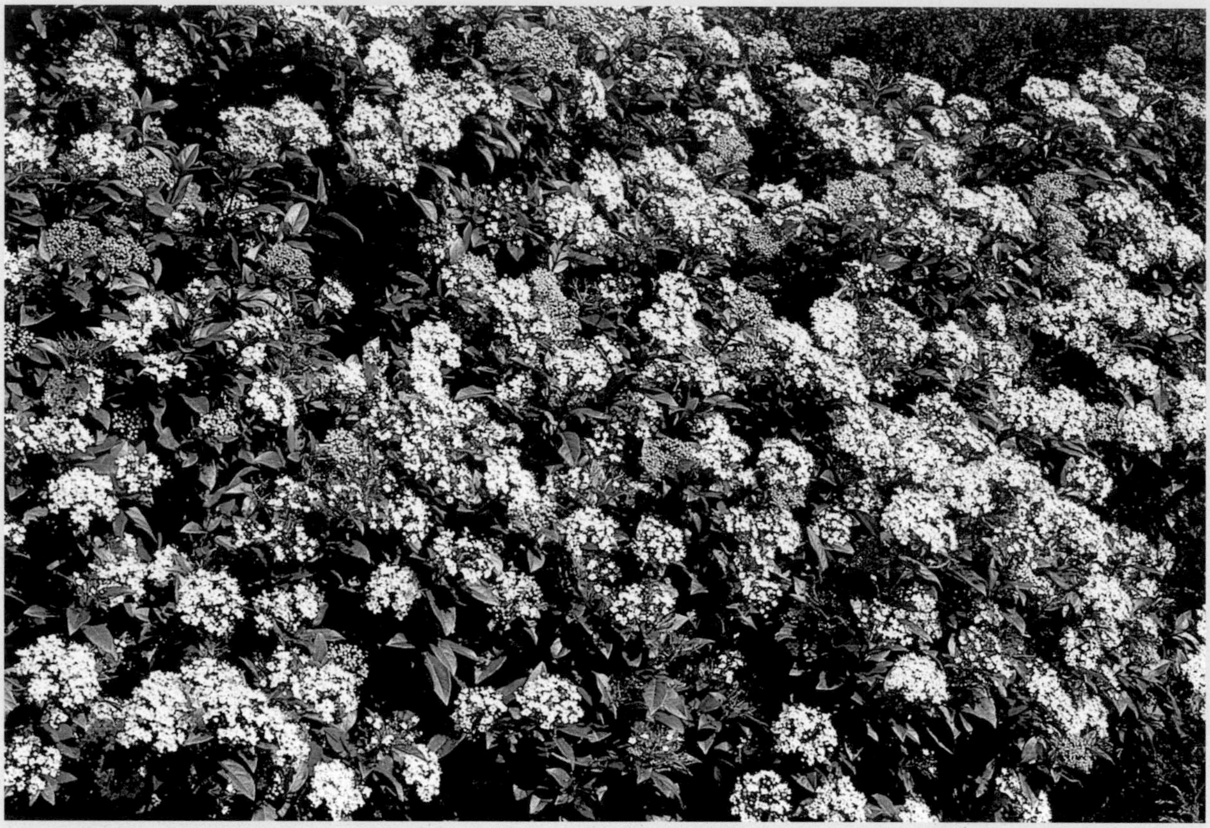

Viburnum tinus

Flowers: pink in bud opening white, in flat heads up to about 10cm (4in) across, appearing from late autumn throughout the winter into early spring.

Fruits: often not borne in profusion, smallish, more or less pear-shaped, metallic-blue becoming almost black.

Cultivation: easy in most soils and situations, tolerant of quite dense shade and coastal exposure, best in a well drained, medium loam in sun or light shade. Makes a good informal hedge or screen. Needs some protection in very cold areas.

Propagation: by cuttings of half-ripened shoots taken in July or August and inserted into sandy compost in a propagator with bottom heat; by layering in autumn.

Varieties: 'Eve Price' is a selected cultivar of very dense habit, with smaller leaves and pinker flowers; 'French White' is a vigorous cultivar with large heads of white flowers; 'Lucidum' is also vigorous, but slightly less hardy, with larger, glossy green leaves and larger heads of flowers, opening in March and April; 'Lucidum Variegatum' is similar, with variegated foliage; 'Purpureum' has leaves tinged purple when young, becoming very dark green; 'Strictum' ('Pyramidale') is very upright in habit; 'Variegatum' has foliage with creamy-yellow variegation, but is less hardy than the type. A number of other cultivars exist and may occasionally be offered by nurseries.

Origin: the Mediterranean region.

V. utile

An elegant, medium shrub of open habit, with long, slender branches bearing small, dark green leaves which are white beneath. Its fragrant white flowers open in April or May and are followed by bluish-black fruits.

Size: up to about 1.8 to 2.1m (6 to 7ft) tall.

Leaves: leathery, oval or broadly elliptical, usually about 5cm (2in) long, dark green above, felted with white hairs beneath.

Flowers: in rounded heads about 5 to 7.5cm (2 to 3in) across, white, sweetly scented, opening in April or May.

Fruits: ripening in late summer and early autumn, reddish at first then bluish-black.

Cultivation: easy in most soils and situations, prefers a medium loam in sun or light shade.

Propagation: as for *V. atrocyaneum*.

Origin: China.

V. x burkwoodii

A medium shrub of fairly open habit producing fragrant flowers, pink in bud but opening white, from as early as January until May. It does not normally produce fruits.

Size: usually attaining about 1.8 to 2.4m (6 to 8ft) in height and as much across.

Leaves: oval, about 7.5 to 10cm (3 to 4in) long, dark green above, felted with brownish-grey hairs beneath.

Flowers: in rounded heads up to 10cm (4in) across, pink in bud, opening white, fragrant, opening from as early as January, more usually March, until May.

Cultivation: easy and vigorous, not fussy about soil or position, but best in medium loam in sun or light shade.

Propagation: as for *V. atrocyaneum*, but cannot be propagated by seed.

Varieties: 'Anne Russell', 'Chenaultii', 'Fulbrook' and 'Park Farm Hybrid' are all selected cultivars of this hybrid group, differing in minor respects. 'Park Farm Hybrid' is particularly vigorous, with a spreading habit.

Origin: a garden hybrid between the deciduous *V. carlesii* and *V. utile*, first raised in 1924.

V. x globosum 'Jermyn's Globe'

A small shrub of dense, rounded habit with foliage rather like that of *V. tinus*.

Size: usually up to about 1.2 to 1.5m (4 to 5ft) high and as much in width.

Leaves: leathery, elliptical to lanceolate, about 7.5 to 10cm (3 to 4in) long, dark green.

Flowers: in domed heads about 7.5cm (3in) across, white, opening in June and July.

Fruits: ripening in autumn, bluish-black.

Cultivation: easy in most soils and situations, best in medium loam in sun or partial shade.

Propagation: as for *V. atrocyaneum*, but will not come true from seed.

Origin: a garden hybrid between *V. calvum* and *V. davidii*, which originated in 1964.

V. 'Pragense'

A highly ornamental, medium to large, spreading shrub, resembling *V. rhytidophyllum*, one of its parents. It is very hardy.

Size: up to about 2.4 to 3m (8 to 10ft) tall and more or less as wide.

Leaves: elliptical, similar to those of *V. rhytidophyllum* but smaller, about 5 to 10cm (2 to 4in) long.

Flowers: pink in bud, but opening to a creamy-white in May.

Cultivation: vigorous and easy in most soils and situations. Best in medium, humus-rich loam in light shade.

Propagation: as for *V. atrocyaneum*, but will not come true from seed.

Origin: a garden hybrid between *V. rhytidophyllum* and *V. utile*, raised in Prague.

V. awabuki (V. odoratissimum var. awabuki) is a fine, large shrub or small tree with creamy-white flowers in May and fruits ripening through red to black; **V. chingii** is a large shrub with white flowers early in the year and red fruits; **V. cylindricum** is a large shrub or small tree with tubular, white flowers from late summer into autumn, but is not very hardy; **V. propinquum** is a small to medium shrub of dense habit with greenish-white flowers in summer followed by bluish-black fruits. A few other evergreen viburnums are in cultivation and may occasionally be offered by nurseries.

SHRUBS WITH SHOWY FRUITS

ARBUTUS

See entry under TREES.

AUCUBA

See entry under SHRUBS for most soils, mainly for foliage effect.

BERBERIS

See entry under SHRUBS for most soils, with showy or strongly scented flowers.

COTONEASTER

A moderately large genus of deciduous and evergreen shrubs, belonging to the rose family. Cotoneasters are widespread in northern temperate regions of Europe and Asia, but particularly numerous in the Himalayan region and western China. All are ornamental, with fairly small, white or pink, hawthorn-like flowers with five petals, followed by berries that are usually red or orange but sometimes yellow. The flowers attract bees and the fruits are often eaten by birds, though they usually survive for a reasonable time on the shrub.

Cotoneasters are not very fussy about soils and conditions and are among some of the most useful evergreen shrubs for any garden. Most are deciduous or only semi-evergreen, but a substantial minority are hardy evergreens. They vary in habit from prostrate to tall: a few will make small trees. Some are good hedging plants, particularly for informal hedges.

Cotoneasters hybridize readily and plants grown from seed are often crosses. Partly because of this, there has been considerable confusion about the naming of cotoneasters in cultivation and it is very likely that many are not correctly named.

C. conspicuus

A medium shrub with very small leaves and arching branches, often wider than it is high. The flowers are white, opening all along the branches in early summer, followed by bright red fruits.

Size: usually up to between 1.5 and 1.8m (5 to 6ft) high and more across.

Leaves: obovate, not more than about 12mm (1/2in) long, dark green above, covered with short whitish hairs beneath, thick and stiff.

Flowers: borne singly or sometimes in clusters of two or three but very numerous along the branches, white, 12mm (1/2in) across, opening in May to June.

Fruits: round, bright red, rather more than 6mm (1/4in) in diameter, usually freely produced, ripening in autumn and often lasting well into winter.

Cultivation: easy, not very fussy about soils, but best in a fertile medium loam in full sun or partial shade.

Propagation: by layering in spring; by cuttings inserted into sandy compost under glass in September; by seeds sown in autumn in a frame or outside in late winter.

Varieties: 'Decorus' is the most commonly grown cultivar, usually not more than 1.2 to 1.5m (4 to 5ft) tall and spreading to as much as 2.4m (8ft) or so across. Several other selected cultivars exist but are scarce at present.

Origin: south-east Tibet.

C. glaucophyllus

A large shrub flowering in mid-summer, the berries ripening late. Tends to be only semi-evergreen in cold winters.

Size: usually up to about 3m (10ft) high.

Leaves: elliptical to oval, about 5cm (2in) long, dark green above, whitish beneath.

Flowers: in domed clusters of 30 or more, white, opening in July.

Fruits: ripening in late autumn to early winter, round or pear-shaped, about 6mm (1/4in) in diameter, and orange-red.

Cultivation: easy in most soils and situations, but prefers a medium loam in a sunny or partly shady position.

Propagation: as for *C. conspicuus*.

Origin: south-west China.

C. harrovianus

A medium shrub with slender, arching branches, very fine in flower, with fruits ripening to red late in the year.

Size: usually up to about 1.8 to 2.1m (6 to 7ft) tall.

Leaves: elliptical to oval, 2.5 to 5cm (1 to 2in) long, leathery, dark green above, whitish beneath.

Flowers: many in dense heads about 2.5cm (1in) across, white, usually freely borne, opening in May or June.

Fruits: dark red, borne in dense clusters, ripening in early winter.

Cultivation: not very fussy about soil and conditions, prefers a sunny or lightly shaded site in medium loam.

Propagation: as for *C. conspicuus*.

Origin: south-west China.

C. henryanus (C. salicifolius var. henryanus)

A large, spreading shrub with more or less pendulous branches, long, crinkled leaves and crimson fruits. Sometimes semi-evergreen in cold winters.

Size: up to about 3m (10ft) tall and usually as wide.

Leaves: about 7.5 to 10cm (3 to 4in) long, elliptical to broadly lanceolate, crinkled, dark green above, downy and whitish beneath.

Flowers: in dense clusters of 30 or more, white, opening in June.

Fruits: crimson, in dense clusters, ripening in late autumn to early winter.

Cultivation: easy in most soils and situations, prefers medium loam and full sun or light shade.

Propagation: as for *C. conspicuus*.

Origin: central China.

C. lacteus

One of the most commonly grown evergreen cotoneasters, a large shrub with pendulous branches, quite big leaves and broad clusters of small red fruits. It makes a good hedge.

Size: usually up to about 3m (10ft) tall and almost as wide.

Cotoneaster lacteus

Cotoneaster microphyllus

Leaves: about 5 to 7.5cm (2 to 3in) long, oval to elliptical, leathery, dark green above, felted with whitish or yellowish woolly hairs beneath.

Flowers: in large, hanging clusters along the branches, white, opening in June or July.

Fruits: individually small but usually abundant, ripening in late autumn or early winter, red.

Cultivation: easy, will grow in most soils except very wet ones, in sun or moderate shade.

Propagation: as for *C. conspicuus*.

Origin: south-west China.

C. microphyllus

A low-growing, spreading shrub with tiny dark green leaves and showy, bright crimson berries.

Size: up to about 60cm (2ft) tall and about three times as wide.

Leaves: obovate, less than 12mm (1/2in) long, dark green.

Flowers: borne singly or in twos and threes all along the branches in May, white, rather less than 12mm (1/2in) across.

Fruits: round, bright crimson berries about 7mm (1/4in) in diameter ripen in autumn and usually last well into winter.

Cultivation: easy in most soils if they are well drained, best in light, fertile loam, in full sun to light shade.

Propagation: as for *C. conspicuus*.

Origin: the Himalayan region and south-west China.

C. pannosus

A medium shrub with graceful, arching branches, small leaves, clusters of white flowers in summer and deep red fruits from autumn into winter.

Size: up to about 1.8 to 2.1m (6 to 7ft) tall and almost as wide.

Leaves: up to about 2.5cm (1in) long, oval to elliptical, greyish-green above and covered with woolly white hairs beneath.

Flowers: in small clusters of just a few to about 20 all along the branches, white, opening in June or July.

Fruits: small, about 6mm (1/4in) across, more or less round, ripening in late autumn to deep red.

Cultivation: likes a well-drained soil in full sun or light shade.

Propagation: as for *C. conspicuus*.

Origin: south-west China.

Cotoneaster salicifolius

C. salicifolius

An excellent, tall, graceful shrub, with narrow, pointed leaves and plentiful bright red fruits in autumn. It is the parent of many hybrids, and several distinct cultivars have been selected from it.

Size: usually up to 3m (10ft) tall and almost as much across, fast growing.

Leaves: elliptical to lanceolate, about 5 to 7.5cm (2 to 3in) long, somewhat crinkled, dark, shining green above, whitish beneath.

Flowers: in large, dense clusters, white, opening in June.

Fruits: small, round, ripening to bright red in autumn.

Cultivation: easy, will grow well in any reasonable garden soil, preferably a medium loam, in full sun to moderate shade.

Propagation: as for *C. conspicuus*.

Varieties: 'Exburyensis' has apricot-yellow fruits, often tinged pink when fully ripe; 'Fructu Luteo' has yellow fruits; 'Rothschildianus' has creamy-yellow fruits. There are also several prostrate cultivars.

Origin: western and central China.

C. serotinus (C. glaucophyllus f. serotinus) is very similar to *C. glaucophyllus*, but grows taller and has shorter, more rounded leaves and larger clusters of flowers; **C. vestitus (C. glaucophyllus var. vestitus)** is another similar shrub, with smaller leaves densely clothed with yellowish-white woolly hairs beneath. **C. x watereri** is the name for a variable group of hybrids, often semi-evergreen, between *C. henryanus, C. salicifolius* and the deciduous *C. frigidus*; 'John Waterer' is a large, spreading shrub with bunches of red fruits in autumn; 'Pink Champagne' is large, vigorous and dense with arching branches and foliage similar to that of *C. salicifolius*, bearing small yellow fruits with a pink tinge.

DANAE

(sometimes included in **Ruscus**)

A genus of only one species, differing from *Ruscus* chiefly in floral details, but of more elegant appearance.

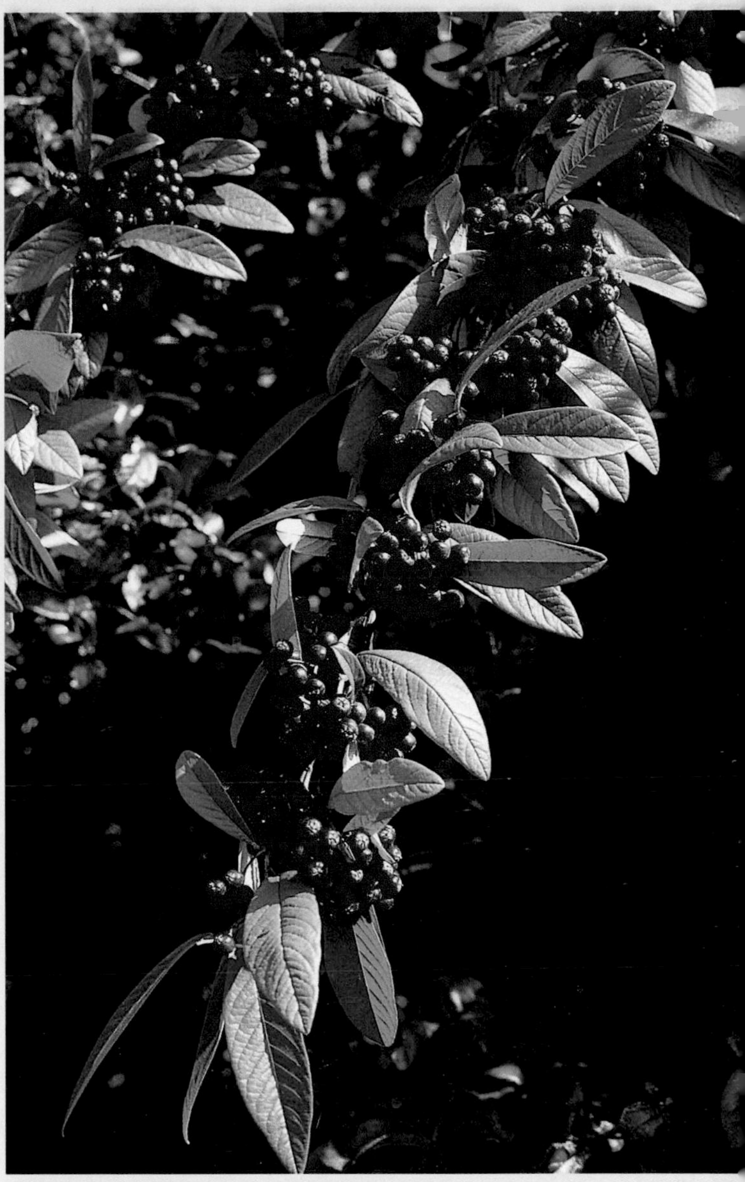

***Cotoneaster x watereri* 'John Waterer'**

D. racemosa (Ruscus racemosus),
the Alexandrian Laurel

A small shrub with erect, leafy shoots reminiscent of bamboo. It is tolerant of deep shade. The flowers are small and greenish, of little decorative value. The orange-red berries would be very attractive if they were borne more freely. A hot summer is needed for any quantity of them to develop.

Size: up to about 90cm (3ft) tall, spreading slowly by basal suckers.

Leaves: oval to lanceolate, about 2.5cm (1in) or so long, mid-green.

Fruits: round, almost 12mm (1/2in) across, orange-red, ripening in autumn and usually persisting well into winter, but rarely abundant.

Cultivation: a woodland plant, good in moderate to deep shade, preferably in a moist loam mixed with plenty of humus.

Propagation: most easily propagated by division in spring; seed, if available, should be sown in autumn and exposed to frost and should then germinate the following spring.

Origin: Turkey to Iran.

DAPHNE

See entry under SHRUBS for most soils, with showy or strongly scented flowers.

EUONYMUS

See entry under SHRUBS for most soils, mainly for foliage effect.

Ilex aquifolium

GAULTHERIA

See entry under SHRUBS requiring acid soils.

ILEX

A large genus of about 400 evergreen and deciduous trees and shrubs occurring more or less throughout the world, except for sub-Saharan Africa. They are most numerous in tropical to temperate regions of Asia. Many species are not hardy, but one is native to northern Europe, including Britain.

Many hollies make excellent, dense hedges. They are generally easy and not very fussy about soil or position, though they can be slow to establish and are often slow-growing. Male and female flowers are normally borne on separate plants. Females need a male to pollinate them if they are to produce berries. Some plants never fruit prolifically, so it is worth selecting good, free-berrying cultivars for the best effect in the garden. Different species will usually cross-pollinate, so one male plant of any species or hybrid should be adequate to allow berrying on several females of any kind of holly.

I. aquifolium, the Common Holly

A very variable plant, usually seen as a large shrub or small tree but, given time and reasonably favourable conditions, capable of becoming a medium tree. The leaves are usually edged with spines, but on older plants they may become more or less spineless, especially on higher branches. The flowers are small and insignificant among the dark green foliage, but a female plant with many berries can be highly decorative. The berries are eaten by birds but often survive at least until Christmas.

There are several dozen different cultivars of this species, many of them with variegated leaves. The Common Holly is one of the best hedging plants for areas with colder climates such as Britain, hardy almost everywhere, wind resistant and dense, with prickly leaves. It may take several years to grow to the required height, but its slow growth is an advantage later, as less trimming is needed.

Size: usually up to about 4.5 to 6m (15 to 20ft) tall, but can attain 18 to 21m (60 or 70ft) after many years.

Leaves: usually more or less elliptical to oval, about

***Ilex aquifolium* 'Ferox Argentea'**

5 to 7.5cm (2 to 3in) long, or sometimes rather larger, dark green and leathery, with a spiny tip and crinkled margins bearing another dozen or so spines, but sometimes with few or no spines.

Fruits: round berries about 6mm (1/4in) in diameter, usually crimson, but some cultivars have orange or yellow fruits, ripening in autumn and often persisting well into winter.

Cultivation: easy in most soils and situations as long as drainage is reasonably good, hardy, tolerant of sun or shade. A fertile medium loam will give excellent results. It is best to acquire pot-grown plants not more than 60cm (2ft) tall and to plant in late autumn or early spring, because hollies dislike root disturbance, particularly during the growing season. Water well until they become established. Holly hedges should be clipped in summer. Cultivars with variegated foliage usually need a sunny position to colour well, though they tolerate shade. Some are prone to produce occasional shoots with ordinary, plain green leaves: these should be pruned out as soon as they appear.

Propagation: by cuttings of half-ripened side shoots with a heel of old wood, taken in late summer and inserted into sandy compost, preferably in a closed propagator with bottom heat, or of ripe new wood taken in winter and kept shaded, under glass; by layering in autumn (holly branches that touch the ground will often root naturally); by seed, sown in autumn as soon as ripe and exposed to frost during the winter. Note that seed-grown plants may be variable in quality.

Varieties: 'Amber' is a female cultivar with bronze-yellow fruits; 'Angustifolia' is of neat, pyramidal habit and slow growth, with small, narrow, prickly leaves and may be either male or female; 'Argentea Marginata' is a name that has been used for both male and female plants with leaves which have creamy-white margins, but is now usually applied to a free-berrying female cultivar; 'Argentea Marginata Pendula' is similar, female and free-fruiting, with strongly weeping branches; 'Aurea Marginata' has yellow-edged leaves; 'Bacciflava' ('Fructu Luteo') has bright yellow berries; 'Crispa' has distorted, twisted leaves and is male; 'Crispa Aureopicta' is similar, with a central splash of yellow and pale green on each leaf; 'Ferox' has small, very spiny leaves, with spines on

Ilex aquifolium 'Silver Queen'

the surface as well as on the margins (male); 'Ferox Argentea' is similar, with creamy-white leaf margins; 'Ferox Aurea' is also similar, but with the centres of the leaves splashed with yellow; 'Flavescens', the Moonlight Holly, is a female cultivar with leaves suffused with yellow and gold; 'Fructo Aurantiaco' has orange berries; 'Golden Milkboy' has large leaves which are gold with a green margin (male); 'Golden Queen' is oddly named, as it is male, and has broad yellow margins to the leaves; 'Golden van Tol' has gold-margined leaves with few or no spines and often berries well; 'Handsworth New Silver' has a dense, upright habit, leaves margined with creamy white and purple young stems (female, often berrying freely); 'J. C. van Tol' has more or less spineless leaves and usually produces a good crop of berries (some growers claim that this cultivar bears both male and female flowers and self-pollinates, but this does not seem to be true of all plants given this name); 'Madame Briot' has purple stems and spiny leaves with yellow margins (female, and often berrying freely); 'Myrtifolia' has purple stems and small, dark green leaves (male); 'Myrtifolia Aurea Maculata' is dense and compact with small leaves splashed with gold (again male); 'Pendula' is female and free-fruiting, with dense foliage on weeping branches; 'Pyramidalis' is upright in growth, especially when young, with leaves either spiny or smooth, and usually fruits abundantly; 'Pyramidalis Fructu Luteo' is similar, with bright yellow fruits; 'Silver Queen' has purple stems and leaves with cream margins, often pinkish when young (male, despite the name). There are a considerable number of other cultivars in existence, and more are still being developed.

Origin: widespread in Europe and a British native.

I. cornuta

A dense, slow-growing shrub with squarish leaves usually with five spines. It can, in favourable conditions, become a large shrub, but more often remains smaller. It is not as hardy as Common Holly. Berries are rarely produced abundantly.

Size: usually not more than about 2.4m (8ft) tall, often less, slow-growing.

Leaves: about 5 to 7.5cm (2 to 3in) long, almost rectangular, with a sharp, downward-pointing spine at the tip and two or sometimes three other spines on each margin, stiffly leathery, dark green.

Fruits: rarely borne in any quantity, round and red.

Cultivation: not as hardy as Common Holly. Best in a warm, sheltered position in light shade or full sun, in a moist, fertile loamy soil.

Propagation: as for *I. aquifolium.*

Varieties: 'Burfordii' is a small, very dense, often freely fruiting cultivar with leaves that have no marginal spines; 'Ira S. Nelson' and 'O. Spring' are variegated female cultivars. A few other cultivars exist but most are rare in cultivation in Britain.

Origin: China.

I. crenata, the Box-leaved Holly

A holly with small, spineless leaves and black fruits, not looking very much like other hollies. It is eventually a large shrub, but is slow-growing.

Size: up to as much as 6m (20ft) tall, but taking many years to attain more than half that height.

Leaves: elliptical to obovate, up to about 2.5cm (1in) long, dark green and leathery, with many rounded teeth on the margins.

Fruits: small, round, black berries.

Cultivation: fairly adaptable, but best in a moist, humus-rich loam in a sunny to partly shady position. Slow-growing. Stands clipping well and will make an excellent low hedge.

Propagation: as for *I. aquifolium.*

Varieties: 'Convexa' is a free-fruiting cultivar of more compact growth; 'Fastigiata' is of upright habit; 'Golden Gem' is dwarf and very dense, with yellow leaves; 'Helleri' is also dwarf, with very small leaves; 'Mariesii' is very dwarf, with tiny, round leaves; 'Shiro-fukurin' ('Snowflake') has leaves splashed with white; 'Variegata' has leaves that are yellowish in spring, becoming pale green later; f. *watanabeana* has yellow fruits. A number of other cultivars exist, of varying size and habit.

Origin: China, Japan, Korea and the Himalayan region.

I. kingiana

In the wild this is an evergreen tree which reaches more than 10m (30ft) in height, but in cultivation it is usually much smaller, rarely more than a large shrub. The leaves are large and very ornamental.

Size: usually up to about 3m (10ft) tall in cultivation, but can eventually become larger in favourable conditions.

Leaves: up to as much as 22.5cm (9in) long, elliptical to broadly elliptical, thick and leathery, with sharply toothed margins on young plants, tending to be almost untoothed on more mature plants.

Fruits: red, round, and up to almost 12mm (1/2in) in diameter.

Cultivation: not hardy enough for very cold areas. Best in a warm, sheltered position in moist, humus-rich soil in sun or light shade, but will also tolerate deep shade.

Propagation: as for *I. aquifolium.*

Origin: the Himalayan region.

I. latifolia

Another fine species with attractive large leaves, which will grow into a large shrub or small tree in regions with cool climates, such as Britain. It will often fruit abundantly.

Size: usually up to about 3.6 to 4.5m (12 to 15ft) in height, but may eventually attain more in very favourable conditions.

Leaves: up to about 17.5cm (7in) long, broadly elliptical, dark, glossy green and leathery, and with toothed margins.

Fruits: about 6mm (1/4in) in diameter, orange-red.

Cultivation: reasonably hardy, but best in a sheltered situation, in sun or partial shade, though it will tolerate deep shade. Prefers a fertile, humus-rich soil.

Propagation: as for *I. aquifolium.*

Origin: Japan and eastern China.

Ilex pernyi

I. myrtifolia

A medium to large shrub with rather small leaves and red, or sometimes yellow, fruits. It is not suitable for chalky soils.

Size: up to about 3m (10ft) tall, sometimes rather more in favourable conditions.

Leaves: rather narrow, oval to elliptical, about 2.5 to 5cm (1 to 2in) long.

Fruits: small, round berries, usually red, but plants with yellow fruits exist.

Cultivation: requires a neutral to acid soil, preferably a moist, fertile loam, and a sheltered situation in full sun or a little shade.

Propagation: as for *I. aquifolium*.

Origin: south-eastern United States.

I. pernyi

An unusual and attractive large shrub or small tree with small, spiny leaves and bright red fruits.

Size: usually up to about 4.5m (15ft) tall, sometimes more, but quite slow-growing.

Leaves: more or less oval but looking very angular because of the projecting marginal spines, about 2.5cm (1in) long, dark green, shiny and leathery. The leaf tip is drawn out into a long spine, with usually two, less often one or three, pairs of prominent spines on the margins.

Fruits: small, round, red berries, usually borne in moderate quantities on female plants.

Cultivation: fairly easy and adaptable, but best with some shelter, in a fertile, humus-rich soil, in sun or light shade.

Propagation: as for *I. aquifolium*.

Origin: China.

I. yunnanensis

A medium to large, bushy shrub with spineless leaves reminiscent of those of some cotoneasters, and with small red fruits.

Size: usually up to about 4.5m (15ft) tall, but may attain more in favourable conditions.

Leaves: more or less oval, about 2.5cm (1in) or a little more in length, with finely toothed but spineless margins, glossy green.

Fruits: small, round, red berries on female plants, often not very abundant.

Cultivation: prefers a humus-rich soil with plenty of moisture and some shelter, in sun or shade.

Propagation: as for *I. aquifolium*.

Origin: western China.

I. x altaclerensis, the Highclere Holly

A group of hybrids generally similar to the Common Holly (*I. aquifolium*), which is one of their parents, but generally of more vigorous growth. Most are large shrubs or sometimes small trees with larger leaves than the Common Holly.

Size: usually up to about 4.5 to 6m (15 to 20ft) tall, but sometimes more.

Leaves: rather variable, generally similar to those of *I. aquifolium* but larger, often with few spines.

Fruits: red fruits like those of *I. aquifolium*, often freely borne on female plants.

Cultivation: generally easy in most soils and positions, faster growing than most other hollies, fairly tolerant of pollution and coastal exposure.

***Ilex* x *altaclerensis* 'Hodginsii'**

Propagation: as for *I. aquifolium*, but, being hybrids, will not come true from seed.

Varieties: 'Balearica' (*I. balearica*) is hardy and vigorous, eventually becoming a medium tree, with few-spined leaves, usually free-fruiting; 'Belgica Aurea' ('Silver Sentinel') is vigorous and erect, with few-spined leaves up to about 10cm (4in) long, margined with cream or yellow (female); 'Camelliifolia' has large, often spineless leaves, purple stems and large fruits; 'Golden King' has broad, more or less spineless leaves with gold margins and is female, despite the name; 'Hodginsii' is a strong-growing male cultivar with large, broad leaves that are variably spiny, though tending to be few-spined on older plants; 'Lawsoniana' is a female cultivar with large, often spineless leaves with a central splash of gold; 'Wilsonii' is another female cultivar which has green stems and large, spiny leaves. There are several other cultivars that are mainly less common in cultivation than those included in this list.

Origin: garden hybrids, the parents being *I. aquifolium* and *I. perado* (or *I. perado* subsp. *platyphylla*), a rather tender holly from the Canary Islands and the Azores.

I. x koehneana

An attractive hybrid with quite big leaves with spine-toothed margins, growing into a large shrub or small tree. The fruits are large.

Size: up to about 6m (20ft) high.

Leaves: up to as much as 12.5 to 15cm (5 or 6in) long, elliptical and leathery, with spiny teeth all along the margins.

Fruits: large red berries are often freely produced on female plants.

Cultivation: generally robust and easy in most soils and positions.

Propagation: as for *I.* x *altaclerensis*.

Varieties: 'Chestnut Leaf' is a vigorous female cultivar with yellowish-green leaves.

Origin: a garden hybrid, the parents being *I. aquifolium* and *I. latifolia*.

I. x meserveae

A small group of very fine hybrids, vigorous but generally smaller than *I.* x *altaclerensis*. The foliage usually has a bluish tinge and the stems are purplish. They flower well. Male plants are good pollinators of other hollies and females berry profusely, as long as there is a male to pollinate them. They are very good for hedging but are less prickly than Common Holly.

Size: up to about 3m (10ft) high and wide.

Leaves: small, about 2.5 to 5cm (1 to 2in) long, oval to elliptical, dark, shiny, bluish-green, with spiny teeth on the margins.

Fruits: round, red berries, often abundantly produced.

Cultivation: easy and tolerant of a range of conditions, but best in a moist, fertile loam in full sun or partial shade. Dislikes coastal exposure.

Propagation: as for *I.* x *altaclerensis*, but note that some cultivars of this group may be subject to Plant Breeder's Rights (see page 6).

Varieties: Blue Angel is a compact, female cultivar; Blue Prince is male and a very good pollinator of other hollies; Blue Princess is a very fine female cultivar, probably the most free-berrying of any holly. A few other cultivars exist and more are currently being developed.

Origin: a garden hybrid between *I. aquifolium* and *I. rugosa*.

I. bioritsensis, I. dimorphophylla, I. fargesii, I. opaca and a number of other species are in cultivation in Britain, and all have some qualities to recommend them, as have the two hybrids **I. x aquipernyi** (*I. aquifolium* crossed with *I. pernyi*) and **I. x attenuata** (a natural hybrid between the two American species *I. cassine* and *I. opaca*).

NANDINA

See entry under SHRUBS for most soils, with showy or strongly scented flowers.

PHOTINIA (including **Stranvaesia**)

A genus of about 70 species of deciduous and evergreen trees and shrubs from southern and eastern Asia, closely related to *Cotoneaster*, *Pyracantha* and *Crataegus*. Many are from China and are sometimes

Photinia davidiana

called Chinese hawthorns. Most occur in warm temperate to subtropical regions and are too tender to be reliable garden plants in Britain and countries with similar cooler climates. There are a few, however, which are sufficiently hardy to flourish in all but the coldest areas, especially if given a little shelter. The flowers are very similar to those of hawthorn, though with less scent, and the usually red fruits often persist well into winter, being less attractive to birds than many other berries.

P. davidiana (Stranvaesia davidiana)

A very vigorous, erect, large shrub or small tree bearing clusters of white flowers in June followed by bunches of red fruits. On mature plants the oldest leaves turn red in autumn. Tends to be semi-evergreen in cold winters.

Size: about 6 to 9m (20 to 30ft) tall, upright in habit.

Leaves: lanceolate to oblanceolate, about 7.5 to 12.5cm (3 to 5in) long, smooth, with untoothed margins, and dark green.

Flowers: in large, domed clusters up to about 10cm (4in) across, white, opening in May or June.

Fruits: round, red berries about 6cm (1/4in) in diameter are borne in large bunches in autumn and persist well into winter.

Cultivation: tough and easy, tolerant of pollution, coastal exposure, chalky soils and clay. Best in a medium to light loam in sun to moderate shade. Makes a good screening plant and is also useful as a tall hedge.

Propagation: by cuttings of half-ripened shoots taken in summer and inserted into sandy compost in a propagator with bottom heat, or taken in winter and kept in shade under glass.

Varieties: 'Palette' has leaves splashed with cream and pink, bears pink berries and is not as large and vigorous as the type; var. *undulata* is smaller, usually only of medium size, and wide spreading, often twice as wide as high; var. *undulata* 'Fructu Luteo' is similar in habit, with bright yellow fruits.

Origin: China.

P. glabra

A medium to large shrub with reddish-bronze young growth and red fruits in autumn and winter. Tends not to flower or fruit very freely in cultivation.

Size: usually about 2.4 to 3.6m (8 to 12ft) tall, but sometimes more.

Leaves: about 7.5cm (3in) long, elliptical to obovate, leathery, with very small teeth on the margins.

Flowers: white, in large clusters up to about 10cm (4in) across, opening in May or June.

Fruits: red berries in large bunches from autumn, persisting into winter.

Cultivation: not sufficiently hardy for very cold areas and is best given some shelter in all but the mildest districts. A fertile, humus-rich soil will give the best results, though it will tolerate most garden soils, including chalky ones. Shade is also tolerated, but sun will encourage flowering.

Propagation: as for *P. davidiana.*

Varieties: 'Parfait' ('Pink Lady', 'Variegata') has variegated foliage.

Origin: Japan, China, Thailand and Burma.

P. serratifolia (P. serrulata)

A large shrub or small tree with large leaves. The young growths are coppery-red. Tends not to flower or fruit very freely in cultivation in Britain.

Size: usually up to about 6m (20ft) tall, but may eventually reach 9m (30ft) in favourable conditions.

Leaves: very striking, up to 22.5cm (9in) long, stiff and leathery with sharply toothed margins, dark green, reddish when young. The red young growths appear over a long period and are highly ornamental. They are remarkably frost-resistant.

Flowers: white, in large clusters up to about 15cm (6in) across, opening in April or May.

Fruits: small, round, red berries ripen in autumn and persist into winter.

Cultivation: tolerant of a range of soils and conditions, but best in a moist, humus-rich soil in full sun to partial shade, with some shelter, especially in cold districts. A fine shrub for chalky soils.

Propagation: as for *P. davidiana.*

Origin: China and Japan.

P. x fraseri

A group of rather variable hybrids, principally grown for their reddish young growths, as flowers are rarely produced in any quantity and fruits scarcely at all. Most plants of this parentage resemble *P. glabra*, but usually have redder young shoots.

Size: usually up to about 4.5m (15ft) tall, but the different cultivars vary somewhat in size.

Leaves: similar to those of *P. glabra*, but often larger, up to about 15cm (6in) long.

Flowers: white, in domed clusters that are up to about 10cm (4in) across, opening in May or June, but rarely very abundant.

Fruits: very rarely seen.

Cultivation: easy in most soils and situations, reasonably hardy, but often comes into growth very early and the young shoots may be damaged by late frosts. Recovery from such damage is normally good, however. Best in a moist, medium loam in full sun or partial shade, with a little shelter. Stands clipping well and will make a good informal or even formal hedge. The production of the red young growths can be encouraged by clipping two or three times a year.

Propagation: as for *P. davidiana.*

Varieties: 'Birmingham' is very similar to *P. glabra*, with bright coppery-red young shoots; 'Red Robin' has bright red young shoots and quite large, lanceolate leaves; 'Robusta' is vigorous and hardy with bright coppery-red young growths and large leaves similar to those of *P. serratifolia*; 'Rubens' is very similar to *P. glabra* with very bright red young shoots.

Origin: a garden hybrid between *P. glabra* and *P. serratifolia.*

PRUNUS

See entry under SHRUBS for most soils, mainly for foliage effect.

PYRACANTHA, the Firethorns

A small genus of only about ten species, one from Europe, but mostly occurring in the Far East and elsewhere in Asia. Firethorns are generally similar to cotoneasters, but have thorny stems and a distinctive angular habit of growth, the side shoots growing more or less at right angles to the branches. They are generally robust, easy to grow and very decorative. They dislike any root disturbance, however, and are best acquired in pots and planted either in autumn or early spring.

As they have quite small leaves, stand clipping well and are densely branched and thorny, many firethorns make excellent hedges. They should preferably be clipped in early spring. Although they are often grown as wall shrubs, and are very good on north- and east-facing walls, most do not need the support or protection of a wall. The flowers are usually produced in abundance and have a scent like that of hawthorn. They are followed by large bunches of red, orange or yellow fruits, which are often eaten by birds early in winter. Yellow fruits seem to be eaten less readily than the red or orange ones. Some firethorns are very susceptible to scab and fire-blight diseases. The best way to avoid disease problems is to plant resistant

Pyracantha coccinea

Pyracantha 'Orange Glow'

Pyracantha 'Orange Glow' in flower

varieties. There are a large and increasing number of hybrid firethorns of uncertain parentage, some of which are more resistant to diseases than the species.

P. angustifolia

A medium to large shrub with orange fruits and narrow leaves that are woolly-hairy beneath.

Size: usually up to about 3m (10ft) tall, but sometimes rather more.

Leaves: narrowly elliptical, small, not more than 5cm (2in) long, covered all over with greyish woolly hairs when young, the upper surface becoming hairless and dark green.

Flowers: white, in small clusters up to about 5cm (2in) across, produced all along the branches in May or June.

Fruits: yellowish-orange, often lasting well into winter.

Cultivation: not as hardy as most other firethorns and requires some protection in cold districts, but otherwise easy and vigorous. Not very fussy about soil, but a fertile, well-drained medium loam is best. Tolerates full sun to moderate shade. Good as a wall shrub.

Propagation: by cuttings of nearly ripe young shoots inserted into sandy compost in shade under glass during late summer; by seed sown in late winter in a cool greenhouse or frame.

Origin: western China.

P. atalantioides (P. discolor)

A large, vigorous shrub or even a small tree, with comparatively large leaves and scarlet fruits.

Size: up to as much as 6m (20ft) tall.

Leaves: usually rather less than 5cm (2in) long, oval to broadly elliptical, dark, glossy green.

Flowers: white, in small clusters up to about 5cm (2in) across, abundantly produced in May to early June.

Fruits: scarlet berries in bunches ripen in autumn and often last well into winter.

Cultivation: strong-growing and easy in most soils and positions, best in a well-drained fertile loam in either sun or shade. Will grow well on a sunless wall.

Propagation: as for *P. angustifolia.*

Varieties: 'Aurea' ('Flava') has yellow berries.

Origin: China.

Pyracantha **'Soleil d'Or'**

P. coccinea (Cotoneaster pyracantha)

A large shrub with small leaves and bright red to orange-red fruits.

Size: up to about 3 to 4.5m (10 to 15ft) tall.

Leaves: oval to obovate, about 2.5cm (1in) or a little more in length, deep green, with finely toothed margins.

Flowers: creamy-white, in small clusters all along the branches, opening in May or June.

Fruits: small, bright coral-red, ripening in autumn and attractive to birds.

Cultivation: fairly vigorous and easy in most soils and situations, but prefers a well-drained, fertile loam in sun or partial shade. Tends to be susceptible to scab and fire-blight.

Propagation: as for *P. angustifolia.*

Varieties: 'Lalandei' is more vigorous and erect than the type, with masses of orange-red fruits; 'Red Column' is also erect, with blood-red berries, probably the reddest produced by any firethorn, and is resistant to fire-blight.

Origin: southern Europe and Asia Minor.

P. rogersiana (P. crenulata var. rogersiana)

A large, erect shrub bearing masses of attractive reddish-orange fruits.

Size: up to about 3 to 3.6m (10 to 12ft) tall and almost as wide.

Leaves: oblanceolate, about 2.5 to 5cm (1 to 2in) long, dark green, with small teeth running along the margins.

Flowers: white, in clusters all along the branches, opening in May.

Fruits: reddish-orange, often borne in profusion.

Cultivation: vigorous and easy in most soils and situations, best in well-drained, fertile loam in either sun or shade. Makes an excellent hedge.

Propagation: as for *P. angustifolia.*

Varieties: 'Flava' has bright yellow berries.

Origin: south-west China.

Pyracantha 'Buttercup' is of spreading habit and has yellow fruits; 'Knap Hill Lemon' has lemon-yellow fruits; 'Mohave' has orange-red berries and is resistant to scab and fire-blight; 'Mohave Silver' is smaller and less vigorous than most firethorns and has foliage variegated with greyish-silver, but unfortunately tends not to fruit freely; 'Orange Glow' is dense, vigorous and free-fruiting with reddish-orange berries, and is resistant to scab; 'Shawnee' bears masses of yellow to light orange berries and is resistant to scab and fire-blight; 'Soleil d'Or' is of upright habit and bears golden-yellow fruits; 'Teton' is vigorous and upright with small, disease-resistant leaves and yellow-orange berries; 'Watereri' is vigorous, dense and upright with masses of flowers followed by equally abundant bright red fruits. There are a number of other hybrid firethorns, most of which make excellent garden plants, and more continue to be produced and marketed all the time.

RHAMNUS

See entry under SHRUBS for most soils, mainly for foliage effect.

RUSCUS

A genus of only about half a dozen species of peculiar small shrubs which have very tiny, scale-like true leaves and flattened stems with the shape and appearance of leaves. The tiny flowers are borne in the middle of these false leaves, followed by showy fruits. Plants may bear only male or only female flowers or sometimes both (hermaphrodite). These last are the most desirable in gardens as male plants do not produce fruits and females require pollination by a male. All plants of the genus are very tolerant of shade and dry conditions and will grow under trees where little else will survive.

R. aculeatus, the Butcher's Broom

A small shrub sending up stiff, erect, branched shoots from underground stems. Female and hermaphrodite plants bear red berries from autumn into winter.

Size: between about 30 and 90cm (1 and 3ft) in height, the clumps of dark green, erect shoots slowly spreading in circumference.

Leaves: the true leaves are very tiny and quite inconspicuous, but flattened stems which look like leaves are oval, about 2.5cm (1in) long, stiff and dark green with a sharply pointed tip.

Fruits: attractive round red berries about 12mm (1/2in) across ripen in autumn on female and hermaphrodite plants. Plants bearing only female flowers require pollination by a male plant.

Cultivation: very tough and easy in most soils and conditions, will grow in dense shade under trees where the ground is very dry. Best in prepared fertile loam in moderate to deep shade.

Propagation: established plants can be divided in the spring, or rooted suckers can be dug up from the edge of a clump and grown on.

Varieties: var. *angustifolius* has narrower false leaves. Some nurseries offer plants that are labelled male, female or hermaphrodite.

Origin: southern Europe, including southern England.

R. hypoglossum, the Large Butcher's Broom, is very similar to the above, but lower growing, to only about 37.5cm (15in) tall. It usually has unbranched shoots, with larger false leaves and fruits. **R. hypophyllum**, the Spanish Butcher's Broom, is similar to *R. hypoglossum*, but is taller, up to more than 60cm (2ft) in height. **R. x microglossum** is a hybrid between *R. hypophyllum* and *R. hypoglossum*, about 60cm (2ft) tall and spreading quite rapidly, but rarely or never fruiting (cultivated plants may all be male).

SKIMMIA

A small genus of evergreen shrubs and small trees, native to the Himalayan region and east Asia. Those in cultivation are mainly grown for their decorative value in winter, either for their red berries or colourful flower buds. The flowers open in early spring. Male and female flowers are usually carried on separate plants. Only the female produce berries, but need to be pollinated by a male. One male plant will, however, pollinate at least two or three females. Skimmias are very susceptible to magnesium deficiency problems, the first sign being yellowing of older leaves. The application of small quantities of magnesium sulphate (Epsom salts) around the roots will remedy this. Otherwise these are generally very adaptable shrubs, suitable for most soils in either sun or shade.

Ruscus aculeatus

Skimmia japonica subsp. *reevesiana*

Skimmia japonica 'Rubella'

S. japonica

A very variable, small to medium or large shrub with leathery leaves and large clusters of white flowers at the ends of the branches in spring. Female plants, if pollinated by a male, carry red berries from autumn through the winter.

Size: usually up to about 1.2m (4ft) high and wide, but at least some cultivars may grow considerably larger, up to as much as 6m (20ft) in height and the same in spread.

Leaves: elliptical to obovate, usually about 10cm (4in) long, stiff, leathery and dark green.

Flowers: individually quite small, but borne in large clusters at the ends of branches, white, usually opening in April, but often decorative when still in bud, the buds being carried throughout winter. Both male and female flowers, usually borne on separate plants, are decorative.

Fruits: round to more or less pear-shaped, red, rather less than 12mm (1/2in) in diameter, borne in clusters at the ends of the branches, ripening in autumn and persisting throughout winter.

Cultivation: most cultivars are very adaptable and will grow in almost any soil, even chalky ones, in full sun or deep shade, but ideal conditions are a moist, humus-rich soil in partial shade.

Propagation: by cuttings of ripe shoots inserted into loamy compost in a propagator with bottom heat during spring and early summer; by layering in autumn; by seeds sown during winter in sandy compost in a cold frame. Named cultivars will not come true from seed.

Varieties: 'Fragrans' is an excellent male clone with flowers smelling like Lily of the Valley; 'Nymans' is a free-berrying female clone with comparatively large fruits; 'Rubella' is a male clone with red flower buds that are conspicuous throughout winter; 'Veitchii' ('Foremanii') is a vigorous female clone with large bunches of showy berries; 'Wakehurst White' ('Fructu Albo') has white berries, but is of rather weak constitution; subsp. *reevesiana* usually has both male and female flowers on the same plant and dark red fruits that are often still present when the white flowers open in May, but it will not flourish on chalk. Several other named cultivars exist, some very compact and small, or distinct in other ways.

Origin: Japan (the typical plant); China (subsp. *reevesiana*).

S. laureola

A small, dense shrub with dark green foliage and greenish yellow flowers in spring. Female plants, if pollinated by a male, bear bright red fruits.

Size: usually up to about 0.9 to 1.2m (3 to 4ft) high and wide, but may grow taller.

Leaves: lanceolate to obovate, usually about 10 to 15cm (4 to 6in) long, dark green, tending to be clustered at the ends of the branches like those of some daphnes.

Flowers: clusters of greenish-yellow flowers open in spring, usually April, and are sweetly scented.

Fruits: bright red, similar to those of *S. japonica.*

Cultivation: best in a moist, woodland soil in semi-shade, but, like *S. japonica*, is generally tolerant.

Propagation: as for *S. japonica.*

Origin: the Himalayan region.

S. x confusa

Similar to *S. laureola*, but with creamy-white flowers.

Size: up to as much as 3m (10ft) tall and about half as wide, but often attaining no more than 1.2 to 1.5m (4 to 5ft) high.

Leaves: similar to those of *S. laureola.*

Flowers: similar to those of *S. laureola*, but much whiter in hue.

Fruits: similar to those of *S. laureola.*

Cultivation: as for *S. laureola.*

Propagation: as for *S. japonica*, but, as a hybrid, it will not come true from seed.

Varieties: 'Kew Green' is a selected male cultivar, which will pollinate female plants of other skimmias.

Origin: a garden hybrid, the parents being *S. japonica* and *S. laureola*

Skimmia anquetilia bears yellowish flowers in spring followed by scarlet berries and grows to about 1.2m (4ft) tall and 1.8m (6ft) wide.

VIBURNUM

See entry under SHRUBS for most soils, with showy or strongly scented flowers.

Skimmia laureola

SHRUBS REQUIRING ACID SOILS

CAMELLIA

A fairly large genus of evergreen shrubs and trees, mainly from tropical and subtropical parts of east and south-east Asia. Only a few species are sufficiently hardy for outdoor cultivation in colder climates which get regular frost and snow in winter, but a very large number of cultivars has been developed from these species by selection and hybridization. They are some of the most beautiful of all flowering shrubs, especially valuable because most of them bloom during winter and early spring or in autumn, when large and colourful flowers are very welcome.

Camellias neither need nor like very acid conditions and should flourish in most soils with a pH of about 5.5 to 6.5. Even with soil reactions of up to pH7 (neutral) problems should be slight and treatable either by applying ferrous sulphate to the soil or by applying chelated trace elements, or both. (See Section 1 for more about soil treatments.) Very acid soils can be treated with dolomitic limestone. Camellias are commercially important. In the Far East, cooking oil is pressed from the seeds of several species and tea is produced from a camellia.

C. japonica

One of the hardiest species, suffering serious damage only in severe winters. A medium to large shrub or small tree with dark green, glossy foliage and moderately large, red to pink or white flowers which open in late winter to spring, depending on the cultivar.

Size: eventually up to as much as 9m (30ft) tall, but takes many years to reach such a size and can easily be kept pruned to no more than 3m (10ft).

Leaves: about 10cm (4in) long, oval to obovate, leathery, dark, shiny green above, paler beneath, with finely toothed margins.

Flowers: very variable, according to the cultivar, usually about 7.5 to 10cm (3 to 4in) in diameter, single to semi-double with a central bundle of yellow stamens, double with a central mass of small petals mixed with stamens or with a few stamens mixed among many large petals, or formally double with few or no stamens. The colour may be pure white or various shades of pink to dark red. Most *C. japonica* cultivars have quite a long flowering period, from as early as February to about mid-May, some being earlier to bloom, others later.

Cultivation: Camellias are very special plants and it is worthwhile making an effort to select and prepare a position in the garden for them where they will flourish. They are best given some shelter and partial shade, with as little exposure to morning sun as possible. Cold or salty winds will cause damage. Evergreen hedges or screens to break the wind and some overhead shade from trees are ideal. Soil should be well dug to a good depth and have plenty of compost, very well-rotted manure (horse manure is good), leaf-mould, composted bark or similar humus-rich material mixed into it. If the soil is heavy, good drainage should be ensured. Mix in sharp sand and grit or create a raised bed, if necessary.

Camellias are best planted in spring and must be kept well watered until established. They dislike root competition from other plants and should be kept weeded and mulched. Shredded bark is excellent for this. Do not plant ground-cover plants around them. They are particularly susceptible to damage by late frosts in spring, which may brown the flowers and kill young growth. It is worth keeping some horticultural fleece to wrap them in if a late frost seems likely. If planting close to buildings, check that the soil has not got limy builders' rubble (pieces of mortar, cement, concrete, plaster or similar) in it. If it has, it is best to dig out a large hole and replace the soil completely. Mix some slow-release fertilizer into the soil when planting, but do not overdo it. Too much nitrogenous fertilizer will cause an excess of weak growth at the expense of flowering. In later years, an occasional light feed with a balanced fertilizer is all that is needed. When more mulch needs to be applied around the base of the plant, mix a little slow-release fertilizer with it.

Propagation: by cuttings of almost ripened new growth taken in late summer and inserted into a humus-rich but open and free-draining compost (three parts of ericaceous compost mixed with one part of sharp sand is good), preferably in a closed propagator with bottom heat, or taken in late autumn and treated similarly; by layering, if suitable branches that can be bent down to the ground are available; or by air-layering (a technique much used by the Chinese for propagating camellias), which will usually produce a good plant more rapidly than other methods.

Varieties: there are now many hundreds of cultivars of *C. japonica*. Only a small selection of the best and most readily available ones, covering most of the major variations in colour and flower form, can be included here. Note that the form and colour of the flowers sometimes varies slightly according to growing conditions.

'Adolphe Audusson' has large, semi-double, dark red flowers, opening in early spring; 'Akashigata' ('Lady Clare') usually grows strongly, with a somewhat weeping habit, and has deep rose semi-double flowers, opening in late winter to early spring; 'Alba Plena' has very formal double white flowers and blooms in late winter to early spring; 'Alba Simplex' has single white flowers in spring; 'Apollo' has rose red, semi-double flowers, sometimes blotched with white, and is vigorous; 'Brushfield's Yellow' has creamy-white flowers with a central mass of small, pale yellow petals; 'C. M. Hovey' ('Colonel Firey') has formal double, vermilion flowers in late spring; 'Debutante' has pale pink, loose double flowers, with some stamens, in early spring, and is of strong, upright growth; 'Drama Girl' has very large, semi-double, deep salmon flowers that last a long time in spring, but are easily weather damaged; 'Elegans' ('Chandleri Elegans') has large, deep pink flowers, with a central mass of small petals that are often marked with white, blooming in early spring; 'Hagoromo' ('Magnoliiflora') has very pale pink, semi-double flowers in early spring; 'Jupiter' has single to semi-double flowers that are bright scarlet, sometimes marked with white, and is of vigorous, upright growth; 'Kramer's Supreme' has large, red, loosely double, fragrant flowers with golden stamens among the petals in early spring; 'Lady Vansittart' is slow growing and bears variable semi-double flowers, that are usually white striped with pink, in late spring; 'Mercury' has large, semi-double, light red flowers, often freely produced; 'Nobilissima' has loosely double, white flowers tinged with yellow and blooms very early; 'Silver Anniversary' has white, semi-double flowers in early spring and is vigorous and erect; 'Tricolor' ('Sieboldii') has semi-double flowers that are white, streaked with carmine, in early spring and is of compact habit. A few cultivars have variegated foliage.

Origin: Japan, China.

***Camellia japonica*: wild plants would be very similar to this cultivar with its single red flowers, here growing in a Chinese garden**

C. rusticana (C. japonica var. rusticana), the Snow Camellia

Very similar to *C. japonica* and formerly much confused with it, this is a very hardy species from northern Japan.

Size: up to about 4.5m (15ft) tall and often more or less as wide.

Leaves: about 10cm (4in) long, oval to obovate, thick and leathery, dark, shiny green above, paler beneath, with toothed margins.

Flowers: variable, usually red, similar to the flowers of *C. japonica*.

Cultivation: as for *C. japonica*, but just a little tougher.

Propagation: as for *C. japonica*.

Varieties: probably involved in the parentage of many camellias considered to be varieties of *C. japonica*. Only a few cultivars are considered with any certainty to belong to this species, the most commonly grown being the fine, strong-growing 'Arajishi', which has loosely double, rose-red flowers in early spring.

Origin: Japan.

C. saluenensis

A medium to large shrub with dark green foliage and quite large, pink flowers.

Size: up to about 4.5m (15ft) tall and rather more than half as wide.

Leaves: elliptical, about 5cm (2in) long, dark green above, lighter beneath, with finely toothed margins.

Flowers: pink, single, with six or seven petals and a central bunch of yellow stamens, about 6cm (2½in) across, often profusely borne, opening in early spring.

Cultivation: as for *C. japonica*.

Propagation: as for *C. japonica*.

Varieties: a few selected cultivars exist, varying mainly in flower colour, such as 'Trewithen Red' and 'William's Lavender'.

Origin: south-west China.

C. sasanqua

A medium to large shrub or even a small tree, with small leaves and flowers, opening in autumn and winter. Less hardy and reliable than *C. japonica*, but worth making an effort to grow.

Size: up to about 4.5m (15ft) tall, of quite open habit.

Leaves: elliptical, about 5 to 7.5cm (2 to 3in) long, dark, shiny green above, paler beneath, with finely toothed margins.

Camellia saluenensis

Flowers: usually quite small, about 5cm (2in) across, but larger in some cultivars, white, pink or red, opening in late autumn or winter.

Cultivation: as for *C. japonica*, but likes more sun and is not as hardy. Not really suitable for colder areas of Britain or countries with similar climates. It is best grown on a west-facing wall, except in very mild areas. It is a good wall shrub, with long, slender branches that can be trained as required.

Propagation: as for *C. japonica*.

Varieties: there are not as many cultivars derived from this species as there are from *C. japonica*. Most have white or pink flowers, but there are a few good reds.

'Crimson King' has bright red, single flowers; 'Fukuzutsumi' ('Apple Blossom') has single white flowers with a tinge of pink; 'Hugh Evans' is tall with weeping branches and single pink flowers; 'Jean May' is bushy with shell-pink, semi-double flowers; 'Narumigata' is vigorous and upright with large, white, single flowers shaded with pink; 'Rainbow' is vigorous with large, white, single flowers with a red border to each petal. A few dozen other cultivars are grown in Britain.

Origin: Japan.

C. sinensis (C. thea, Thea sinensis), the Tea Plant

This species has been cultivated in China for many centuries and is the original source of tea. Many cultivars have been bred in tea plantations, but these are generally of little interest to gardeners, as they have been selected for the quality and flavour of their leaves as tea, rather than for any ornamental value. What is of interest to gardeners, however, is that the cultivation of tea has spread northwards in China from the original home of the plant in the south of the country. This spread implies that hardier cultivars of the tea plant have been developed. Early introductions of *C. sinensis* into Britain were distinctly tender, but hardier cultivars have quite recently been imported and seem to be at least reasonably successful.

The flowers of this camellia are smaller and less showy than those of the other camellias described here, but this is nevertheless an attractive shrub and makes an interesting talking point in the garden.

Camellia sinensis: **foliage of a hardy form**

Size: in the wild it may grow into a small tree, but cultivated varieties are generally smaller. In Britain and countries with similar climates it is unlikely to exceed 1.5 to 1.8m (5 or 6ft) in height, except possibly after many years, in very favourable conditions.

Leaves: elliptical, about 5 to 10cm (2 to 4in) long, dark green, with toothed margins.

Flowers: more or less cup-shaped, with five or six white petals and a central mass of yellow stamens, about 4cm (1½in) across, nodding and often rather hidden by the leaves, opening usually in late winter to early spring, sometimes at other times of year.

Cultivation: only the hardier forms of this plant are suitable for outdoor culture in cool climates. It generally shares the requirements of *C. japonica*, but a little more shelter is probably a wise precaution. Rather more shade would certainly be tolerated, though this might tend to discourage flowering. The hardier forms of this species have not been grown in countries with relatively cold climates, such as Britain, for long enough for their needs to be precisely assessed.

Propagation: as for *C. japonica*.

Origin: China.

Camellia x *williamsii* 'Anticipation'

C. x williamsii

Most of the best camellias for general planting in cooler climates belong to this group of hybrids. They are among the hardiest and most vigorous of camellias, suitable for all but very cold districts. Their foliage tends to resemble that of *C. japonica*, while their flowers are closer to those of *C. saluenensis*. So far, no really good red-flowered plant of this group has been developed. Most of the cultivars have flowers of varying shades of pink.

Size: up to about 4.5 to 6m (15 to 20ft) tall and about half as wide.

Leaves: somewhat variable, usually similar to those of *C. japonica*, but in some cultivars they are smaller, intermediate between those of *C. japonica* and *C. saluenensis*.

Flowers: usually pink, sometimes white and in a few cultivars almost red, single to fully double, about 7.5cm (3in) across, more in a few cultivars, opening in winter or spring.

Cultivation: as for *C. japonica*, but rather tougher and easier than most other camellias and usually vigorous and free-flowering.

Propagation: as for *C. japonica*.

Varieties: 'Anticipation' has flowers that are almost red and fully double, opening in early spring; 'Ballet Queen' has large, salmon-pink, double flowers with a central mass of small petals in late spring; 'Bow Bells' has bright rose-pink, semi-double flowers opening over a long period in spring; 'Brigadoon' has large, rose-pink, semi-double flowers in early spring; 'China Clay' has white, semi-double flowers; 'Daintiness' has large, salmon-pink, semi-double flowers; 'Debbie' has double or sometimes semi-double, clear pink flowers; 'Donation' is vigorous, erect and usually free-flowering, with large, semi-double pink blooms with darker veining, opening in early spring; 'E. G. Waterhouse' has light pink, formal double flowers in late spring; 'Elegant Beauty' has large, deep rose-pink, double flowers with a central mass of small petals, blooming in late spring; 'Elsie Jury' has large, fully and loosely double, deep pink flowers in late spring; 'Francis Hanger' has single, white flowers in mid-spring and is of erect habit; 'Golden Spangles' has small, single, pink flowers and leaves with a central blotch of yellow; 'J. C. Williams' has single, pale pink flowers over a long period in spring – this was the first named cultivar of this group; 'Jury's Yellow' is not quite what it claims, bearing white flowers with a central mass of small, pale yellow petals, opening over a long period in spring; 'Mary Christian' has small, clear pink, single flowers in early spring and is of vigorous growth; 'Mary Phoebe Taylor' has very large, light rose-pink, double flowers opening in early spring and is erect in habit; 'November Pink' has single, pink flowers that will sometimes open as early as November, but more often in late winter; 'Saint Ewe' has single, rose-pink flowers in early spring; 'Water Lily' has formal double, pink flowers of very attractive shape in early spring.

Origin: hybrids between the various cultivars of *C. japonica* and *C. saluenensis*.

C. reticulata has the largest flowers of any camellia, but unfortunately is not very hardy. It is suitable for growing outdoors in only the mildest districts, or on a warm, preferably west-facing, wall in favoured areas. The flowers begin to open as early as January and are very susceptible to frost damage. Several dozen cultivars have been developed from this species, the older ones in China and more recent ones in Australia and the southern USA. Only a few are usually available in Britain. Attempts have been made to breed plants with at least some of the qualities of

C.reticulata, but with greater hardiness, by hybridization with other, hardier, camellias. Among the best results have been **C. 'Black Lace'**, with dark velvet red, double flowers (a hybrid between *C. reticulata* and a *C.* x *williamsii* cultivar); **C. 'Inspiration'**, with large, pink, semi-double flowers (*C. reticulata* crossed with *C. saluenensis*); **C. 'Leonard Messel'**, with large, semi-double, rose-pink flowers, opening over a long period (another hybrid with *C.* x *williamsii*); and **C. 'Salutation'**, with large, single to semi-double, pale pink flowers (*C. saluenensis* crossed with *C. reticulata*).

C. 'Cornish Snow' is a lovely hybrid between the small-flowered species *C. cuspidata* and *C. saluenensis*, with masses of quite small, white, single flowers covering the branches over a long period in spring; **C. 'Freedom Bell'** is a hybrid of unknown parentage, with quite small, bright coral-red, semi-double flowers in late winter to early spring. Both these plants are vigorous in growth and do well in cooler conditions.

ERICA

A fairly small genus of mostly dwarf and small shrubs, occurring principally in the Mediterranean region and South Africa. The South African species are not hardy outdoors in colder climates such as that of Britain, except perhaps in the very mildest districts. Some of the Mediterranean species, especially the larger ones, are on the borderline of hardiness. This is the type genus of the family Ericaceae, comprising the heaths, heathers, rhododendrons and their relatives, plants which form the great majority of ornamentals that flourish on acid soils. The heaths are very distinct in appearance, with their tiny needle-like leaves densely covering the younger branches and individually very small flowers borne in profusion towards the ends of the shoots. They vary considerably in their tolerance of lime in the soil. None will grow successfully in very limy soils, but some are perfectly happy with soils close to neutral.

***Camellia* x *williamsii* 'Ballet Queen'**

E. arborea, the Tree Heath

A large shrub or even a small tree, densely branched and covered with fragrant, white flowers in early spring. Moderately hardy, but not recommended for cold, inland areas.

Size: usually up to about 3.6m (12ft) tall, but can grow into a small tree 6m (20ft) high, especially in mild districts.

Leaves: very small, less than 6mm (1/4in) long, needle-like, dark green, usually in whorls of four, densely clothing the younger branches and shoots.

Erica arborea

Flowers: broadly bell-shaped, very small, white, in dense, spike-like clusters at the ends of branches, fragrant, opening during March and April.

Cultivation: likes sandy soil, but will flourish in any light, free-draining soil, preferably in full sun with some shelter. Not hardy enough for cold areas with hard winter frosts. Does not require strongly acid soil.

Propagation: by cuttings of young, half-ripened shoots taken in summer and inserted into a sandy compost, preferably in a closed propagator with bottom heat.

Varieties: var. *alpina* is hardier and smaller, to about 1.8m (6ft) tall and very erect.

Origin: the Mediterranean region.

E. australis, the Spanish Heath

A bushy, erect, medium shrub with reddish-pink flowers in spring. This is one of the loveliest of the large heaths.

Size: up to about 1.8m (6ft) high or a little more.

Leaves: similar to those of *E. arborea*.

Flowers: comparatively large, between 6 and 12mm (1/4 and 1/2in) long, tubular, deep reddish-pink, fragrant, in small clusters at the tips of shoots, opening in April and May.

Cultivation: as for *E. arborea*, but rather less hardy.

Propagation: as for *E. arborea*.

Varieties: 'Mr. Robert' has white flowers; 'Riverslea' has reddish-purple flowers. One or two other selected cultivars, with flowers of different colours, also exist.

Origin: Spain and Portugal.

E. lusitanica, the Portuguese Heath, is very like *E. arborea*, but with pink-tinged flowers, opening during winter and spring; **E. scoparia**, the Besom Heath, is a medium shrub, probably the least attractive of the large heaths, with green flowers, sometimes with a reddish tinge, opening in May and June; **E. terminalis**, the Corsican Heath, is very similar to *E. australis*, but with bright pink, slightly smaller

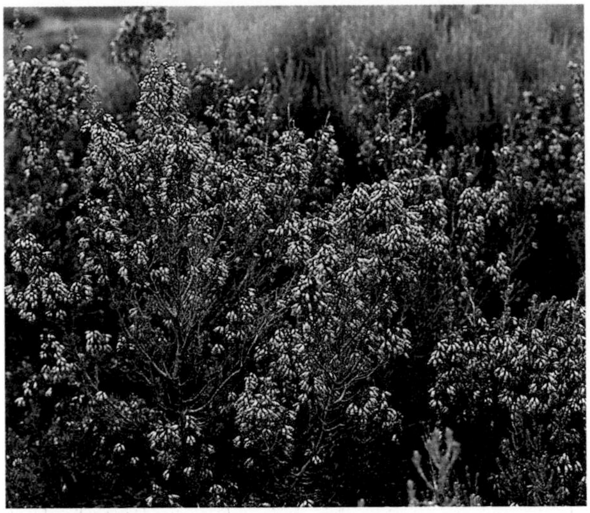

Erica australis

flowers, opening in late summer, and is lime-tolerant; **E. x veitchii** is a hybrid between *E. arborea* and *E. lusitanica*, a medium shrub with white or pink flowers in spring.

GAULTHERIA

(including **Pernettya, x Gaulnettya** and **x Gaulthettya**)

Also belonging to the family Ericaceae, this is a genus of moderate size and wide distribution, occurring in Australia, New Zealand, North and South America and Asia. Many gaultherias are dwarf shrubs and shrublets, however, and are not included here. Others are omitted because they are not very hardy. The flowers are small, white or pink and usually urn-shaped (rather like the flowers of Lily of the Valley). In many species the fruits are as decorative as the flowers.

G. fragrantissima

One of the best of the larger species, a medium shrub bearing narrow leaves, fragrant flowers and lovely bright blue fruits.

Size: usually up to about 1.8m (6ft) tall, sometimes more in favourable conditions.

Leaves: lanceolate to narrowly elliptical, about 5 to 10cm (2 to 4in) long, leathery, with toothed margins.

Flowers: borne in spikes about 5cm (2in) long in the leaf axils and at the ends of shoots, very small, white, fragrant, opening in May or June.

Fruits: fleshy and berry-like, about 6mm (1/4in) in diameter, bright blue to bluish-black, ripening in late summer to autumn.

Cultivation: likes a very moist, preferably peaty, acid soil in light to moderate shade. If the soil is not naturally peaty, very large quantities of humus should be dug in. Composted bark is excellent for this. Probably only really successful in wet areas.

Propagation: most easily propagated by digging up rooted suckers from the base of the plant, separating them and growing them on.

Origin: the Himalayan region, Burma, China, India and Sri Lanka.

G. mucronata (Pernettya mucronata)

A small shrub with erect shoots, spreading by underground runners. One of the showiest of all berrying shrubs, producing fruits in a range of colours. Although not lime-tolerant, it does not require very acid conditions and should grow in any soil of pH7 or below, provided it is sufficiently moist. Individual plants tend to produce flowers of one sex only, though some are hermaphrodite. In order to ensure a good crop of berries, it is best to plant at least one male plant among each group of females.

Size: up to as much as 1.2 or 1.5m (4 or 5ft) tall, but more often about 60 to 90cm (2 to 3ft), spreading indefinitely by underground runners, but not very invasive and easily controlled.

Leaves: small, about 12mm (1/2in) long, elliptical, dark green, with finely toothed margins.

Flowers: individually very small, but produced in large quantities over a long period from late spring into summer, white.

Fruits: round fruits like berries, almost 12mm (1/2in) in diameter, white to pink, red or purple, persisting for a long period through autumn well into winter.

Cultivation: easy and vigorous in the right conditions, it requires a very humus-rich, neutral to acid, moist

Gaultheria mucronata

soil. Dig in large amounts of composted bark, with some leaf-mould if available, and add some ferrous sulphate if the soil is close to pH7. Keep very well watered until established, with rainwater unless the local tap water is not limy, and water again during any dry spells. Full sun is tolerated, and may promote heavy fruiting, but some shade is desirable for the best growth, at least in warmer and drier areas. If plants begin to spread beyond the space they have been allocated, they can be kept under control by chopping off the runners with a spade.

Propagation: easily propagated by digging up rooted runners and growing them on.

Varieties: 'Bell's Seedling' has reddish young stems and large, dark red fruits and is at least partly self-fertile; 'Lilacina' usually produces an abundance of lilac-red fruits; 'Lilian' has pink fruits; 'Mulberry Wine' has large, magenta to deep purple fruits; 'Parelmoer' ('Mother of Pearl') has pale pink fruits; 'Pink Pearl' has pinkish-lilac fruits; 'Sea Shell' has quite large fruits that are pale pink at first, darkening with age; 'Signal' has deep red fruits; 'Thymifolia' is a low-growing, small-leaved male cultivar; 'Wintertime' has white fruits. There are more than a dozen other selected cultivars with fruits of varying colours.

Origin: South America.

G. x wisleyensis (x Gaulnettya wisleyensis, x Gaulthettya wisleyensis)

A vigorous hybrid, with larger leaves than *G. mucronata* and usually rather taller, bearing red or pink fruits.

Size: usually about 1.2 or 1.5m (4 or 5ft) tall, forming a dense thicket and spreading indefinitely.

Leaves: varying in different cultivars, usually between 2.5 and 5cm (1 to 2in) long, elliptical and dark green.

Flowers: white or pink, in dense spikes in the leaf axils and at the ends of shoots, starting to open from late May and lasting through June.

Fruits: very abundant on some cultivars, lasting from autumn well into winter.

Cultivation: as for *G. mucronata*, but more robust and vigorous in growth.

Propagation: as for *G. mucronata.*

Varieties: 'Pink Pixie' has pink flowers; 'Wisley Pearl' has white flowers and dark, blood-red fruits.

Origin: a garden hybrid between *G. shallon* and *G. mucronata.*

G. forrestii, about 0.9 to 1.2m (3 to 4ft) tall, has conspicuous white, fragrant flowers and blue fruits, but is scarce in cultivation. ***G. shallon*** is included only as a warning, as it is very invasive, forming dense thickets up to about 1.5m (5ft) high and spreading by underground runners. It is completely unsuitable for most gardens.

KALMIA

A small genus of the family Ericaceae with only a few species, all from North America. Kalmias resemble rhododendrons and require similar growing conditions, but bear clusters of small, upward-facing, cup-shaped flowers. The fruits are not ornamental.

K. latifolia, the Calico Bush or American Laurel

A very attractive medium to large shrub, with usually pink, sometimes white or red, flowers.

Size: up to as much as 3m (10ft) high and wide, but slow-growing and often rather less.

Leaves: more or less elliptical, about 7.5 to 13cm (3 to 5in) long, dark, glossy green.

Flowers: individually small, but borne in flattened clusters about 5 to 7.5cm (2 to 3in) across and often very abundant, usually pink but white or red in some of the cultivars.

Cultivation: requires a moist, humus-rich, acid soil. Flowering is likely to be more profuse in full sun or very light shade, but partial shade may be better away from areas with high rainfall. Very hardy.

Propagation: by cuttings taken in spring or summer and inserted into sandy but humus-rich compost, preferably placed in a closed propagator with bottom heat; by layering.

Varieties: 'Freckles' has very pale pink flowers marked with deeper pink; 'Minuet' has cinnamon-maroon flowers and is small, up to about 90cm (3ft) high; 'Ostbo Red' has flowers red in bud, opening to deep pink; 'Pink Charm' has dark pink buds opening to rich pink with maroon markings; 'Sarah' has red flowers and is strong growing; 'Snowdrift' has white flowers. There are more than two dozen other cultivars, varying mainly in flower colour, but also in size.

Origin: eastern North America.

K. angustifolia is similar but smaller, usually less than 90cm (3ft) tall, with rosy-red flowers.

LEUCOTHOE

A fairly small genus of the family Ericaceae, comprising a few dozen species occurring in the Americas and eastern Asia. Many are from warm temperate to subtropical areas and are not hardy in colder climates. Only about half a dozen species are in cultivation, some of them dwarf. They are closely related to pieris but look rather more like their slightly more distant relatives, gaultherias, requiring similar growing conditions, but tolerating shade. They do not bear ornamental fruits.

L. walteri (L. fontanesiana)

An elegant small shrub with arching, zigzagged branches, bunches of small, white flowers and foliage that is often colourful.

Size: up to as much as 1.5m (5ft) tall but usually rather less, spreading by suckers to form a gradually expanding mound of shoots.

Leaves: lanceolate, about 4cm (1½in) long, green and slightly leathery, often turning reddish in winter.

Flowers: white, urn-shaped, hanging downwards in spikes borne all along the branches from May to June.

Cultivation: requires similar conditions to gaultherias, but tolerant of considerable shade.

Propagation: most easily propagated either by division in spring or by digging up rooted suckers, either in autumn or spring.

Varieties: 'Rainbow' has leaves splashed with yellow, cream and pink. There are a few other selected cultivars available.

Origin: south-eastern USA.

L. davisiae is rarely as much as 90cm (3ft) tall, and bears spikes of creamy-white flowers at the ends of shoots in June and July; **L. 'Zeblid' (Scarletta)**, a hybrid with colourful foliage, is now one of the most popular garden plants of this genus.

MYRICA

A widespread genus of moderate size belonging to a family with only one other member. It occurs mainly in tropical to subtropical regions, more or less throughout the world, with a few species from cooler areas that are hardy in colder climates such as that of Britain. The foliage of many species is aromatic. The flowers are of little ornamental value, but the fruits are pleasantly decorative.

M. californica, the Californian Bayberry

A medium to large shrub with glossy, rather pale green foliage and small, dark purple fruits.

Size: up to about 4.5m (15ft) tall.

Leaves: oblanceolate, about 5 to 10cm (2 to 4in) long, shiny, apple-green, with toothed margins.

Fruits: small, round, dark purple, persisting until mid-winter, making an attractive display.

Cultivation: not absolutely hardy and so cannot be recommended for very cold districts. Tolerates permanently damp conditions. Best in a moist, acid loam, in sun or moderate shade.

Propagation: by cuttings, taken in autumn and inserted into sandy compost, either outdoors or under glass; by layering.

Origin: western USA.

M. cerifera, the Wax Myrtle, is similar, but hardier and taller, with fruits covered with greyish-white wax that can be made into candles.

PIERIS

A small genus of only about half a dozen species belonging to the family Ericaceae, with erect spikes of white or pink flowers looking rather like those of Lily of the Valley. The young growth in spring is often colourful, especially in selected cultivars. Most species are from eastern Asia and the Himalayan region, with a minority from North America.

P. formosa

A very lovely, large shrub which unfortunately is not absolutely hardy in Britain, though it is rarely damaged by winters in southern England and mild

Pieris formosa

***Pieris japonica* 'Debutante'**

***Pieris japonica* 'Red Mill'**

parts of Scotland and Wales. It has dark, glossy green foliage with bronze to red young growths and white flowers in spring. The fruits are not showy. An excellent plant for open woodland.

Size: up to about 3.6m (12ft) tall and about half to two-thirds as wide.

Leaves: lanceolate to elliptical, up to about 10cm (4in) long, dark, glossy green, with finely toothed margins. Young leaves in spring are coppery to dark red.

Flowers: white, in long spikes clustered at the ends of branches, opening in April or May.

Cultivation: requires similar conditions to rhododendrons. Good in woodland, in light to moderate shade, in a moist, humus-rich, acid soil. Usually quite slow-growing. The young shoots in early spring are susceptible to frost damage and overhead protection from trees is very valuable in limiting this. However, if the young growth is killed, new shoots usually appear later. Shelter from cold winds is also appreciated at all seasons.

Propagation: by cuttings of half-ripened wood taken in May or June and inserted into sandy compost in a closed propagator with bottom heat; by layering.

Varieties: var. *forrestii* is the best variety to grow, slightly hardier than the type and with redder young growths; 'Jermyns' is a selected cultivar of this variety, with wine-red young shoots; 'Wakehurst' is another similar cultivar, vigorous, with broader leaves that are bright red when young.

Origin: the eastern Himalayan region and China.

P. japonica

A small to medium or large shrub with smaller leaves than *P. formosa* and somewhat hardier, but otherwise very similar.

Size: up to about 3.6m (12ft) tall, but often less, and about as wide as it is high.

Leaves: elliptical to lanceolate, about 7.5cm (3in) long, dark green, with finely toothed or more or less untoothed margins. Young leaves in spring are bronze to pink or red, often becoming creamy-yellow before finally turning green.

Flowers: similar to those of *P. formosa*, opening during March and April, or sometimes earlier.

Cultivation: as for *P. formosa*, but this species is rather hardier and happier in full sun. The young growth is just as susceptible to damage by any late frosts, however.

Propagation: as for *P. formosa*.

Varieties: 'Blush' has pink-tinged white flowers borne on red flower stems from February to March; 'Christmas Cheer' is very hardy, with white flowers that are pink at the tip and open early, though rarely as early as Christmas; 'Daisen' has entirely pink flowers; 'Debutante' usually flowers profusely, with pure white flowers on green stems, and is small and compact, reaching about 1.2m (4ft) high and wide; 'Little Heath' is a dwarf cultivar with variegated leaves which rarely flowers; 'Little Heath Green' is very similar, but with green leaves; 'Mountain Fire' has coppery-red young growth and pure white flowers and grows to about 1.5 to 1.8m (5 to 6ft) high and wide; 'Purity' bears large, entirely white flowers; 'Red Mill' has white flowers and bright red young growths that become yellow and cream before turning green; 'Valley Rose' has pink flowers and grows to about 1.5 or 1.8m (5 or 6ft) tall and rather more across; 'White Rim' has leaves bordered with creamy-white, flushed pink when young, and is slow-growing. There are several dozen other cultivars, varying mainly in the colour of the young foliage and the flowers.

Origin: Japan and China.

P. floribunda is very similar to *P. japonica*, but rather less decorative, with smaller flowers and less colourful young growth. **P. 'Forest Flame'**, a cross between *P. formosa* var. *forrestii* 'Wakehurst' and *P. japonica*, is a large shrub with bright red young shoots. The leaves turn from red to pink and cream before becoming green. **P. 'Flaming Silver'** is also of hybrid origin and has leaves variegated with creamy-white.

RHODODENDRON
(including **Azalea**)

One of the largest of all genera, with at least 700 species, mainly from eastern Asia, with smaller numbers occuring elsewhere in Asia, in North America and in Europe. One species grows in northern Australia. The great centre of the genus is the eastern Himalayan region through south-west China to south-east Asia, where at least two-thirds of all rhododendrons are found.

Most species are evergreen, with a considerable minority that are deciduous. As they are generally showy in flower and range from tiny creeping shrublets to small or medium trees, they have inevitably become very important in gardens. They vary greatly in hardiness, some requiring the protection of a cool glasshouse in winter, while others will survive the worst frosts, winds and snows. Some are, in fact, among the hardiest of all broad-leaved evergreen shrubs and would be worth growing on that account alone, even if they did not also produce lovely flowers. The only serious problem with rhododendrons is their requirement for acid soil. Very few of them will flourish in soils of pH6.5 or higher, the ideal acidity being around pH5.5 or even below. This rules them out completely for many gardeners, at least as open garden plants. Attempts to breed hybrid rhododendrons that are lime-tolerant have so far had only limited success. A lesser drawback is their need for plenty of water, especially in summer, so that in drier areas they will often require watering, even in short dry spells. Rhododendrons are generally shallow rooting and do not send roots deep into the earth, where moisture remains for longer than in the top few inches of soil.

Many rhododendrons are naturally woodland plants and are happiest given at least a little shade. Too much shade, however, usually means greatly reduced flowering. As a rough guide, it can be assumed that rhododendrons with small leaves will be happy in full sun or with just a little shade, while those with larger leaves will require more shade. Very large-leaved rhododendrons usually require moderate shade and shelter from wind, as well as plenty of moisture, and are likely to look very unhappy unless the right conditions can be provided. Most rhododendrons are quite easy to grow, however, provided that their requirements for acid soil and plenty of water can be met. The fact that *R. ponticum* has become naturalized in large parts of Britain where soils are acid and rainfall is high, to the extent of becoming a real weed, indicates just how readily they can take to British conditions. As a rule, once a site has been prepared for rhododendrons and they have been planted, they require very little attention. It is beneficial to mulch around them every year, preferably in autumn, to a depth of no more than 5 to 7.5cm (2 to 3in). Rotted leaf-mould and composted bark are excellent for mulching. Removing dead flowers encourages the formation of flower buds for the following year. Otherwise, the only care they will usually require will be watering in dry periods.

The great number of hardy, evergreen rhododendron species has been vastly augmented by a huge and ever-expanding range of hybrids. These are now much more often grown than most of the species they were

Rhododendron arboreum

derived from. Many of the species are at least as fine as their hybrid offspring, however, and are well worth a place in any rhododendron garden. Although the great majority of rhododendrons flower in mid-spring to early summer, some flower as early as January or even December, and others bloom late, in July or August. It is not at all hard to have rhododendrons flowering in the garden for six months of the year, or even as long as nine months in mild districts. The range of flower colours is almost unlimited. The only deficiency is a really good blue, though several rhododendrons bear flowers that come very close to blue. The decorative value of the foliage should also not be overlooked. Many rhododendrons have fine foliage, particularly those which have a covering of scales or hairs on the lower surface of the leaves, known as indumentum. This indumentum is often very attractive, especially on young growth. There are also rhododendrons with decorative bark.

There are many specialist publications dealing solely with rhododendrons. It is impossible to include here more than a small selection of the best and most commonly cultivated species and hybrids.

R. arboreum

In the wild, this is probably the largest of all rhododendrons, growing into a tree 30m (100ft) tall or more. In cultivation it rarely becomes more than a large shrub or small tree. It is variable, with flowers that may be anything from blood-red to white and leaf indumentum that may be whitish to rust-coloured. Unfortunately most forms of this very fine plant are less than absolutely hardy. To be seen at its best, this rhododendron requires woodland conditions in areas of high rainfall.

Size: usually up to about 9m (30ft) in cultivation, but can attain more in favourable conditions.

Leaves: up to 20cm (8in) long, elliptical or oval, dark green above with the veins impressed into the surface, with whitish to rusty-brown indumentum beneath.

Flowers: in dense round heads of a dozen or more at the ends of the branches. Individual flowers are narrowly bell-shaped, about 5cm (2in) long, varying from blood-red to white. Pale-flowered forms are

Rhododendron augustinii

often the hardiest. The flowering period also varies, from as early as January until April.

Cultivation: requires an acid, humus-rich, moisture-retentive soil and is best planted in open woodland. Not recommended for drier areas as it will only flourish in moist, humid conditions. Some forms of this plant are not very hardy and are only really suitable for growing in mild areas. The flowers of all forms are susceptible to being browned by frost. While frost damage is, of course, a greater problem with those forms that flower very early, late frosts after mild weather can cause serious damage to any.

Propagation: by seed: rhododendron species, and some hybrids, readily produce large quantities of very tiny seeds which will usually germinate well if sown in late winter on the surface of a moisture-retentive, acid compost and kept covered with glass or clear plastic, but hybridization occurs very readily and seedlings may well not be identical with the parent plant; by cuttings of firm young shoots taken in July or August, the leaves trimmed to half their length or rather less, and inserted into an acid compost containing plenty of sand as well as humus in a closed propagator with bottom heat; by layering.

Varieties: subsp. *cinnamomeum* has reddish-brown leaf indumentum, flowers that are usually pink, sometimes white, and is generally fairly hardy; subsp. *delavayi* has smaller leaves with a whitish to fawn indumentum and red flowers, but is not very hardy. There are a number of selected forms of these and other subspecies in cultivation today.

Origin: the Himalayan region, south-west China, Burma, India and Sri Lanka.

R. augustinii

One of the loveliest species, with flowers that are as near to blue as any in the genus. A large shrub with small leaves, of fairly vigorous growth. Its only defect is that it is not quite hardy, though some forms are hardier than others, but it should usually suffer little or no damage in most winters, especially if it can be given some shelter among trees or other large shrubs. Some forms tend to be semi-evergreen in cold winters.

Size: usually up to about 3 to 3.6m (10 to 12ft) tall, though sometimes more, fairly erect in habit.

Leaves: narrowly elliptical to elliptical, about 5 to 10cm (2 to 4in) long, mid-green.

Flowers: openly funnel-shaped, about 2.5 to 4cm (1 to 1½in) across, in clusters of about three, often very abundant, purple, mauve or lavender to very nearly blue or sometimes white or pink, opening in April to May.

Cultivation: best in open woodland but may also flourish among other large shrubs or in the shade of buildings. Constant heavy shade will greatly reduce flowering, however. Most forms are not absolutely hardy and cannot be recommended for cold districts.

Requires acid, humus-rich soil and moderate to plentiful moisture.

Propagation: as for *R. arboreum*, but roots more easily from cuttings, and a closed propagator with bottom heat is not essential.

Varieties: subsp. *chasmanthum* has pale to dark lavender or mauvish-lavender flowers, which usually appear in May; subsp. *rubrum* has reddish-purple flowers; 'Electra' is a cultivar derived from crossing the typical plant and subsp. *chasmanthum*, and has flowers of a very striking bluish-violet with paler markings. Several selected forms exist, not all formally named.

Origin: western China.

R. auriculatum

A beautiful large shrub or occasionally a small tree with large, white flowers. It is very hardy and has large leaves, but is of most value in the garden because it flowers in July and August, one of the latest rhododendrons to bloom.

Size: can attain as much as 6m (20ft) in height after many years, if growing conditions are very good, but usually grows slowly to no more than about 3 to 3.6m (10 to 12ft) tall.

Leaves: broadly elliptical to oblanceolate, up to 20 or 22.5cm (8 or 9in) long, hairy beneath.

Flowers: large, 7.5 to 10cm (3 to 4in) across, funnel-shaped, with seven lobes, white, scented, in clusters of about 10 to 12 at the ends of branches, opening in July and August.

Cultivation: ideally needs woodland conditions, or at least partial shade and shelter from strong winds, in a humus-rich, moist acid soil.

Propagation: as for *R. arboreum*.

Origin: western China.

R. barbatum

A very fine large shrub or occasionally a small tree, with brilliant crimson flowers very early in spring and peeling bark. The smooth main branches are grey, shaded with pink and reddish-brown and are decorative at all times of year.

Size: usually up to about 3.6m (12ft) tall but may attain more in favourable conditions.

Leaves: elliptical to obovate, up to as much as 20cm (8in) long, dark green. The leaf stalks are usually bristly.

Flowers: bell-shaped, about 4cm (1½in) across, crimson to blood-red, in dense clusters of up to 20 at the ends of branches, opening in late February or March.

Cultivation: prefers light shade and some shelter in open woodland or among other large shrubs, in a humus-rich, acid, moist soil. Not absolutely hardy throughout the whole of Britain, but can be grown successfully in some parts of Scotland.

Propagation: as for *R. arboreum*.

Origin: the Himalayan region.

R. bureaui

A medium shrub, not exceptional for its flowers, but with outstanding foliage. Old leaves are dark green with a rusty-red indumentum on the underside and the young shoots are entirely covered with fawn to rusty felt.

Size: up to about 3 to 3.6m (10 to 12ft) tall.

Leaves: elliptical, about 10cm (4in) long, dark green above and with a dense rusty-red indumentum beneath when mature, entirely covered with paler, fawn to pinkish felting when young.

Flowers: bell-shaped, about 4cm (1½in) across, very pale pink tinged with deeper pink, in tight clusters of about a dozen at the ends of the branches, opening in April to May.

Cultivation: very hardy, prefers light shade among other shrubs or in woodland, in a moist, humus-rich, acid soil.

Propagation: as for *R. arboreum*.

Origin: south-west China.

R. calophytum

A large shrub or small tree with long leaves and very big clusters of white or pink flowers. One of the hardiest of large-leaved rhododendrons, which may be grown almost anywhere in Britain. It does need to be sheltered from wind, however, which will damage the foliage.

Size: may attain as much as 6m (20ft) in height, or even more in very favourable conditions, but much more commonly grows to about 3 to 4.5m (10 to 15ft) tall.

Leaves: oblanceolate, up to about 30cm (12in) long, dark green above, paler beneath.

Flowers: broadly bell-shaped, about 5cm (2in) across, white to pale pink spotted with purple, in clusters of as many as 30 at the ends of the branches, opening from February to April.

Cultivation: very hardy but needs protection from wind because of its large leaves and some shelter to prevent frost damage to its early flowers. It is naturally a woodland plant and is at its best in woodland conditions. A humus-rich, moist, acid soil is ideal.

Propagation: as for *R. arboreum*.

Varieties: var. *openshawianum* is very similar, but with shorter leaves, needing less shelter.

Origin: south-west China.

R. campanulatum

A variable, medium to large shrub, with fairly large leaves with a striking, reddish-brown indumentum. Flowers pink, lavender, mauve or sometimes white.

Size: usually up to about 3 to 3.6m (10 to 12ft) high.

Leaves: oval to broadly elliptical, about 10 to 12.5cm (4 or 5in) long, dark green above, covered with a dense, reddish-brown, suede-like indumentum beneath, young growths more or less entirely covered with similar indumentum.

Flowers: broadly bell-shaped, about 5 to 7.5cm (2 to 3in) across, appearing in clusters of about a dozen at the ends of branches, and opening in April and May. The colour varies from pink to lavender or mauve, sometimes white, usually with small flecks of purple.

Rhododendron calophytum

Cultivation: hardy, happy in full sun or partial shade in a moist, humus-rich, acid soil.

Propagation: as for *R. arboreum*.

Varieties: 'Knap Hill' has lavender-blue flowers; subsp. *aeruginosum* is smaller, slow-growing and compact, with very attractive bluish-green young shoots and lilac or mauve flowers. Selected forms with white flowers are also available.

Origin: the Himalayan region.

R. campylocarpum

A very attractive, medium to large shrub with yellow flowers. This is one of the best yellow-flowered rhododendrons for general planting, though it tends not to bloom when young.

Size: usually up to about 3m (10ft) tall, can occasionally grow larger.

Leaves: broadly elliptical to rounded, about 7.5 to 10cm (3 to 4in) long, glossy green above, duller and paler beneath.

Flowers: lemon-yellow, bell-shaped, about 4cm (1½in) across, in clusters of up to about 10 to 12, opening in April to May.

Cultivation: hardy enough to succeed in most of Britain, especially if given some shelter by trees or other shrubs. Likes a little shade and a moist, humus-rich, acid soil.

Propagation: as for *R. arboreum*, but cuttings will root more easily and bottom heat is not essential, though useful if available.

Varieties: subsp. *caloxanthum* has very broad, almost round, leaves.

Origin: the Himalayan region and south-west China.

R. cinnabarinum

A very variable medium to large shrub of great beauty. Unfortunately this is not the easiest of rhododendrons to grow well, tending to be susceptible to powdery mildew.

Rhododendron cinnabarinum

Size: usually up to about 2.4 to 3m (8 to 10ft) tall, though possibly twice as high in very favourable growing conditions.

Leaves: broadly to narrowly elliptical, about 5 to 7.5cm (2 to 3in) long, green in some forms of the species, glaucous in other forms.

Flowers: more or less tubular or narrowly bell-shaped, hanging downwards, about 4cm (1½in) long, in small clusters of about five at the ends of branches, opening in April, May or June. The colour varies greatly, from plum-crimson through various shades of red to orange and yellow, or red and yellow combined.

Cultivation: hardy, but prefers some shelter and light shade. Must have plenty of moisture during the growing season and a humus-rich, acid soil. If mildew is a problem, spraying with a fungicide will usually give good control.

Propagation: as for *R. arboreum*.

Varieties: 'Aestivale' has red flowers tipped with orange in June; the Blandfordiiflorum Group has lovely red and yellow flowers in May or June, but also great susceptibility to powdery mildew; 'Nepal' has yellow and red flowers; the Roylei Group has glaucous foliage and plum-crimson flowers in May; 'Vin Rosé' has clear red flowers and very attractive glaucous foliage; subsp. *xanthocodon* is fairly resistant to powdery mildew and has shorter, more bell-shaped, yellow flowers in May to June; the Concatenans Group of this subspecies has lovely, silvery bluish-green foliage and pinkish-orange flowers; the Purpurellum Group of this subspecies has small leaves and purple flowers. Other forms, varying in flower colour and foliage, also exist. All are very lovely plants.

Origin: the Himalayan region.

R. concinnum

A very hardy and easily grown medium to large shrub with flowers in various shades of reddish-purple.

Size: up to about 3m (10ft) tall, often rather less, and almost as wide as high.

Leaves: oval to elliptical, about 5cm (2in) long, dark green and often somewhat scaly above, grey or brownish beneath.

Flowers: openly funnel-shaped, carried in small clusters of about three, each about 4cm (1½in) across, often covering the plant, varying in colour from deep reddish-purple to almost red, opening in April to May.

Cultivation: hardy and quite easy, happy in any moist, acid soil in full sun or partial shade.

Propagation: as for *R. augustinii.*

Origin: western China.

R. dauricum

A very hardy, erect, small to medium shrub, sometimes semi-evergreen or even deciduous, but extremely valuable as its flowers open in winter.

Size: usually up to 1.5m (5ft) tall, sometimes more.

Leaves: dark green, stiff, oval to elliptical, about 2.5 to 4cm (1 to 1½in) long.

Flowers: openly funnel-shaped, about 2.5cm (1in) across, purplish-pink or white, opening from as early as late December until February or March.

Cultivation: easy in most reasonably humus-rich, free-draining, acid soils, in full sun or partial shade. The flowers will withstand some frost, even after opening.

Propagation: as for *R. augustinii.*

Varieties: 'Arctic Pearl' has white flowers, usually in March; 'Dark St. Andrews' has large, dark pinkish-purple flowers in February to March; 'Hokkaido' has white flowers; 'Midwinter' is more or less deciduous but early flowering, often in January. Other selected cultivars, varying in size and flower colour, exist.

Origin: Siberia, Mongolia, north-east China and northern Japan.

R. decorum

A very beautiful, vigorous, easy and hardy species of large size, with big, white or pale pink flowers that are fragrant.

Size: up to about 4.8m (16ft) tall.

Leaves: oblanceolate to elliptical, up to about 15cm (6in) long, mid- to dark green.

Flowers: more or less openly bell-shaped, with six or seven lobes, about 5cm (2in) across, in loose clusters of about eight to ten at the ends of branches, white to pale pink, sometimes flecked with green or red inside, and sweetly scented.

Cultivation: vigorous and easy, tolerant of drier conditions than most rhododendrons, happy in reasonably humus-rich, acid soils, in sun or partial shade.

Propagation: as for *R. arboreum.*

Varieties: subsp. *diaprepes* has larger leaves and flowers.

Origin: south-west China and north-east Burma.

R. falconeri

A large shrub or small tree with impressive foliage and creamy-yellow flowers.

Size: usually up to about 6m (20ft) tall, but can attain twice that height under favourable conditions.

Leaves: broadly elliptical to obovate, up to 30cm (1ft) or sometimes rather more in length, dark green and puckered above, with a dense rufous indumentum beneath.

Flowers: bell-shaped, about 5cm (2in) across, with usually eight lobes, pale creamy-yellow with a dark purple basal blotch, in large clusters of about 15 to 20 at the ends of branches, opening in April to May, or sometimes June.

Cultivation: best in woodland conditions in a moist, humus-rich, acid soil. Needs shelter from winds to prevent damage to the large leaves. Not absolutely hardy everywhere in Britain, but can be grown in parts of Scotland.

Propagation: as for *R. arboreum*.

Varieties: subsp. *eximium* has pink flowers.

Origin: the Himalayan region.

R. ferrugineum, the Alpen Rose

A small, spreading shrub with dark green, shiny foliage and deep pink flowers.

Size: usually up to about 0.9 or 1.2m (3 or 4ft) tall, sometimes a little more, and often wider than high.

Leaves: elliptical, about 25 to 38mm (1 to 1 1/2in) long, dark, shiny green above, rusty beneath.

Flowers: narrowly bell-shaped, about 1.5cm (3/4in) across, deep crimson-pink, in heads at the ends of branches, opening in May or June.

Cultivation: likes a very free-draining but moist and humus-rich, acid soil, in full sun or a little shade. A very hardy species.

Propagation: can usually be propagated fairly easily by layering, though patience is needed for this method as rooting can take a long time. Can also be propagated quite easily by cuttings taken in July or August and inserted into sandy, acid compost; or by seed, as for *R. arboreum*.

Varieties: there is a rare, white-flowered form. A few other selected forms are occasionally grown.

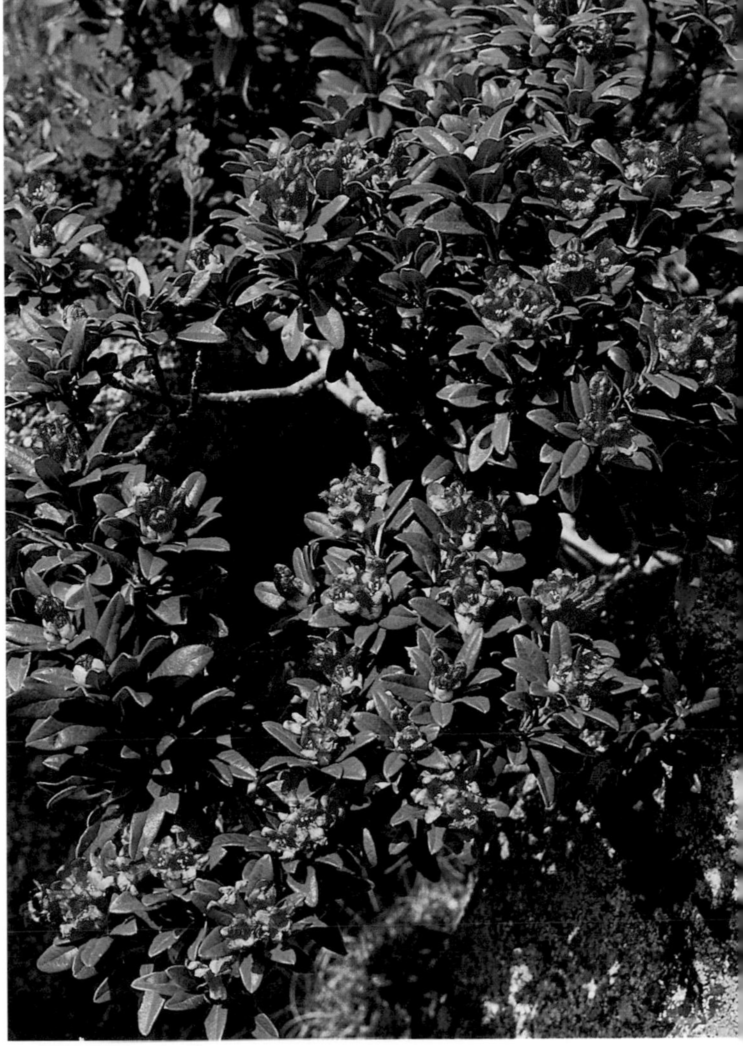

Rhododendron ferrugineum

Origin: the European Alps and Pyrenees.

R. fortunei

A large shrub or small tree with fine foliage and big, pink, fragrant flowers. Very hardy and the parent of many fine hybrids.

Size: usually up to about 3 to 3.6m (10 to 12ft) tall, but can grow larger.

Leaves: more or less obovate, up to about 17.5cm (7in) long, dark green above, paler beneath. The leaf stalks are often purple.

Flowers: broadly bell-shaped, about 7.5cm (3in) across, with seven lobes, pale pink or lavender-pink, sometimes almost white, fragrant, borne in clusters of about 6 to 12 at the ends of branches, opening in May or June.

Cultivation: easy in any acid, reasonably humus-rich soil with moderate amounts of moisture, preferably in light shade and with some shelter from other shrubs and trees. This is a very hardy species which usually flowers late enough to miss any late frosts.

Propagation: as for *R. arboreum*.

Varieties: 'Sir Charles Butler' ('Mrs. Charles Butler') has very pale pink flowers that fade to almost white; subsp. *discolor* has narrower leaves and white to pale pink flowers, opening later, in June or July. A few other variations have been named.

Origin: south China.

R. haematodes

One of the most beautiful of all rhododendrons. A small, compact shrub with attractive foliage and stunning, bright crimson flowers. Usually slow-growing.

Size: usually up to about 0.9 to 1.2m (3 to 4ft) tall, but can reach 1.8m (6ft) after many years, compact, forming a rounded mound at least as wide as high.

Leaves: obovate to elliptical, about 5 to 7.5cm (2 to 3in) long, dark green above, densely felted with a cinnamon to rufous indumentum beneath.

Flowers: bell-shaped, about 4cm (1 1/2in) across, bright crimson, in clusters of about half a dozen at the ends of shoots, opening in May.

Cultivation: needs plenty of moisture during the growing season to do really well: not recommended for dry areas. Will enjoy full sun in cooler, damper areas of Britain, but elsewhere is best given partial shade. A humus-rich, acid soil is essential.

Propagation: as for *R. arboreum*.

Varieties: subsp. *chaetomallum* has slightly larger leaves with a paler indumentum and bristly leaf stalks and flowers earlier, from March to April.

Origin: south-west China and north-east Burma.

R. hippophaeoides

A very attractive, fairly erect small shrub with lavender-blue flowers. Very hardy and tolerant of a wide range of soil conditions.

Size: up to 0.9 to 1.2m (3 to 4ft) tall, fairly erect.

Rhododendron haematodes

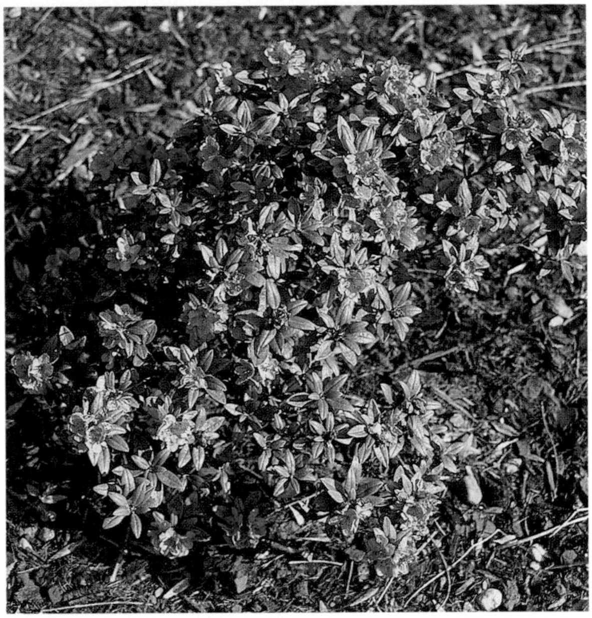

Rhododendron hippophaeoides

Leaves: small, up to about 2.5cm (1in) long, broadly elliptical, greyish-green above, buff beneath.

Flowers: opening almost flat, about 12mm (1/2in) across, in dense clusters of about five or six, lavender-blue to greyish-blue or bluish-purple, opening in April to May and very tolerant of frost.

Cultivation: reasonably easy, tolerating a range of soil conditions as long as the soil is acid, even surviving in quite boggy ground. Best in full sun to light shade in reasonably humus-rich soil with moderate amounts of water during the growing season.

Propagation: as for *R. augustinii*.

Varieties: 'Haba Shan' ('Bei-ma-shan') is erect, with greyish-blue flowers; 'Inshriach' has lavender-mauve flowers with dark margins; Yu 13845 is smaller, up to about 60cm (2ft) tall.

Origin: south-west China.

R. hirsutum

A small shrub, similar to *R. ferrugineum* but with paler pink flowers and with very hairy foliage. It is one of the most lime-tolerant of all rhododendrons.

Size: up to about 60 to 90cm (2 to 3ft) high and wide.

Leaves: obovate, up to about 2.5cm (1in) long, clothed with stiff hairs, mid-green.

Flowers: like those of *R. ferrugineum*, but bright rose-pink, opening in June to July.

Cultivation: as for *R. ferrugineum*, but very lime-tolerant for a rhododendron and should be happy in soils up to pH7 (neutral).

Varieties: 'Flore Pleno' has double flowers; f. *albiflorum* has white flowers.

Origin: Europe (the Alps).

R. lutescens

A slender, rather open, medium to large shrub, related to *R. augustinii*, *R. concinnum* and *R. triflorum*, with pale yellow flowers early in the year. It is reasonably hardy but needs shelter to prevent frost damaging the flowers.

Size: up to about 3 to 4.5m (10 to 15ft) tall, fairly erect, with slender branches.

Leaves: lanceolate or almost elliptical, about 5 to 7.5cm (2 to 3in) long, mid-green, often reddish when young.

Flowers: similar to those of *R. concinnum* but pale yellow, opening from as early as February until April.

Cultivation: reasonably easy and adaptable, but best in a moist, humus-rich, acid soil in open woodland.

Rhododendron lutescens **'Bagshot Sands'**

Not hardy enough for very cold districts, and at least some shelter is needed almost anywhere in Britain to prevent the early flowers being destroyed by frost.

Propagation: as for *R. augustinii*.

Varieties: 'Bagshot Sands' is a selected cultivar with good foliage and flowers.

Origin: western China.

R. makinoi (R. yakushimanum subsp. makinoi)

A very hardy, medium shrub with decorative foliage and pale pink flowers.

Size: usually up to 1.5m (5ft) tall and about as wide.

Leaves: lanceolate, up to 20cm (8in) long, dark green above with a thick fawn indumentum beneath. A paler indumentum often entirely covers the young shoots, which are very decorative.

Flowers: bell-shaped, about 4cm (1 1/2in) across, pale pink, in clusters of about eight at the ends of the branches, opening in May to June.

Cultivation: very hardy, reasonably adaptable, best in a humus-rich, moist, acid soil in full sun to light shade.

Propagation: as for *R. arboreum*.

Origin: Japan.

R. moupinense

A charming, early flowering, small shrub, often of open habit, with bristly young branches. It is the parent of many fine hybrids.

Size: up to about 0.9 to 1.2m (3 to 4ft) tall.

Leaves: more or less elliptical or oval, about 4cm (1 1/2in) long, blunt-tipped.

Flowers: quite large for a small shrub, up to about 5cm (2in) across, openly bell-shaped, white or pale pink flushed with darker pink and often spotted with red, borne singly or in pairs, opening in February to March.

Cultivation: in the wild this species often grows on fallen tree trunks or on branches of living trees in very humid areas. It likes an open, humus-rich, acid soil, but tolerates dry conditions better than most rhododendrons. It prefers light shade. The flowers are more likely to suffer damage if morning sun falls on them before overnight frost has thawed.

Propagation: as for *R. augustinii*.

Varieties: Distinct pink- and white-flowered forms exist.

Origin: western China.

R. oreodoxa

A medium to large shrub, usually producing an abundance of large pink flowers in early spring, even on young plants.

Rhododendron oreodoxa* var. *fargesii

Size: usually up to about 3 to 4.5m (10 to 15ft) tall, fairly erect in habit.

Leaves: more or less elliptical, about 7.5cm (3in) long, dark green above, glaucous beneath.

Flowers: bell-shaped, with six or seven lobes, pink, up to 5cm (2in) across, in large, loose clusters of about half a dozen at the ends of branches, opening in March to April. The flowers may be damaged by frosts once they have opened, though the buds are frost-resistant.

Cultivation: quite easy, best in a moist, humus-rich, acid soil in a little shade, but happy in full sun, at least in cooler, moister areas of Britain.

Propagation: as for *R. arboreum*.

Varieties: var. *fargesii* is more commonly cultivated than the type, from which it differs only in very minor details.

Origin: western China.

R. ponticum

In mild, wet areas of Britain this rhododendron has become naturalized and is sometimes a serious weed, smothering more delicate plants. It is, however, a vigorous and easy species for areas where rhododendrons are more difficult to grow and should not be overlooked simply because it is common. It has leaves of medium size and no especial beauty and mauve flowers in late spring. Useful for sheltering more delicate rhododendrons; can make an excellent informal hedge.

Size: up to about 3 to 4.5m (10 to 15ft) tall.

Leaves: oblanceolate to broadly elliptical, up to about 17.5cm (7in) long, mid-green above, paler beneath.

Flowers: bell-shaped, up to about 5cm (2in) across, mauve, sometimes lilac or purple, in large heads of up to 20 at the ends of branches, opening in May to June.

Cultivation: one of the easiest of all rhododendrons, which will grow even in dry shade, but is best in a reasonably moist, humus-rich, acid soil in partial shade. Where rhododendrons do well, it should be avoided as it is very likely to become a weed. In areas where they need more care and attention, it can be very useful for giving shelter to choicer species and hybrids and filling difficult corners of the garden. It can make a fine, large hedge, hardier than Cherry Laurel, and produces plenty of flowers if it can be left more or less untrimmed.

***Rhododendron racemosum* 'Rock Rose'**

Propagation: very easy from seed, though seedlings are likely to be hybrids; cuttings and layers usually root well; basal suckers may be produced on older plants and can be separated and grown on.

Varieties: 'Variegatum' has leaves margined with creamy-white. A few other named forms exist.

Origin: south-west and south-east Europe, Turkey and the Caucasus region.

R. racemosum

A lovely small shrub producing masses of pink flowers in spring.

Size: variable, usually up to about 1.2 to 1.5m (4 to 5ft) tall, but both taller and dwarf forms exist.

Leaves: broadly obovate to elliptical, up to about 5cm (2in) long, greyish-green above, often with a reddish tinge, white beneath.

Flowers: small, funnel-shaped, up to about 1.5cm (3/4in) across, pale to bright pink or sometimes white, very numerous, borne not only at the ends of branches but also in the upper leaf axils, opening in March to April or May.

Cultivation: fairly easy, likes full sun provided the soil does not dry out. It does not require such a humus-rich soil as other rhododendrons.

Propagation: as for *R. augustinii*.

Varieties: 'Rock Rose' is an erect cultivar with bright pink flowers. A couple of other named cultivars exist but are rare in gardens.

Origin: south-west China.

R. rubiginosum

A vigorous large shrub, or occasionally a small tree, which withstands wind well and usually flowers profusely.

Size: up to about 6m (20ft) tall.

Leaves: more or less elliptical, about 5 to 10cm (2 to 4in) long, dark green above, covered with brown scales beneath.

Flowers: openly funnel-shaped, about 2.5cm (1in) or rather more across, pink, pinkish-lilac, mauve-pink or occasionally white, in clusters of up to ten at the ends of branches, often borne in abundance, opening in March, April or May.

Cultivation: easy, likes a moist, humus-rich, acid soil with a little shade, but is very wind-resistant and will stand full sun in more humid parts of Britain.

Propagation: as for *R. augustinii*.

Varieties: forms with flowers of various colours exist, most of them not formally named.

Origin: south-west China.

R. russatum

A small, easily grown shrub happy in full sun or part shade, covering itself with purple flowers in spring.

Size: up to 0.9 to 1.2m (3 to 4ft) tall and as wide.

Leaves: quite small, up to 4cm (1½in) long, elliptical, dark green above, usually pale green with scattered reddish-brown scales beneath, but the scales sometimes denser and almost entirely covering the lower surface.

Flowers: similar to those of *R. hippophaeoides*, but usually darker and more purple.

Cultivation: one of the easiest species to grow, hardy, tolerant of quite dry conditions, at its best in a fairly moist, humus-rich, acid soil in full sun or light shade.

Rhododendron russatum **(Waterer form)**

Rhododendron thomsonii

Propagation: as for *R. augustinii.*

Varieties: many selected colour forms exist, including a rare white form, most of them not formally named.

Origin: south-west China.

R. thomsonii

A very desirable medium to large shrub with attractive, smooth, reddish-brown bark, rounded, dark green leaves and blood-red flowers, often borne in profusion.

Size: usually up to about 2.4 to 3m (8 to 10ft) tall, but can attain more in favourable conditions.

Leaves: obovate to almost round, about 7.5cm (3in) long, dark green above, paler beneath, glaucous when young.

Flowers: bell-shaped, up to about 5cm (2in) long, deep crimson, in loose clusters of about half a dozen at the ends of branches, opening in April to May.

Cultivation: not suitable for very dry areas because it needs abundant moisture during the growing season. In the wild it often grows in very wet places, with running water around the roots, particularly in summer. Best in very moist, humus-rich, acid soil in full sun to light shade. Susceptible to powdery mildew and may need to be sprayed with a fungicide from time to time. Appreciates an annual feed, using a balanced fertilizer without too much nitrogen, and regular mulching.

Propagation: as for *R. arboreum.*

Varieties: subsp. *lopsangianum* is smaller, up to about 1.8m (6ft) tall, and flowers earlier, in March to April.

Origin: the Himalayan region.

R. trichostomum

A small shrub with aromatic foliage and round heads of usually pink, daphne-like flowers in spring.

Size: up to about 90cm (3ft) tall, sometimes a little more, and usually as wide.

Leaves: small and narrow, up to about 2.5cm (1in) long, linear to oblanceolate, dark green above, usually covered with pale brown scales beneath, aromatic.

Flowers: individually small, less than 12mm (1/2in) long and wide, shaped rather like a Cowslip flower, borne in dense, rounded heads at the ends of branches, often very abundant, usually pink, but sometimes white, opening in May to June.

Rhododendron trichostomum

Cultivation: likes a moist, humus-rich, acid soil in full sun or a little shade.

Propagation: as for *R. augustinii.*

Origin: south-west China.

R. triflorum

A medium to large shrub with attractive peeling bark and pale yellow flowers. Related to R. *augustinii*, R. *concinnum* and R. *lutescens* and generally similar in habit and form.

Size: usually up to about 2.4 to 3m (8 to 10ft) tall, upright, rather open in habit.

Leaves: oval to lanceolate, about 5cm (2in) in length, dark green above, with greyish-brown scales beneath.

Flowers: similar to those of R. *lutescens*, but usually very pale yellow, sometimes blotched or suffused with reddish-brown. They also open much later, usually in May to June.

Cultivation: fairly easy, best in open woodland, but will flourish in more open situations, especially if given some shelter from other shrubs, buildings, hedges or screens. Likes a moist, humus-rich, acid soil and a little shade.

Propagation: as for R. *augustinii*.

Varieties: the Mahogani Group has flowers variously shaded with brownish-red that are really more unusual than attractive; var. *bauhiniiflorum* has flowers that are more open, almost flat.

Origin: the Himalayan region and India.

***Rhododendron triflorum* var. *triflorum* (Mahogani Group)**

Rhododendron wardii

R. wardii

A very lovely yellow-flowered rhododendron of medium to large size, related to R. *campylocarpum* but with more widely open flowers, usually of slightly deeper colour.

Size: up to about 3m (10ft) tall, but may grow larger under favourable conditions.

Leaves: rather variable, from narrowly obovate to broadly ovate, about 5 to 10cm (2 to 4in) long, dark green above, paler green or sometimes glaucous below.

Flowers: saucer-shaped, about 5 to 7.5cm (2 to 3in) across, varying from pale to sulphur yellow, or sometimes white, with or without a purple-red basal blotch, in clusters of about six to 12 at the ends of branches, opening in May or June.

Cultivation: not quite as adaptable and easy as R. *campylocarpum*. Hardy, but likes some shelter and a little shade. A humus-rich, acid soil and plenty of moisture in the growing season are essential. In parts of Britain some forms of this species may fail to flower well due to a lack of magnesium, which can be remedied by applying small amounts of Epsom salts to the soil around the base of the plant.

Propagation: as for R. *campylocarpum*.

Varieties: a number of variant forms exist, with flowers of different shades of yellow and with or without crimson markings; var. *puralbum* has pure white flowers.

Origin: south-west China.

R. williamsianum

A very attractive small, spreading shrub with rounded leaves and large, nodding, bell-shaped, pale pink or sometimes white flowers.

Size: usually up to about 90cm to 1.2m (3 or 4ft) high, but occasionally a little more. Usually wider than high.

Leaves: rounded, about 2.5 to 5cm (1 to 2in) long and almost as wide, mid-green above, whitish beneath. Young shoots are bronze-red.

Flowers: bell-shaped, nodding, large, about 38mm (1 1/2in) long, pale pink or sometimes white, in small clusters of two or three at the ends of branches, opening in April or May.

Cultivation: fairly easy in a moist, humus-rich, acid soil in full sun or a little shade, but both the flowers and the young shoots, which begin to grow early, are very susceptible to damage by late frosts.

Propagation: as for *R. campylocarpum*.

Varieties: there are selected forms that are not formally named, with white or particularly large attractive flowers.

Origin: western China.

Rhododendron williamsianum

R. yakushimanum

An extremely hardy, small, compact, dome-shaped shrub with very ornamental foliage and attractive pink and white flowers. The parent of a large group of fine hybrids.

Size: usually up to about 90cm (3ft) high, sometimes rather more, and often rather wider than high.

Leaves: elliptical to broadly elliptical, about 10 to 12.5cm (4 or 5in) long, leathery, dark, glossy green above, densely felted beneath with reddish-brown indumentum. Young growths are wholly covered with whitish felting.

Flowers: more or less bell-shaped, pink in bud, opening pale pink or white tinged with pink and often fading to white, or sometimes more or less pure white, in compact clusters of about five to ten at the ends of branches, opening in May.

Cultivation: fairly tough and easy, though usually quite slow-growing. Best in a humus-rich, moist, acid soil in full sun or light shade. More or less completely hardy throughout Britain.

Propagation: as for *R. campylocarpum*.

Varieties: a few selected, named cultivars exist, mainly differing in flower colour, from pink to white. There are also variants without formal names.

Origin: Japan (Yakushima Island).

R. yunnanense

A variable, very floriferous medium to large shrub, of fairly erect habit, related to *R. triflorum*. The flowers are usually a shade of pink.

Size: up to about 3 to 4.5m (10 to 15ft) tall.

Leaves: elliptical or lanceolate, about 5cm (2in) long, mid- to dark green above, paler and scaly beneath, sometimes partly deciduous or even entirely deciduous in very cold winters.

***Rhododendron* 'Cilpinense'**

Flowers: similar in shape to those of *R. augustinii* or *R. concinnum*, about 38mm (1½in) across, usually pink, but also white or lavender, variously spotted and blotched, often borne in profusion, opening in May.

Cultivation: fairly tough and easy in any reasonably humus-rich, acid soil with moderate amounts of water during the growing season, preferably in full sun or just a little shade in a sheltered position. Shelter is particularly important in colder districts.

Propagation: as for *R. augustinii*.

Varieties: a number of selected forms exist, mainly varying in flower colour. A few have been given formal cultivar names.

Origin: south-west China and north-east Burma.

Other species: R. anwheiense is a small to medium, dome-shaped bush bearing rounded clusters of quite frost-resistant, white flowers with a pink tinge in April or May; **R. catawbiense** is similar to its relative, *R. ponticum*, and is very hardy and vigorous, with flowers in shades of purplish-lilac to pink or white; **R. davidsonianum** is similar to *R. concinnum*, but with pink or mauve flowers; **R. griersonianum** is a very distinct species with bright scarlet, narrowly bell-shaped flowers that open in June and leaves with attractive buff indumentum beneath, but unfortunately is not hardy enough for very cold districts; **R. johnstoneanum** is a medium or sometimes large shrub with lovely, big, fragrant, creamy-yellow flowers in May, not absolutely hardy but can be grown outdoors successfully even as far north as Scotland; **R. morii** is medium to large and exceptionally free-flowering, bearing masses of white flowers spotted with crimson in April to May;

R. pachysanthum is a fairly recent introduction from Taiwan but has quickly become popular as it has very fine leaves with silvery to brown indumentum on both surfaces, which are darker beneath, and white to pink flowers from March to April; **R. primuliflorum** is very like *R. trichostomum* but usually grows taller and has white or pale pink flowers; **R. serotinum** is a rather obscure species, very little known as a wild plant, resembling *R. decorum*, bearing white flowers with a pink flush and dark red blotch. It is valuable in the garden as it flowers very late, sometimes into September. There are many other lovely rhododendron species.

Hybrids: R. 'Addy Werry' is a Japanese azalea growing to about 1.5m (5ft) tall with glossy, dark green leaves and masses of bright, orange-red flowers in April to May; **R. 'Anna Rose Whitney'** is a tall and vigorous hybrid with very large clusters of deep pink flowers in May or June; **R. 'Bashful'** is a Yakushimanum hybrid with deep pink flowers and compact, rounded habit; **R. 'Betty Wormald'** is of medium to large size with big, deep pink flowers heavily marked with dark crimson; **R. 'Blaauw's Pink'** is a Kurume azalea, growing to about 1.2m (4ft) tall, with very small, dark green leaves and masses of vivid salmon-pink flowers in April to May; **R. 'Blue Danube'** is a Japanese Azalea with large, bluish-violet flowers, of spreading habit, reaching about 90cm to 1.2m (3 to 4ft) in height; **R. 'Blue Peter'** is a medium to large shrub about as wide as high, with bluish violet flowers in April to May; **R. 'Bow Bells'** is a hybrid of *R. williamsianum*, low-growing, with pink, bell-shaped flowers in April to May; **R. 'Britannia'** is compact and slow-growing, forming a mound of pale green foliage up to about 1.8m (6ft) tall, usually wider than high, with glowing scarlet flowers in May to June; **R. 'Caroline Allbrook'** is a very hardy and vigorous Yakushimanum hybrid growing to about 1.2m (4ft) tall, with abundant lavender flowers in May to June; **R. 'Christmas Cheer'** is very hardy and up to about 1.8m (6ft) tall, usually producing its pink flowers in March but sometimes earlier (though it really needs forcing under glass to flower at Christmas); **R. 'Cilpinense'** is the result of crossing *R. moupinense* with *R. ciliatum* and is a free-flowering bush up to about 90cm (3ft) tall and often wider, with large, white and pink flowers in March; **R. 'Crest'** is a fine hybrid of *R. wardii* growing to about 3.6m (12ft) tall, with very large yellow flowers; **R. 'Cunningham's White'** is a *R. ponticum* hybrid, very hardy and robust, of medium size, with white flowers opening in May to June; **R. 'Cynthia'** is large, vigorous and adaptable, with big clusters of rose-red flowers in May to June; **R. 'Doc'** is a Yakushimanum hybrid growing to about 1.2m (4ft) high and wide, with large clusters of rose-pink flowers in May; **R. 'Doncaster'** is a hybrid of *R. arboreum* of small to medium size, with very dark green foliage and bright crimson flowers in May to June; **R. 'Dopey'** is another Yakushimanum hybrid of compact growth with deep red flowers in June; **R. 'Fastuosum Flore Pleno'** is a large, hardy and vigorous hybrid of *R. ponticum* with semi-double, bluish-mauve flowers in May to June; **R. 'Furnivall's Daughter'** is large and quite vigorous, with big pink flowers with darker markings in May to June; **R. 'Golden Torch'** is a vigorous, easily grown Yakushimanum hybrid growing to about 1.2m (4ft) tall, with pink and pale yellow flowers; **R. 'Gomer Waterer'** is a large shrub with white flowers flushed mauve-pink in June; **R. 'Hotei'** is compact and of medium size with deep yellow flowers in May to June; **R. 'Hydon Dawn'** is one of the best Yakushimanum hybrids, growing to about 1.5m (5ft) tall, with dark foliage powdered with silver and pale pink flowers fading to almost white in May to June; **R. 'Hydon Hunter'** is of exactly the same parentage as the preceding, but is more upright in habit with deeper pink flowers with some orange spotting; **R. 'Lady Clementine Mitford'** is large, with glossy green foliage and peach-pink flowers in May to June; **R. 'Lavender Girl'** is of medium size, compact and vigorous, with an abundance of pale lavender, fragrant flowers in June; **R. 'Lee's Dark Purple'** is a tall, tough hybrid bearing dense clusters of deep purple flowers in May to June; **R. 'Lord Roberts'** is tall and erect, with deep crimson flowers in rounded clusters in June; **R. 'Markeeta's Prize'** is tall with dark green foliage and bright scarlet flowers in May and will stand full sun, even in warm areas; **R. 'May Day'** is a hybrid of *R. haematodes* growing to about 1.5m (5ft) tall, with bright signal red, narrowly bell-shaped flowers in May; **R. 'Morning Cloud'** is a low-growing Yakushimanum hybrid with white flowers with a flush of pink; **R. 'Mrs. T. H. Lowinsky'** is tall with white flowers tinged with pink in June; **R. 'Nobleanum Album'** is large, a *R. arboreum* hybrid, with white flowers often flushed pink, opening in January to March (there are other Nobleanum hybrids with pink and red blooms, all of

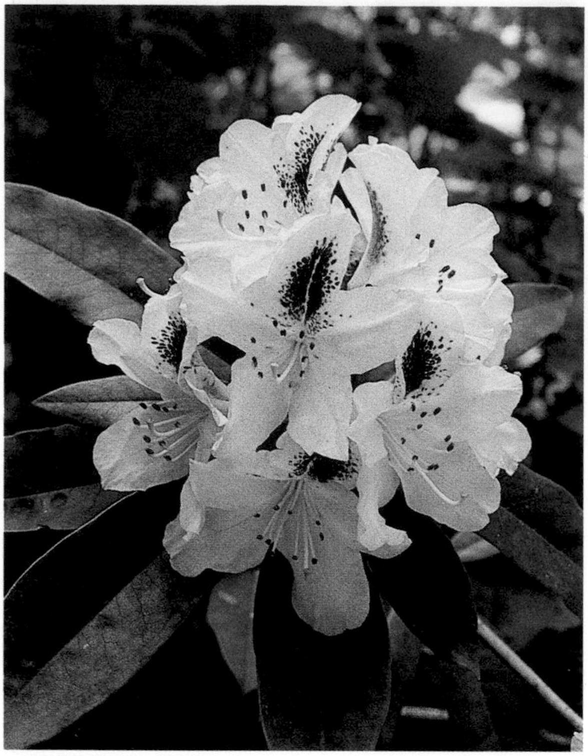

***Rhododendron* 'Sappho'**

which are early flowering); **R. 'Palestrina'** is an azalea with white flowers in late spring, growing to about 1.2m (4ft) tall; **R. 'Percy Wiseman'** is a very fine Yakushimanum hybrid, low-growing, with masses of pink and cream flowers in May; **R. 'Pink Pearl'** is an old but still very popular hybrid, tall and vigorous, with deep pink flowers in May to June; **R. 'Purple Splendour'** is a large hybrid of *R. ponticum* with deep purple flowers in May to June; **R. 'Sappho'** is vigorous, growing into a rounded bush about 3m (10ft) tall, with white flowers blotched with dark purple in June; **R. 'Sneezy'** is a very hardy Yakushimanum hybrid of vigorous growth to about 1.2m (4ft) tall, with rose-red flowers and silvery new growth; **R. 'Susan'**, a *R. campanulatum* hybrid, is medium to tall and bushy, with dark foliage and large clusters of bluish-mauve flowers in April to May; **R. 'Titian Beauty'** is a very lovely Yakushimanum hybrid growing to about 1.5m (5ft) tall, with waxy red flowers on a compact bush in May to June; **R. 'Unique'** is a very attractive *R. campylocarpum* hybrid of medium size and dense habit, with shiny rounded leaves and flowers peach in bud, opening cream. There are hundreds of other hybrids, available in all sizes and forms, with flowers of a wide range of colours.

VACCINIUM

A large genus of mainly evergreen, but also deciduous, shrubs and small trees. Although usually included in the same family as the heathers and rhododendrons, some botanists consider vacciniums sufficiently distinct to place them in a separate family.

Most of the species occur in tropical mountainous regions in south-east Asia and South America and are not very hardy. A number of species are native to northern temperate regions, in North America, Asia and Europe, and some of these are attractive, hardy shrubs, suitable for growing in similar conditions to rhododendrons. Several species are prostrate or dwarf and are not included here. A number of species bear edible fruits that have some commercial value, especially in North America. They are the blueberries, whortleberries, bilberries and cranberries.

V. delavayi

A compact, slow-growing, box-like shrub with small leaves. It bears pinkish-white flowers followed by bluish-purple berries, but these are rarely abundant. Its bronze-red young shoots are the main attraction of this plant.

Size: slowly growing to about 90cm (3ft) tall and about half as wide again.

Leaves: obovate, about 12mm (1/2in) long, blunt tipped, thick, leathery and dark green. Young shoots are tinged reddish-brown.

Flowers: small, in short spikes borne on the ends of old branches, white flushed with pink. The flowers usually open in May or June, at the same time that the colourful young shoots are growing, but they are rarely freely produced and are usually rather hidden by the foliage.

Fruits: round, 6mm (1/4in) in diameter, dark bluish-purple,fruits ripening in late summer to early autumn.

Cultivation: best given some shade, in a moist but free-draining, humus-rich, acid soil. Not absolutely hardy and needs shelter in colder parts of Britain.

Propagation: by cuttings taken in summer, of half-ripened shoots, inserted into a sandy, humus-rich compost under glass; by seed, sown in spring in similar

Vaccinium delavayi

compost; rooted basal shoots can sometimes be divided from the parent plant and grown on.

Origin: south-west China, north-east Burma.

V. glaucoalbum

A small shrub with very attractive foliage and pink flower spikes followed by bluish-black berries.

Size: usually about 90cm to 1.2m (3 to 4ft) tall, occasionally a little more, and spreading by suckering to form slowly expanding thickets, but not very invasive.

Leaves: large for a vaccinium, about 5cm (2in) long, elliptical or oval, somewhat leathery, greyish-green above, bluish-white beneath.

Flowers: borne in the leaf axils on mature wood, white with a pink tinge, in spikes among rosy bracts, opening in May to June.

Fruits: round, about 6mm (1/4in) in diameter, black with a blue bloom, ripening in late summer to early autumn and often lasting well into winter, edible.

Cultivation: requires a moist, humus-rich, acid soil, preferably with some shade and shelter. An excellent woodland plant. Not absolutely hardy and may suffer frost damage in cold districts.

Propagation: most easily propagated by removing suckers from the parent plant.

Origin: the Himalayan region and south-west China.

V. ovatum is of medium size and dense habit, with coppery-red young foliage, becoming dark, glossy green. Its white to pink flowers hang beneath the arching branches and are followed by berries that ripen from red to black.

CLIMBERS

CLEMATIS

A large genus of climbers, shrubs, sub-shrubs and herbaceous plants, occurring more or less throughout the world, though with a high proportion of species from eastern Asia. Most are woody climbers, but comparatively few are evergreen and only a couple of the evergreens are hardy enough to be grown outdoors in regions with cooler climates such as Britain.

Clematis usually support themselves by twisting their leaf stalks around the branches of shrubs or trees. The leaf stalks are not long enough to twist around anything very thick, so if they are grown against a wall it is best to fix wire mesh to it, preferably on a wooden frame which holds the wire a couple of inches away from the wall, so that they can easily cling to the wire. Clematis can also be encouraged to climb wooden fences and tree trunks by attaching wire mesh. Though principally grown for their flowers, the seeds each have a long, hairy tail and the seed-heads are often quite attractive. Clematis flowers do not have true petals. What appear to be petals are actually colourful sepals, but for simplicity they will be referred to as petals here.

Clematis cirrhosa

C. armandii

A vigorous, tall climber with dark green foliage and clusters of white or pinkish flowers in early spring. Not absolutely hardy.

Size: will grow to a height of about 6m (20ft), or even rather more, and requires considerable space.

Leaves: divided into three leaflets, each leaflet being more or less narrowly oval, about 7.5 to 12.5cm (3 to 5in) long, quite leathery and glossy dark green.

Flowers: each flower is about 5cm (2in) or a little more in diameter, with four or sometimes five white petals, often flushed with pink, in loose clusters of 40 or 50. They are borne usually on the upper portions of the stems, opening during late March to April or early May.

Cultivation: robust and easy in any reasonable garden soil in full sun or light shade, preferably with some shelter or, in colder areas, on a warm, south- or west-facing wall. Not hardy enough for very cold areas with regular hard frosts.

Propagation: by cuttings of young growth taken in late spring and inserted into sandy compost in a closed propagator, preferably with bottom heat.

Varieties: 'Apple Blossom' has large, pink-tinged flowers; 'Snowdrift' is early-flowering with pure white blooms. There are a few other selected cultivars.

Origin: China.

C. cirrhosa, the Virgin's Bower

Not one of the most spectacular clematis in flower, but blooms in winter when any flowers are welcome. The shiny green leaves are variably divided and lobed. Not too large and vigorous, suitable for small gardens.

Size: up to about 3 to 3.6m (10 to 12ft) high.

Leaves: variable, either divided into three leaflets or divided into three and then three again, or undivided but deeply three-lobed, or neither divided nor lobed, but always with toothed margins, usually about 5cm (2in) long, shiny green.

Flowers: nodding, borne singly in upper leaf axils, about 5cm (2in) in diameter, yellowish-white, often with dark red spots, opening throughout winter.

Cultivation: quite easy in any reasonable garden soil, preferably in a sunny position. Lack of sun will result in poor flowering and straggly growth. Not absolutely hardy and needs protection in colder parts of Britain, where it is best grown on a warm wall.

Propagation: by cuttings taken in early spring and inserted into sandy compost in a closed propagator, with bottom heat.

Varieties: 'Freckles' has flowers with plenty of red spots; 'Jingle Bells' has unspotted, yellowish flowers; 'Wisley Cream' has plain, creamy-white flowers; var. *balearica* always has leaves divided into several leaflets, often turning bronze-red in winter.

Origin: the Mediterranean region.

C. 'Blaaval' (Avalanche, C. x cartmanii 'Avalanche')

A fairly new hybrid with attractive foliage and lovely white flowers. Very fine, but of unproven hardiness.

Size: fairly vigorous but of quite modest size, up to about 3 to 3.6m (10 to 12ft) high.

Leaves: about 7.5 to 10cm (3 to 4in) long, divided into three leaflets or into three and then three again, the individual leaflets deeply toothed and lobed, dark green and stiff.

Flowers: about 7.5cm (3in) across, white, with six petals and a central boss of yellow stamens, in loose clusters of a few to several in the upper leaf axils, opening in March to April.

Cultivation: fairly easy in any reasonable garden soil in a sunny position. Probably at least as hardy as either of the two species described above, but until it has been grown for longer and its exact hardiness assessed it would be wise to grow it on a warm wall, at least in colder areas.

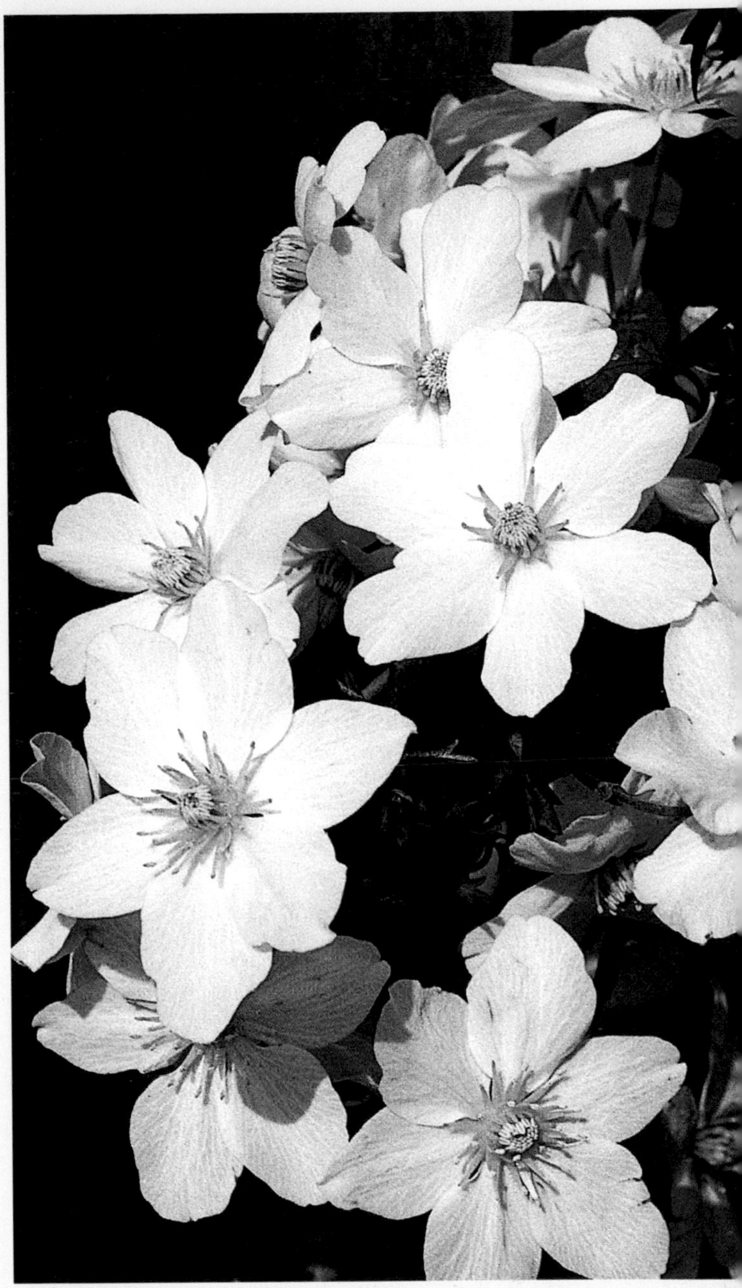

Clematis 'Blaaval'

Propagation: subject to Plant Breeder's Rights (see page 6).

Origin: a garden hybrid between two New Zealand species, *Clematis paniculata* and *C. marmoraria*.

C. fasciculiflora is quite a recent introduction to cultivation in Britain from China and has dark green leaves with paler markings and nodding, greenish-white flowers. It is not very hardy and needs a sheltered position in all but the mildest locations.

DECUMARIA

A very small genus of evergreen and semi-evergreen climbers, related to hydrangeas but looking very different in flower.

D. sinensis

An attractive climber that deserves to be more often grown, with heads of whitish, very sweetly scented flowers in late spring.

Size: grows quite slowly, at least until well established, reaching a height of about 4.5m (15ft) or a little more.

Leaves: elliptical to obovate, about 5 to 7.5cm (2 to 3in) long, somewhat leathery, often with margins toothed towards the tip.

Flowers: individually small, green and white, in dense, rounded heads about 7.5cm (3in) across, smelling strongly of honey, opening in May.

Cultivation: likes a free-draining but humus-rich, fertile soil. Will tolerate both sun and shade. Clings by aerial roots, like climbing hydrangeas or ivy, and will grow up a wall or a tree.

Propagation: by cuttings, taken in summer and inserted into any reasonable compost or soil, preferably under glass; by layering.

Origin: central China.

Ercilla volubilis

ERCILLA

A very small genus of climbers from South America.

E. volubilis

An unusual climber with quite small, rounded leaves and downward-pointing spikes of small, purplish flowers in spring. The flowers are followed by black fruits, but neither flowers nor fruits are very showy.

Size: up to about 3.6m (12ft) high.

Leaves: rounded, about 2.5 to 5cm (1 to 2in) long, somewhat leathery.

Flowers: individually very small, purplish-white, borne in small, dense spikes growing downwards from the leaf axils, opening in April or May.

Cultivation: likes a light loam and a sunny position. Best on a south-facing wall, but can also be grown up trees, especially in warmer areas. It clings by aerial roots, like ivy. Hardy enough to be grown in colder areas such as parts of Scotland, especially on a warm wall.

Propagation: by cuttings taken in autumn and inserted into any reasonable soil or compost; by layering.

Origin: Chile.

EUONYMUS

See also entry under SHRUBS for most soils, mainly for foliage effect.

E. fortunei

A very hardy trailing or climbing shrub grown mainly for its foliage and often used as ground cover, but also capable of climbing slowly to 6m (20ft) or more. Like ivies (*Hedera* spp.), it produces both non-flowering, climbing or trailing shoots and mature shoots with somewhat different foliage that bear flowers and fruits. The flowers are small, green and of little ornamental value, though the fruits are colourful. Many cultivars, often with variegated foliage, have been developed from this species. Not all climb and several rarely, if ever, flower. As a climber, it is self-clinging. Trailing shoots will often root where they touch the ground.

Euonymus fortunei 'Emerald 'n' Gold'

Size: will climb slowly to a height of 6m (20ft) or more. As ground cover, will reach a height of between 0.9 and 1.2m (3 to 4ft).

Leaves: more or less elliptical, about 2.5 to 7.5cm (1 to 3in) long, dark green, leathery.

Fruits: borne only on mature shoots, yellowish-pink splitting to reveal orange seeds, up to almost 12mm (1/2in) across, ripening in autumn.

Cultivation: easy in most soils and situations. Tolerant of coastal conditions. The cultivars with variegated foliage usually colour best in sun. It is usually slow to begin climbing and may be encouraged to do so by providing support to which longer shoots can be fastened.

Propagation: most easily propagated by layering, but cuttings taken in autumn and inserted into sandy compost will usually root well.

Varieties: 'Coloratus' has foliage that turns purple in winter, reverting to green in spring, and will climb well; 'Dart's Blanket' has leaves that turn reddish-purple in autumn and is low-growing and wide-spreading as ground cover, and can also be encouraged to climb; 'Emerald 'n' Gold' has broad yellow margins to the leaves, often with a pink tinge in winter, and will climb well, given some encouragement, to about 4.5m (15ft); 'Silver Queen' has leaves with a broad creamy-white margin and will reach 3m (10ft) or more on a wall; 'Variegatus' has greyish-green leaves, margined with creamy-white and often tinged pink, and is a good climber or trailing ground cover; var. *radicans* has rather small leaves, up to about 4cm (1 1/2in) long, and trails or climbs well; var. *vegetus* has broad, sometimes almost round, leaves and trails or

Euonymus fortunei 'Silver Queen'

climbs, also flowering and fruiting well. There are about a couple of dozen other cultivars, many with coloured foliage, most best as ground cover and reluctant to climb.

Origin: China, Japan and Korea.

HEDERA

The ivies are a small genus of about a dozen species, occurring throughout Europe, Asia and north Africa. They include the toughest and hardiest of all evergreen climbers, attaching themselves by means of aerial roots.

Though the number of species is small and the differences between them not very great, there is a very large number of cultivars, varying in habit, vigour, leaf shape and leaf coloration. Even on individual plants there are variations in the leaves. Young, climbing shoots bear leaves of different size and shape to those on mature, flowering shoots. The flowers are not very ornamental, being small and greenish, in rounded heads. The round, usually black, berry-like fruits are only slightly more conspicuous. Ivies are very useful for covering walls and the remains of dead trees, but care should be taken with the more vigorous ones if planting against house walls, as they can block gutters and damage roofs if they are not kept under control. Forms with variegated or coloured leaves are often less vigorous than those with plain green leaves.

Contrary to beliefs still held by some, ivies are not parasitic and cause no harm to trees, though they might tend to smother very small ones. They are very good grown through deciduous hedges, which they will make denser and, of course, evergreen. A strong, chain link or similar fence can also be turned into an evergreen hedge by growing ivy over it. Ivies can also make very good ground cover. They will grow even in very dark, dry places under the shade of trees.

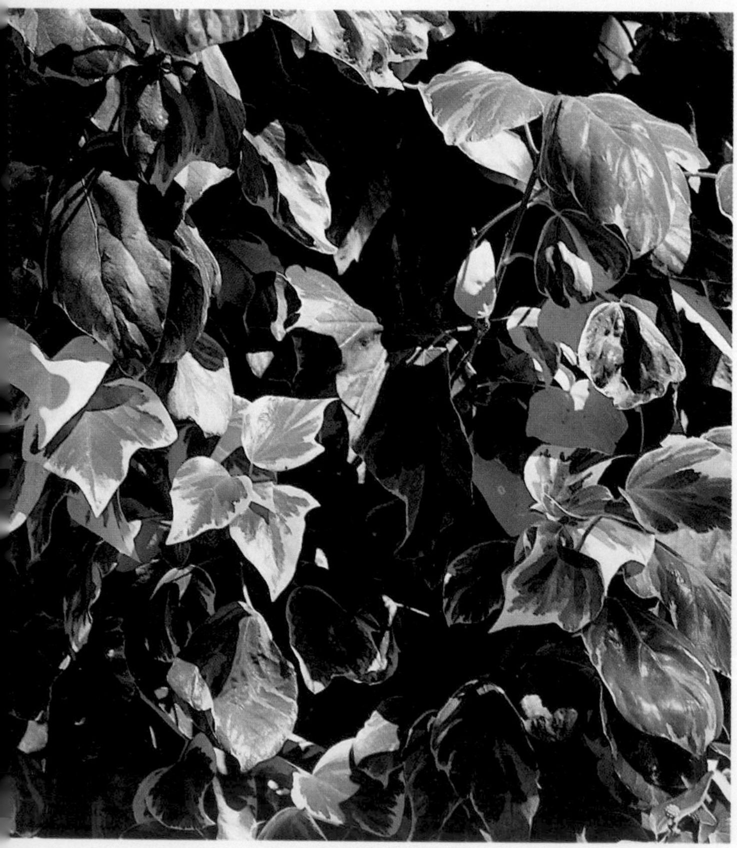

Hedera canariensis **'Gloire de Marengo'**

H. canariensis, the Canary Island Ivy

A vigorous, large-leaved species which is surprisingly hardy, given its origins, but not really suitable for very cold areas. There is some confusion about the naming of this plant, some of the cultivars possibly being of hybrid origin.

Size: will climb quite quickly to 4.5m (15ft) high or even more.

Leaves: on climbing shoots, more or less kidney-shaped, sometimes bluntly three-lobed, about 15cm (6in) or sometimes more across; on flowering shoots the leaves are rounded with a heart-shaped base, bright green in summer and often shaded bronze in winter, especially in a dry situation.

Cultivation: easy in almost any soil and situation, in sun or shade.

Propagation: by cuttings of firm shoots, taken in autumn or winter and inserted into sandy compost, preferably under glass; by layering.

Varieties: 'Gloire de Marengo' ('Variegata') is the most commonly grown cultivar, with leaves that are green in the centre, shading into silvery-grey and then creamy-white around the margins. It is slightly less hardy and vigorous than the type and is often grown as a house plant. There are a few other selected cultivars.

Origin: the Canary Islands, north-west Africa.

***Hedera colchica* 'Dentata Variegata'**

H. colchica, the Persian Ivy

A handsome, vigorous species with the largest leaves in the genus, otherwise similar to the Common Ivy.

Size: will quite quickly attain as much as 6m (20ft) in height and eventually more.

Leaves: on climbing shoots, up to 20cm (8in) long, oval or elliptical and scarcely lobed, dark, shiny green; on flowering shoots, smaller and broader.

Cultivation: easy in almost any soil and situation.

Propagation: as for *H. canariensis*.

Varieties: 'Dentata' has very large leaves that are sometimes three-lobed, with purplish stems and leaf stalks; 'Dentata Variegata' ('Dentata Aurea', 'Variegata') is rather like *H. canariensis* 'Gloire de Marengo', but hardier, with heart-shaped to elliptical leaves; 'Sulphur Heart' ('Paddy's Pride') has broadly oval leaves with an irregular central splash of yellow, shading to pale green and then dark green at the margins, with some leaves almost entirely yellow.

Origin: Turkey and the Caucasus region.

H. helix, the Common Ivy

A familiar plant, both in gardens and in the wild, this is the hardiest evergreen climber, occurring naturally more or less throughout Britain. It is a woodland plant, often growing in dense, dry shade under trees, but climbs to obtain more light and will stand full sun. Its main drawback in the garden is that it can be too rampant and often tends to seed itself profusely. A few hundred cultivars have been developed from the wild plant and many are less vigorous.

Size: will grow up a tree to a height of 9m (30ft) or more.

Leaves: about 5 to 10cm (2 to 4in) long; on climbing shoots, usually more or less heart-shaped, with three or five shallow to deep, pointed lobes; on flowering shoots, oval or elliptical and more or less unlobed.

Cultivation: very easy in almost any soil and situation, very tough and hardy, will tolerate dry shade. Too vigorous to grow on most house walls, but good for covering boundary walls or fences, or growing through hedges to make them denser and evergreen. Some cultivars are much less vigorous. Variegated cultivars often tend to lose their colour in too much

Hedera helix **'Chrysophylla'**

Hedera hibernica

shade and require at least a partly sunny position. They also dislike very acid soils.

Propagation: as for *H. canariensis*, but only the less vigorous cultivars need to be propagated under glass. Common Ivy often self-seeds abundantly.

Varieties: hundreds of cultivars have been developed from this species and only a few are described briefly here. 'Atropurpurea' is vigorous, with dark green leaves that turn purple in winter and have paler green veins; 'Buttercup' is of moderate growth, with broad, shallowly lobed leaves that are almost completely yellow, or yellowish-green in shade, more brightly coloured when young; 'Cavendishii' has small, angular leaves blotched with grey and with creamy-white margins; 'Chrysophylla' is vigorous and has leaves partly or almost entirely coloured yellow, but tends to revert, producing normal shoots with entirely green leaves; 'Erecta' is slow-growing, with stiff, erect shoots and arrow-shaped leaves; 'Glacier' is a moderate grower with leaves that are dark green in the centre shading to greyish-green and then creamy-white at the margins; 'Goldchild' has pale green leaves with broad yellow margins and is small and slow-growing; 'Green Ripple' has small leaves with long, narrow, pointed lobes; 'Ivalace' is compact, with dark green, crinkled leaves with paler veins; 'Luzii' ('Marmorata') has small leaves irregularly splashed with cream and grey, sometimes also with pink; 'Oro di Bogliasco' ('Goldheart', 'Jubiläum Goldherz', 'Jubilee') has leaves with a central splash of yellow; 'Parsley Crested' ('Cristata') has pale green, twisted and crinkled leaves; 'Pedata' ('Caenwoodiana') has small leaves with narrow lobes; 'Sagittifolia' has five-lobed leaves with the main lobe large and pointed; 'Tricolor' has greyish-green leaves with a creamy-white margin, tinged reddish in winter; f. *poetarum* ('Poetica') has bright green, shallowly lobed leaves and yellow fruits.

Origin: Europe, including Britain, and western Asia.

H.azorica, the Azores Ivy, is similar to *H. canariensis*, but has dull, pale green leaves with five to seven blunt lobes; **H. hibernica (H. helix subsp. hibernica)**, the Irish Ivy, is very similar to *H. helix*, but has larger leaves, up to 15cm (6in) long, usually with five broad lobes. There are a number of cultivars of this species, formerly often considered to be cultivars of *H. helix*, including some with variegated leaves, such as 'Anna Marie' and 'Dealbata'; **H. nepalensis**, the Himalayan Ivy, is vigorous and has oval and sometimes three-lobed, greyish-green leaves up to about 12.5cm (5in) long, and large, yellow or sometimes red fruits; **H. rhombea**, the Japanese Ivy, is similar to the preceding, but with narrower, occasionally shallowly lobed leaves and black fruits.

HOLBOELLIA

A small genus of about a dozen species of evergreen, woody climbers from south and east Asia. Most are from subtropical regions and are not hardy in cooler northern climates such as that of Britain, but a few are hardy enough to be grown outdoors, at least in warmer districts. Male and female flowers are borne in separate clusters on the same plant, followed by curious sausage-like fruits. Unfortunately these are rarely produced at all freely in cultivation. Hand-pollinating the flowers encourages fruiting. Holboellias climb by twining.

H. coriacea

Probably the hardiest species, vigorous and reasonably tough, with large, glossy leaves and purplish flowers.

Size: can grow to a height of 6m (20ft) or even rather more.

Leaves: dark, glossy green, leathery, divided into three leaflets, each leaflet with a short stalk and elliptical to obovate, about 10 to 15cm (4 to 6in) long.

Flowers: about 12mm (1/2in) long, with six, thick, coloured petal-like sepals, in loose, hanging clusters each comprising several flowers. Male and female flowers are in separate clusters: the males greenish-white, tinged purple; the females purplish. They open in April to May.

Fruits: fleshy, about 5cm (2in) long, sometimes more, purple, rarely freely borne.

Cultivation: best in a fertile, humus-rich soil, but fairly adaptable. Tolerates sun or shade, but will flower and fruit more freely in sun. Good for growing through large shrubs or into trees. Dislikes cold winds.

Propagation: by cuttings, taken in spring and inserted into sandy compost, preferably in a closed propagator with bottom heat.

Origin: central China.

H. fargesii is similar, but the leaves are divided into three to seven leaflets and the flowers and fruits are larger; **H. latifolia** also has leaves with three to seven leaflets, but is otherwise more like *H. coriacea*: it is less hardy than the two other species.

HYDRANGEA

A genus of moderate size, mainly of deciduous shrubs, but including a number of climbers, a few of them evergreen. Many of the species are from eastern Asia, but others are native to North and South America. The climbing species support themselves by aerial roots.

Holboellia fargesii

H. serratifolia (H. integerrima)

A large, bushy climber with long, leathery leaves and upright clusters of white flowers in late summer.

Size: will grow to a height of 6m (20ft) or more.

Leaves: elliptical to narrowly obovate, up to about 15cm (6in) long, leathery, dark green.

Flowers: individually small, creamy-white, borne in large, almost conical clusters, opening in July to August.

Cultivation: prefers a humus-rich, fertile soil in either sun or shade. Best grown against a wall, but will also climb trees.

Propagation: most easily propagated by layering, but cuttings taken in late summer to early autumn and inserted into an open, humus-rich compost will often root successfully.

Origin: Chile.

LONICERA

See also entry under SHRUBS for most soils, mainly for foliage effect.

Lonicera giraldii

L. acuminata

A very vigorous, often semi-evergreen species with small, reddish flowers.

Size: will climb to a height of 6 to 9m (20 to 30ft) and can also make good, fast-growing ground cover.

Leaves: up to about 10cm (4in) long, oval to lanceolate, very shortly stalked, somewhat leathery and hairy.

Flowers: small, up to about 2.5cm (1in) long, borne in pairs in the upper leaf axils and at the ends of shoots, narrowly funnel-shaped with a large upper lip and a smaller lower lip, creamy-yellow with a reddish tinge, opening in June or July.

Fruits: small, about 6mm (1/4in) in diameter, round, bluish-black, ripening in autumn.

Cultivation: easy in most soils and situations, will tolerate sun or shade, although flowers are less abundant in heavy shade. Good for growing into trees or large shrubs or as ground cover, but fast-growing and rapidly occupying a great deal of space. May suffer frost damage in severe winters, especially if exposed to cold winds.

Propagation: most easily propagated by layering, but cuttings taken in late summer and inserted into sandy compost usually root quite easily.

Origin: the Himalayan region, China and south-east Asia.

L. giraldii

Rather like the above species, but less vigorous and with purplish-red flowers. The whole plant is covered with soft, buff-coloured hairs.

Size: will climb to a height of about 4.5 to 6m (15 to 20ft).

Leaves: about 7.5 to 10cm (3 to 4in) long, lanceolate to narrowly elliptical, heart-shaped at the base, dark green above, paler beneath, very hairy.

Flowers: small, not more than about 2.5cm (1in) long, dark purplish-red, with yellow stamens, borne at and near the ends of the shoots, opening in June or July.

Lonicera implexa

Fruits: small, about 6mm ($^{1}/_{4}$in) in diameter, round, bluish-black, ripening in autumn.

Cultivation: as for *L. acuminata*, but less vigorous and a better plant for smaller gardens. Can be grown over fences to make them look like evergreen hedges, but will not flourish if exposed to strong, cold winds.

Propagation: as for *L. acuminata.*

Origin: western China.

L. implexa, the Menorca Honeysuckle

Generally similar in appearance to the Common Honeysuckle (*L. periclymenum*).

Size: moderately vigorous, will climb to about 4.5m (15ft) high.

Leaves: oval to broadly elliptical, about 7.5cm (3in) long, bluish-green, those near the flowers fused in pairs.

Flowers: narrowly funnel-shaped, about 3.8cm (1$^{1}/_{2}$in) long, creamy-white inside, purplish-pink outside, in clusters at the ends of shoots, fragrant, opening in June to August.

Fruits: rather more than 6mm ($^{1}/_{4}$in) in diameter, round, red, ripening in autumn.

Cultivation: best in full sun in a warm position, tends to be semi-evergreen in cold winters and is not really hardy enough for very cold districts. Prefers a light, free-draining soil, but is fairly adaptable.

Propagation: as for *L. acuminata.*

Origin: the Mediterranean region.

L. japonica, the Japanese Honeysuckle

The most commonly grown evergreen honeysuckle, though it is vigorous to the point of being rampant and cannot be recommended for small gardens. In parts of North America it is now a naturalized weed.

Size: will grow rapidly up to 9m (30ft) in height.

Leaves: oval, sometimes with a few blunt lobes, about 5cm (2in) long, mid-green above, paler beneath.

Flowers: fragrant, about 4cm (1$^{1}/_{2}$in) long, white turning to yellow with age, borne in pairs in the upper leaf axils over a long period from about June onwards, not very showy.

Fruits: small, about 6mm ($^{1}/_{4}$in) in diameter, round, bluish-black, ripening in autumn.

Cultivation: easy in almost any soil and situation, prefers a light loam and full sun. Will make good, rapid ground cover as well as climbing. Is often semi-evergreen in colder winters.

Lonicera similis var. *delavayi*

Propagation: as for *L. acuminata*.

Varieties: 'Aureoreticulata' ('Variegata') has leaves reticulated with yellow and is slightly less vigorous than the type; 'Halliana' is a selected form, differing little from the type; 'Hall's Prolific' is a selection from the preceding, bearing an abundance of fragrant flowers from June to September; 'Horwood Gem' has variegated foliage; var. *repens* (*L. flexuosa*) is distinct, with young shoots and flowers flushed reddish-purple. There are a few other selected cultivars.

Origin: Japan, Korea and China.

L. similis var. delavayi (L. delavayi)

A very attractive, often semi-evergreen climber with quite large, fragrant, white flowers.

Size: moderately vigorous, growing to a height of about 4.5 to 6m (15 to 20ft).

Leaves: oval to lanceolate, up to about 10cm (4in) long, smooth and shiny above when mature, often rather hairy when young.

Flowers: fragrant, about 5cm (2in) long, white ageing to yellow, borne in pairs in the upper leaf axils and in small clusters at the ends of shoots, opening in June to July.

Fruits: rather more than 6mm (1/4in) in diameter, egg-shaped, bluish-black, ripening in autumn.

Cultivation: easy in most soils in a sunny to partly shady position. Not too large and vigorous for most gardens and more showy in flower than most of the evergreen honeysuckles.

Propagation: as for *L. acuminata*.

Origin: China.

L. alseuosmoides is similar to *L. acuminata*, but has narrower, less hairy leaves and yellow and purple flowers; **L. henryi** is also like *L. acuminata*, but is hairy only on young shoots and has rather larger leaves; **L. sempervirens** is a fine species with large, orange-red, scentless flowers, but is unfortunately not very hardy and needs to be grown on a warm wall in all but the mildest parts of Britain.

MUTISIA

A genus of a few dozen species belonging to the Daisy family (Compositae), mainly from tropical and subtropical parts of South America. Only a few species are sufficiently hardy to be grown outdoors in cooler climates such as that of Britain but none is suitable for very cold areas. They climb by means of tendrils. The flowers are quite large and very showy.

M. ilicifolia

Probably the hardiest species, of vigorous growth but, except in very mild areas, it is best grown on a warm wall.

Size: up to about 3 to 4.5m (10 to 15ft) tall.

Leaves: leathery, stalkless, more or less oval with a heart-shaped base, about 2.5 to 5cm (1 to 2in) long, dark green above, covered with whitish or fawn woolly hairs beneath, with spiny teeth on the margins and tipped with a tendril up to 10cm (4in) long.

Flowers: carried singly on short stalks at the ends of shoots, 5 to 7.5cm (2 to 3in) across, with a yellow centre and 8 to 12 pink to pale mauve rays, opening over a long period from summer into autumn.

Cultivation: needs a warm, sunny position with a fertile, free-draining soil, ideally a sandy loam with plenty of humus mixed into it. It will scramble through a large shrub but in cooler areas will need to be grown against a warm wall, preferably one which faces west.

Propagation: by cuttings of half-ripened shoots inserted into a sandy compost in shade under glass during April or May.

Origin: Chile.

M. decurrens is similar but less hardy and vigorous, with longer leaves and flowers up to about 12.5cm (5in) across, orange or vermilion in colour. It is often difficult to establish. **M. oligodon** is even more similar, with flowers of a lovely shade of pink, but grows to only about 1.5m (5ft) tall and forms a clump of suckering shoots. Its foliage is often browned by frost in winter.

PILEOSTEGIA

A very small genus of just a few species, related to hydrangeas but not very similar in general appearance. They climb by means of aerial roots.

P. viburnoides

The only species generally cultivated, a very fine climber for any aspect, in full sun or shade. Can reach a considerable height, but is slow-growing and easily kept under control. The white flowers open during late summer and early autumn.

Size: will climb to as much as 6m (20ft) high, or even more in favourable conditions, but is slow-growing.

Leaves: more or less elliptical, up to about 15cm (6in) long, dark green, leathery, usually untoothed or with a few small marginal teeth towards the tip.

Flowers: individually small, white, borne in large branched clusters at the ends of side shoots, opening in late August to October.

Cultivation: likes a reasonably moist, humus-rich, fertile soil. Will grow and flower in sun or shade and is good on a north wall, though it dislikes exposure to cold winds. It will also grow up trees.

Pileostegia viburnoides

Propagation: by layering; by cuttings of shoots with aerial roots, taken in late autumn and inserted into humus-rich but free-draining compost, kept in shade under glass.

Origin: China, Japan (Ryukyu Islands), north-east India.

RUBUS

A very large genus found more or less all over the world, but mainly in northern temperate regions. The most familiar members are the native British brambles. Very variable in ornamental value, some being very attractive and desirable while others have little to recommend them. Some are invasive weeds. They vary greatly in habit, from tiny, creeping shrublets to erect bushes of varying size and large, scrambling climbers. Many are prickly. A minority are evergreen. They are not self-clinging, relying on their hooked prickles for support from the shrubs through which they naturally grow, and need fastening to a wall or fence.

R. henryi

A species of no great floral beauty, grown mainly for its attractive foliage.

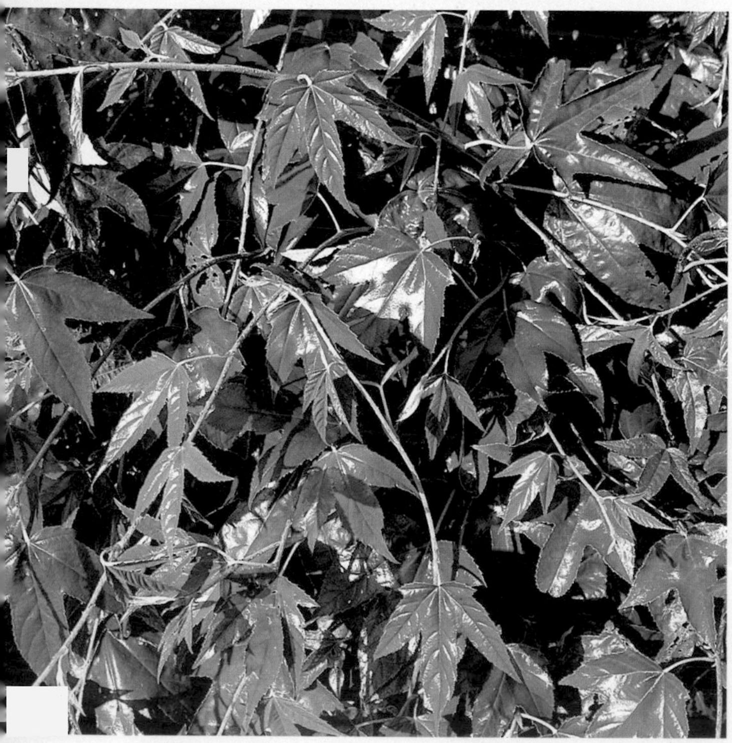

Rubus henryi

Size: will attain about 6m (20ft) in height on a suitable support.

Leaves: quite large, up to about 15cm (6in) long, deeply three-lobed, each lobe more or less lanceolate with toothed margins, leathery, glossy dark green above, felted with white hairs beneath.

Flowers: small, pink, opening in May or June, not very showy.

Fruits: about 12mm (1/2in) or a little more in diameter, black, ripening in late summer.

Cultivation: easy in most soils and situations.

Propagation: by layering.

Varieties: var. *bambusarum* (*R. bambusarum*) has leaves completely divided into three separate leaflets, each one more or less lanceolate and up to almost 15cm (6in) long.

Origin: central and western China.

TRACHELOSPERMUM

A small genus of climbers occurring in eastern Asia. Most are from tropical to subtropical regions and are not very hardy, just a couple of species being suitable for a warm wall in areas with colder climates like Britain. They are very attractive, bearing jasmine-like flowers with a sweet fragrance in summer. They are self-clinging by means of aerial roots and will also twine.

T. asiaticum

A beautiful species with small, glossy leaves and creamy-white, very fragrant flowers.

Size: will reach a height of about 6m (20ft).

Leaves: oval to elliptical, small, about 2.5 to 5cm (1 to 2in) long, dark, glossy green.

Flowers: rather like jasmine flowers, with a narrow tube and five spreading lobes, rather less than 2.5cm (1in) across, creamy-white ageing to yellow, sweetly scented, borne in loose clusters in the leaf axils, opening in July.

Trachelospermum jasminoides

Cultivation: likes a fertile, reasonably humus-rich, well-drained soil and a warm, sunny position. Not suitable for very cold districts.

Propagation: by cuttings of half-ripened shoots, taken in July or August and inserted into sandy compost, preferably in a closed propagator with bottom heat.

Origin: Japan and Korea.

T. jasminoides is very similar to *T. asiaticum*, but rather larger in all its parts and taller growing, with whiter flowers. Unfortunately, it is also a little less hardy. There are several selected cultivars of this species, among them 'Variegatum', which has leaves marked with creamy-white, often tinged red in winter, and 'Wilsonii', which has leaves that vary considerably in width and often turn an attractive dark red during winter.

ABOUT THE AUTHOR

Stephen G. Haw has been writing about plants and gardens for more than 20 years. His articles have appeared in many periodicals, including the Royal Horticultural Society's publications *The Garden* and *The Plantsman* (and *The New Plantsman*), the Alpine Garden Society's *Bulletin, Hortus* and *Country Life*. His first book, *The Lilies of China*, was published by Batsford in 1986 and he has since written contributions to *Plant Life* (Oxford University Press [USA]), *By Pen and By Spade* and *The Generous Garden* (Alan Sutton).

Stephen's interests are not restricted to gardening and botany: he has a degree in Chinese and has lived in China and travelled extensively there, as well as in South-east Asia, Nepal, Bhutan, Central Asia and several European countries. He is the author of *China: a cultural history* (Batsford) and *A Traveller's History of China* (Windrush Press). He is also a professional photographer, whose photographs have been used to illustrate not only his own writings but also other publications. He frequently gives lectures, illustrated with his own colour transparencies, to societies interested in plants and gardens.

Stephen cultivates a large, partly wooded garden in north Oxfordshire where he grows a wide variety of plants, including many broad-leaved evergreens.

GENERAL INDEX

INDEX OF CULTIVARS AND SELLING NAMES

For an explanation of the terms 'cultivar' and 'selling name' see page 6

Titles available from

GMC PUBLICATIONS

BOOKS

WOODCARVING

The Art of the Woodcarver — *GMC Publications*
Carving Architectural Detail in Wood: The Classical Tradition — *Frederick Wilbur*
Carving Birds & Beasts — *GMC Publications*
Carving Nature: Wildlife Studies in Wood — *Frank Fox-Wilson*
Carving Realistic Birds — *David Tippey*
Decorative Woodcarving — *Jeremy Williams*
Elements of Woodcarving — *Chris Pye*
Essential Tips for Woodcarvers — *GMC Publications*
Essential Woodcarving Techniques — *Dick Onians*
Further Useful Tips for Woodcarvers — *GMC Publications*
Lettercarving in Wood: A Practical Course — *Chris Pye*
Making & Using Working Drawings for Realistic Model Animals — *Basil Fordham*
Power Tools for Woodcarving — *David Tippey*
Practical Tips for Turners & Carvers — *GMC Publications*
Relief Carving in Wood: A Practical Introduction — *Chris Pye*
Understanding Woodcarving — *GMC Publications*
Understanding Woodcarving in the Round — *GMC Publications*
Useful Techniques for Woodcarvers — *GMC Publications*
Wildfowl Carving – Volume 1 — *Jim Pearce*
Wildfowl Carving – Volume 2 — *Jim Pearce*
Woodcarving: A Complete Course — *Ron Butterfield*
Woodcarving: A Foundation Course — *Zoë Gertner*
Woodcarving for Beginners — *GMC Publications*
Woodcarving Tools & Equipment Test Reports — *GMC Publications*
Woodcarving Tools, Materials & Equipment — *Chris Pye*

WOODTURNING

Adventures in Woodturning — *David Springett*
Bert Marsh: Woodturner — *Bert Marsh*
Bowl Turning Techniques Masterclass — *Tony Boase*
Colouring Techniques for Woodturners — *Jan Sanders*
The Craftsman Woodturner — *Peter Child*
Decorative Techniques for Woodturners — *Hilary Bowen*
Fun at the Lathe — *R.C. Bell*
Further Useful Tips for Woodturners — *GMC Publications*
Illustrated Woodturning Techniques — *John Hunnex*
Intermediate Woodturning Projects — *GMC Publications*
Keith Rowley's Woodturning Projects — *Keith Rowley*
Practical Tips for Turners & Carvers — *GMC Publications*
Turning Green Wood — *Michael O'Donnell*
Turning Miniatures in Wood — *John Sainsbury*
Turning Pens and Pencils — *Kip Christensen & Rex Burningham*
Understanding Woodturning — *Ann & Bob Phillips*
Useful Techniques for Woodturners — *GMC Publications*
Useful Woodturning Projects — *GMC Publications*
Woodturning: Bowls, Platters, Hollow Forms, Vases, Vessels, Bottles, Flasks, Tankards, Plates — *GMC Publications*
Woodturning: A Foundation Course (New Edition) — *Keith Rowley*
Woodturning: A Fresh Approach — *Robert Chapman*
Woodturning: An Individual Approach — *Dave Regester*
Woodturning: A Source Book of Shapes — *John Hunnex*
Woodturning Jewellery — *Hilary Bowen*
Woodturning Masterclass — *Tony Boase*
Woodturning Techniques — *GMC Publications*
Woodturning Tools & Equipment Test Reports — *GMC Publications*
Woodturning Wizardry — *David Springett*

WOODWORKING

Bird Boxes and Feeders for the Garden — *Dave Mackenzie*
Complete Woodfinishing — *Ian Hosker*
David Charlesworth's Furniture-Making Techniques — *David Charlesworth*
Furniture & Cabinetmaking Projects — *GMC Publications*
Furniture-Making Projects for the Wood Craftsman — *GMC Publications*
Furniture-Making Techniques for the Wood Craftsman — *GMC Publications*
Furniture Projects — *Rod Wales*
Furniture Restoration (Practical Crafts) — *Kevin Jan Bonner*
Furniture Restoration and Repair for Beginners — *Kevin Jan Bonner*
Furniture Restoration Workshop — *Kevin Jan Bonner*
Green Woodwork — *Mike Abbott*
Kevin Ley's Furniture Projects — *Kevin Ley*
Making & Modifying Woodworking Tools — *Jim Kingshott*
Making Chairs and Tables — *GMC Publications*
Making Classic English Furniture — *Paul Richardson*
Making Little Boxes from Wood — *John Bennett*
Making Shaker Furniture — *Barry Jackson*
Making Woodwork Aids and Devices — *Robert Wearing*
Minidrill: Fifteen Projects — *John Everett*
Pine Furniture Projects for the Home — *Dave Mackenzie*
Practical Scrollsaw Patterns — *John Everett*
Router Magic: Jigs, Fixtures and Tricks to Unleash your Router's Full Potential — *Bill Hylton*
Routing for Beginners — *Anthony Bailey*
Scrollsaw Projects — *GMC Publications*
The Scrollsaw: Twenty Projects — *John Everett*
Sharpening: The Complete Guide — *Jim Kingshott*
Sharpening Pocket Reference Book — *Jim Kingshott*
Space-Saving Furniture Projects — *Dave Mackenzie*
Stickmaking: A Complete Course — *Andrew Jones & Clive George*
Stickmaking Handbook — *Andrew Jones & Clive George*
Test Reports: The Router and Furniture & Cabinetmaking — *GMC Publications*
Veneering: A Complete Course — *Ian Hosker*
Woodfinishing Handbook (Practical Crafts) — *Ian Hosker*
Woodworking with the Router: Professional Router Techniques any Woodworker can Use — *Bill Hylton & Fred Matlack*
The Workshop — *Jim Kingshott*

UPHOLSTERY

The Upholsterer's Pocket Reference Book — *David James*
Upholstery: A Complete Course (Revised Edition) — *David James*
Upholstery Restoration — *David James*
Upholstery Techniques & Projects — *David James*
Upholstery Tips and Hints — *David James*

TOYMAKING

Designing & Making Wooden Toys — *Terry Kelly*
Fun to Make Wooden Toys & Games — *Jeff & Jennie Loader*
Restoring Rocking Horses — *Clive Green & Anthony Dew*
Scrollsaw Toy Projects — *Ivor Carlyle*
Scrollsaw Toys for All Ages — *Ivor Carlyle*
Wooden Toy Projects — *GMC Publications*

DOLLS' HOUSES AND MINIATURES

Architecture for Dolls' Houses — *Joyce Percival*
A Beginners' Guide to the Dolls' House Hobby — *Jean Nisbett*
The Complete Dolls' House Book — *Jean Nisbett*
The Dolls' House 1/24 Scale: A Complete Introduction — *Jean Nisbett*
Dolls' House Accessories, Fixtures and Fittings — *Andrea Barham*
Dolls' House Bathrooms: Lots of Little Loos — *Patricia King*
Dolls' House Fireplaces and Stoves — *Patricia King*
Easy to Make Dolls' House Accessories — *Andrea Barham*
Heraldic Miniature Knights — *Peter Greenhill*
Make Your Own Dolls' House Furniture — *Maurice Harper*
Making Dolls' House Furniture — *Patricia King*
Making Georgian Dolls' Houses — *Derek Rowbottom*
Making Miniature Gardens — *Freida Gray*
Making Miniature Oriental Rugs & Carpets — *Meik & Ian McNaughton*
Making Period Dolls' House Accessories — *Andrea Barham*
Making 1/12 Scale Character Figures — *James Carrington*
Making Tudor Dolls' Houses — *Derek Rowbottom*
Making Victorian Dolls' House Furniture — *Patricia King*
Miniature Bobbin Lace — *Roz Snowden*
Miniature Embroidery for the Georgian Dolls' House — *Pamela Warner*